# A NEIGHBORHOOD OF EAGLES

## By Norman Rudi

Copyright © 2003 McMillen Publishing

All rights reserved. No part of this book may be reproduced or transmitted in any form or by any means, electronic or mechanical, including photocopying, recording, or by any information storage and retrieval system, without permission in writing from the publisher.

Publishing Manager: Denise Sundvold

Editor: Bridget Moore

Published, printed, and distributed by:

Library of Congress Control Number: Pending

ISBN: 1-888223-41-3

www.mcmillenbooks.com

All the opinions expressed herein are solely those of the author or subjects and do not necessarily reflect those of McMillen Publishing.

*Editor's note: Text written by subjects (letters, logs, etc.) are mostly unedited so as to preserve the integrity of the writing; any inconsistencies in spelling, capitalization, style, etc., have been left intentionally.*

*For Lauren and Nathan*

*And all children
who wonder why
their grandparents
really care.*

*There are no footprints in the sky
To guide a path for raining death.
And death extends to those up high
Who find their berth in sea and earth.*

*There are no footprints in the sky.*

# TABLE OF CONTENTS

**Introduction** .................................................................................. 7

**Book One: Robert Stafford** B-17 Pilot ................................. 13

**Book Two: Rollen Phillips** B-24 Pilot ................................. 59

**Book Three: Dean Huston** P-51 Pilot .................................. 95

**Book Four: Roman Dankbar** B-24 Bombardier ................ 135

**Book Five: Arthur Ketelsen** B-17 Pilot .............................. 159

**Book Six: Robert Underhill** B-17 Bombardier .................. 183

**Book Seven: Merritt Bailey** S-2 Intelligence ..................... 223

**Book Eight: Floyd Penkhus** B-25 Pilot ............................... 247

**Book Nine: William Singer** B-17 Navigator ....................... 289

**Acknowledgements** ................................................................ 333

**Bibliography** ........................................................................... 333

**About the Author** ................................................................... 334

**Glossary** .................................................................................. 335

# INTRODUCTION

The 1920s have been described by historians as a period of "fads, fancies and mass lunacy." The early 1920s were a period when the young men and women born would ultimately participate in World War II (WWII). They would grow up during a time of social evolution, economic revolution, and a massive conflict fought worldwide. The persons surviving the conflict would return to help build a nation of vitality, strength, and technological achievement that is unparalleled in history.

The subjects in this book were born between 1917 and 1923, and probably do not remember much about the "roaring twenties." However, they all have memories of their teenage years during the Great Depression, and of the technological advancements during the late 1930s. They have particularly vivid recollections of the early 1940s.

The period of "fads, fancies and mass lunacy" had its moments:

The first airmail letter was sent in 1918 from a certain Mr. Bradshaw, Postmaster General in Washington, D.C., to T. B. Payton, Postmaster of New York City. The letter carried a W.W. Wilson autographed stamp, and was placed on an airplane housed in a Washington, D.C., pasture. When the airplane would not start, they discovered it was out of gas. After fueling, the airplane took off and proceeded to get lost while flying over New Jersey. The pilot landed in a cow pasture and took the letter to the nearest train station. The historic letter arrived in New York, and was finally delivered to Mr. Payton at the post office. It was a rather inauspicious start for "airmail."

In 1919, the United States Congress, in their infinite wisdom, passed the Eighteenth Amendment, "Prohibiting the manufacturing, sale, or transportation of intoxicating liquors." By 1933, there were 219,000 illegal speakeasies in the United States freely dispensing the forbidden liquids. The "manufacture, sale and transportation of intoxicating liquors" by illegal means created organized crime in America.

The prosperity of the early 1920s created good economic times and produced a boom in the manufacture of cars and—out of necessity—the building of roads. The movie industry relocated from New Jersey to California, and movie stars influenced the lifestyles of people in all of the states in between.

The 1920s saw a tremendous increase in the "joiners"; the folks who wanted to be Rotarians, Kiwanians, Lions, Elks, Moose, Masons, and Odd Fellows.

In 1920, there were 2,000 golf courses; in 1930, there were 8,000.

In 1920, the population of the United States totaled 106,446,000 people. By 1930, the population had increased to 123,077,000 inhabitants, and by 1940 the population was well over 132,000,000.

In 1922, the Lincoln Memorial was dedicated in Washington, D.C., the *Reader's Digest* began publication, and *Nanook of the North* (a pioneer documentary film) was released.

In 1923, Mah Jongg replaced Parcheesi as the board game of choice. Kewpie dolls were a hot item. Young people sang "Yes, We Have No Bananas," and danced the "Charleston." They watched as Jack Dempsey beat up heavyweight fighters across the country.

1923, a paperhanger in Germany attempted to take over the Socialist Party by force and, failing, was jailed for a year. While incarcerated, the man wrote a book entitled, *Mein Kampf* or "My Struggle." Published in 1924, the book was an odd collection of observations and selective insights that fueled his rise to power, and in 1933 he was elected President of the Third Reich.

In 1923, archaeologist Howard Carter discovered King Tutankhamen's tomb in Egypt, fueling a new interest in antiquity and "Egyptian-style" home decorating.

Cosmetology started in the early 1920s with "beauticians" applying lipstick and face powder. The hot styles would be the "Pageboy" hair style and dresses above the knee with big bows or a sash at the waist.

The Women's Suffrage Movement suffered a setback when "New York State denied the vote to criminals, lunatics, idiots, and women."

In 1920, there were 1,000,000 radios. In 1925, there were 4,000,000 radios. In 1920, there were 22 radio stations. By 1923, there were 576 radio stations.

During the 1920s, elaborate, expensive movie houses were constructed that dazzled movie-goers throughout the country. In 1927, the first "talking" picture, *The Jazz Singer* starring Al Jolson, excited the world of cinema. Technicolor, created in 1922, was still being refined.

In 1925, George Gershwin's *Rhapsody in Blue* premiered, and F. Scott Fitzgerald's *The Great Gatsby* was published.

In 1927, Charles Lindbergh had a plane made to his specifications by the Ryan Company; Lindbergh successfully flew—nonstop—across the Atlantic, from New Jersey to Paris. Eight years later in Germany, Willy Messerschmitt was directed to design and build a fighter plane for supporting ground troops and attacking bombers—the Me-109 was the result.

In 1930, Grant Wood unveiled his *American Gothic* painting.

In 1936, a German scientist, Alexander Lippisch, invented the jet airplane and built a flying model. Hitler decided he wanted it to be a bomber, and eight years were wasted trying to make it efficient enough to carry a bomb load.

In 1934, the Boeing Airplane Company began work on an experimental bomber while the Army and the Navy bickered over the requirements and the purpose of a bomber. Two years later, the B-17 Flying Fortress was improved enough to go into production.

Herbert Hoover was elected President in 1928; thus, he had the misfortune of being President when the stock market crashed in 1929. Hoover had been a successful and competent mining engineer and businessman, as well as a great humanitarian; he bore the blame for the bank failures and economic depression resulting from the "fads, fancies and mass lunacy" of economic expansion in the 1920s.

It was during the period of the 1930s that the young people would "learn to do without." When banks closed, personal investments were lost. Many fathers were without jobs or resources, and there was a major depression in personal spirits, as well as the economy. The government developed programs to "make work," giving hope and a little income to those in need. Such programs helped to develop a work ethic that continued for fifty years. The young people from this era were called upon to fight a war—a war initiated by the unemployed paperhanger in Germany.

In 2001, a biography was written about a young man who served in WWII as a B-24 bomber pilot, became a prisoner of war, returned to successfully operate airport facilities, and was inducted into the Iowa Aviation Hall of Fame. While making a presentation to a local service club about the biography, the speaker recognized six individuals in the audience who had served in the air forces and who lived within two blocks of one another. Certainly, these represented six wartime experiences worth investigating and sharing. The initial group grew to nine people, all who lived in a community where several hundred persons could easily have been included.

The question might be raised as to why persons involved in the WWII air war should be emphasized—thereby overlooking the other branches of service; this exclusion is not deliberate, but is the result of the coincidence of circumstance. This book of the nine airmens' stories was a natural evolvement from research completed for the previous book. In this book, each airman's missions are listed in a separate chapter.

Read the lists of missions very carefully.

The frequency of missions, difficulties encountered, and exposure to peril all tell a good deal about the reliability and character of these young men. Through these stories, one can witness the day-to-day activities, the weather, and even sense the fatigue and fear they experienced. They traveled to places never anticipated by youngsters in rural America, were given responsibility for equipment well beyond their concept of cost, and were thrust into dangerous situations all too frequently.

The records kept by individuals varied, and most not only saved documents from during the war, but added to them as the years passed. Finally, interest in their involvement was renewed when wings, groups, and squadrons started having reunions. Many airmen returned to Europe and toured the old bases, communities, and nearby cemeteries. Some veterans have been involved in restoring and converting control towers into museums depicting the four-year sojourn when thousands of young Americans passed through the area.

The process of interviewing and recording information from the nine airmen was very interesting; their stories are vaguely similar, yet vastly different from one another. Each man's exposure to peril is similar, yet the men's reactions are varied. During the war, adapting to the local environment was often difficult, but faded in importance when faced with the necessity of performing one's duties.

Big bands were very popular during the war, and traveling shows made numerous appearances at camps and bases all over the world. When the airmen were asked what their music preferences were during the war, their answers were—again—similar, but varied. Some liked sentimental tunes, while others liked dance tunes, such as "Frenesi" and "Pennsylvania 6500." "The Air Force Song" was named three times as a favorite. However, the song the airmen mentioned the most was "I'll Be Home for Christmas."

Training in the Air Corps lasted for a little over one year, and a tour of duty was six to eight months. The exposure for the infantry soldier was unique because he went to North Africa in 1941 and returned home in 1945, with extended battle experience during that period.

Some of the nine airmen interviewed were married before entering the service, some were married while in service, and some were married after service. Without dwelling on the apprehension on the homefront, it is not difficult to imagine how those at home must have felt to have a loved one in danger in a land far from home.

While one veteran was being interviewed about his service experience, his wife stated several times, "I'm glad I didn't know him then. I would have been so worried."

Many parents and loved ones who sent a youngster off to war were indeed, "so worried," and all too frequently experienced the loss of that someone who was near and dear. That youngster would never know how much they would be missed, or that they would be perceived as a hero; they would never experience a honeymoon, the birth of a first child, a child's first day of kindergarten, or the raising of a teenager. They would never experience the fears, the tears, the years, and joys of an extended life.

This is the tragedy of sending youngsters off to war!

# BOOK ONE

# STAFFORD

*Lt. Robert W. Stafford*

*B-17 Pilot*

*Eighth Air Force*

*94th Bomb Group*

*333d Squadron*

"Hitler has heard from me now, so watch for the crumbling of Nazi moral[e], defenses, and all. My terms are unconditional surrender."

—Stafford

# STAFFORD
# CHAPTER ONE

331st Sqdn, 94th Bomb Group
Wednesday, August 16, 1944
(Written at Bury St. Edmunds)

Dear Folks

    Uncle Sam can discard the red pencil when marking up my activities: his eighteen month investment is paying dividends. Your little son is now a warrior—tried and true.
    When Atwood called "Bombs Away" on our first mission, my joy and pride hit a new high. It was really a great feeling.
    I felt as peaceful as a dove and harmless as a kitten as we glided along above the clouds. The air was refreshingly cool and the sun shone brightly. We were going to drop our bomb load, but I felt no more malice than a paperboy delivering his papers.
    But the Jerries sometimes misunderstand and when the flak comes up you kind of feel that it serves them right. I want to drop the bombs just as a matter of business, but when they start shooting the bombs drop with a vengeance.
    We had analyzed the psychological aspects of fear and all on coming into combat for the first time and the basis of our deductions was a newspaper article (the British papers have lots of feature writers) which said that only an abnormal person would be fearless on such an occasion.
    As we covered the beautiful European landscape and approached the target, I felt normal and prepared to be scared. I expected to make myself as small a target as possible. I had heard that at times like this I might sweat profusely. I wasn't sweating but expected to start any moment as the target appeared.
    I had all the available protection. Besides the plane's armor plate (with an extra piece stuck under the cushion of my seat), I was wearing my flak suit protecting my chest and belly and my helmet with flaps hinged to go over my earphones. Also I was wearing goggles to protect my eyes from flash burns.
    As we started the bomb run I could see the flak burst ahead. They are little black clouds that hang in the sky for hours and the sky is darkened by each succeeding burst. The Jerries also have rockets that

leave a white smoke trail corkscrewed at the top. All they do is break up in the black pattern.

I felt warm, but I wasn't sweating. I was quite comfortable with the flying activity and cabin heat. I was only wearing the sweater you knitted for me, and my flight jacket.

Finally we came over the target and the flak was there. I waited for the fear and the sweat, but it never came. I was even craning my neck to check up on the flak bursts. I watched the engine instruments which indicate battle damage and soon we were past and out of the danger area.

I am no heavy bomber fan, but I think Boeing is going to have a new convert after a few more missions. The self-sealing gas tanks and the strongly built fuselages are wonderful. The fighter protection is the very best insurance. Good old American P-51s, P-47s, and P-38s—their support is all the papers say it is.

We can send newspaper clippings of our missions, but we can't discuss the military aspects. I am enclosing three of the clippings with other articles from our ETO newspapers, the S&S (Stars and Stripes).

I am on a 48 hour rest leave, but I sent my blouse to the cleaners (finally) so I can't go any place. Frank and Bob went to London. Joe and I are taking it easy around here.

You can watch the exploits of the Eighth Air Force. But of course I only fly part of the time. Jimmie Doolittle is the CO of the Eighth. He's pretty popular in the states.

Our plane is "The Gremlin's Hotel." It's a swell plane and the ground crew is tops. We're thoroughly satisfied on that score as well as believing we've got a damned good [flight] crew.

I've made a few landings coming back from a couple of missions and am doing a lot of flying to make up for the quick B-17 training in the states.

I like the 94th. They seem to use their heads—regardless of Army tradition. We are well informed, equipped and trained.

Have spent several evenings in town, going to movies and the Red Cross Officers Club. In the movie "Tender Comrade" where Ginger Rogers tells her husband not to look at any of those English, Australian or Chinese girls brought down the house.

Hitler has heard from me now so watch for a crumbling of Nazi moral[e], defenses, and all. My terms are unconditional surrender.

Rather busy right now.

Love, Bob

# STAFFORD
## CHAPTER TWO

Graduation at Ames High School was always performed with a great deal of ceremony and importance. Perhaps it was because Ames was a college town—a Big Six college town—and the education of professors' children emphasized preparation for more education. The graduation ceremony in the spring of 1942 had a special meaning because many of the young persons would be directly involved in subduing the Nazis and Japanese in a world conflict.

After the customary opening prayers, musical interludes, speeches, and recognitions, it was time for the class to march on stage and receive their prized diplomas. Proceeding alphabetically, the young smiling faces and ill-fitting robes proceeded across the stage, shaking hands, receiving their diplomas from the Chair of the Board of Education, and repositioning the orange tassels on their mortarboards.

Robert W. Stafford shuffled along awkwardly, trying not to call attention to his crutches. His timing was not the best. Breaking a foot the previous week while running cross country in a track meet was an embarrassment to this modest young man. Bob was a good student, inductee of the National Honor Society, member of the staff of the school paper, and drum player in the school pep band. The quiet, studious young man took his schoolwork and responsibilities seriously. He shook hands with the Superintendent, received his diploma, and (with the help of friends) bounced down the stage stairs, returning to his auditorium chair and the Class of 1942.

Clay Stafford was a respected second-generation banker in the community, trying to recover from the Great Depression that had placed all banks in a bad light. The Depression was difficult for everyone, and the Stafford family was no exception. Clay Stafford and his bride Mabel (Hasbrouck) Stafford were of third generation English and French Huguenot ancestry. They had three children: Richard born in 1920, Margaret (Peggy) born in 1922, and Bob.

Bob, born October 17, 1923, had attended Beardshear Elementary School, seventh and eighth grades under Principal Mrs. Schmidt, and ninth grade at Welch Junior High School where

Principal John Harlan shaped young minds. A new senior high school was dedicated in 1939 at the downtown location of Fifth and Clark. At that time, a serious discussion ensued as to the location of the new high school for Ames; with one group wanting it in the campustown area, and another group thinking that a site just beyond Thirteenth Street would be a good location. Some folks felt that the city limits of Ames would "never extend beyond the potholes and prairies of Thirteenth Street," (although in certain sections it already had) and the school was finally built near the downtown retail area as a compromise between the two factions. Some sixty years later, the community extends two miles north of Thirteenth Street, and in 1980, the stately 1939 structure was converted to a City Hall. Bob's class was the first class to spend all three years of senior high school in the new building.

Bob learned the value of work early in his life, probably because of the Depression years, and had numerous paying jobs from age ten through high school.

After graduating from high school, Bob enrolled at Iowa State College (now University). He joined Beta Theta Pi fraternity, and worked hard to make the transition from high school to college. However, Bob decided to fulfill his service commitment after his first quarter of college, so he enlisted in the Army Air Corps on December 7, 1942.

At his pre-enlistment physical examination at Camp Dodge outside Des Moines, Bob answered the many questions—admitting to allergies, hay fever, and occasional sinus trouble. The doctor added to the list Bob's deviated septum from a broken nose received when Bob tripped over his mother's rocking chair; nasal problems were a serious concern for a prospective aviation cadet. At the exit interview, however, a sergeant asked Bob if he planned to have surgery before enlistments closed in just a week. He recommended that Bob see a Dr. Downing who had been the eye, ear, and nose examiner at his physical. Surgery was quickly scheduled and performed. The next week, with his nose still in bandages, Bob's nasal problems were erased from his record by a colleague of Dr. Downing, who was certain the surgery had corrected all of Bob's nasal deficiencies.

At age nineteen, his enlistment was accepted, and in March 1943, Bob Stafford reported to Jefferson Barracks in Missouri, where he was processed, received shots, and was issued military clothing. The organized chaos for young men making a transition to army life was a story unto itself. The long lines for food, physicals, shots, and shoes seemed never-ending. Learning to march was comedic at first. Knowing why you salute, when to salute, and how to salute seemed mundane, but even one mistake would be corrected and reinforced with a loud and vociferous reminder.

Bob was sent to Moorhead, Minnesota, to a College Training Detachment intended to expedite the two years of college that was a basic requirement for entry into the U.S. Army Air Corps. While there was some military training, most of the time was spent on college-level courses. The training included some exposure to flying, with several hours spent in a Piper Cub. The training did not last long, and in two months they moved along into the cadet pipeline.

Bob left, by train, for Santa Ana, California, for pre-flight training. He was then sent to Thunderbird II training base near Scottsdale, Arizona, for his primary air training. Everything seemed to be going well, but Stafford had one small problem.

Surviving broken noses, operations, and intense hay fever, he soon learned of another affliction. Bob was subject to motion sickness. This was not a mild airsickness. This situation was most disconcerting to his instructors as they were responsible for their equipment and they had to clean the airplane before the next student could have a lesson.

Thunderbird II was a private-contract training facility with one lieutenant assigned to represent the U.S. Army Air Corps (as it was then called). A cadet was required to fly solo within the first twelve hours of pilot training; because flying was continuous, each student had several instructors. Bob approached his twelve-hour limit and had not soloed with his Nisei instructor, so he was scheduled to ride with the Lieutenant in a pass/fail test in which he either soloed or was washed out.

After performing a chandelle (inverted flight and a barrel roll) correctly for the Lieutenant, Bob had to recover from a spin the Lieutenant had reversed after entering—which Bob had detected and properly reversed. The Lieutenant said they would shoot some landings and told Bob to take over after the Lieutenant incorrectly entered the flight pattern. Bob made the correction and landed the plane. Having watched Bob perform satisfactorily, the Lieutenant got out of the airplane and said, "Take it up." Bob taxied to the edge of the field, applied full power, and discovered the thrill of solo flight. He returned to the flight line and the other cadets promptly threw him into the swimming pool—following the local custom.

After soloing in the Stearman bi-wing PT-17 primary trainer, Bob continued to complete his flying requirements. The open cockpit bi-plane became Bob's favorite airplane because of its performance during aerobatics. Pecos, Texas, was the site for Basic

*The crew at Pyote, Texas, in April 1944. Front: Pilot Halm, Co-Pilot Stafford, Navigator Pettigrew, Bombardier Young. Back: Airmen Lucas, Jarvis, Ganry, Waite, Young, and Newman.*

Training flying the Vultee BT-13 and for Advanced Training flying the twin-engine Cessna UC-78 "Bamboo Bomber."

Bob Stafford graduated from Flight School in March 1944, in the Class of 44-C. Since his parents were not available and there was no "femme fatal" in his life, his squadron commander pinned on his pilot's wings. Stafford received a commission as a flight officer (a warrant officer) and not as a second lieutenant. Later, he was pleased to note that as a warrant officer, he drew more overseas pay than a second lieutenant.

Following graduation and his first leave in over a year, Stafford returned to Texas at Pyote Air Force Base where he was assigned as co-pilot in a newly formed crew. The crew continued to train from April 1944 until June 6, 1944. After the training session that day, they retired to the Officer's Club to listen to reports of the landings on the Normandy Coast, D-Day. The day was memorable in many ways.

The crew consisted of Pilot Frank Halm, Co-Pilot Stafford, Navigator Joe Pettigrew, Bombardier Bob Atwood, and Airmen Lucas, Jarvis, Waite, Young, and Newman.

The crew then boarded a train for Kansas and went on to Kilmer, New Jersey, where Bob boarded the Dominion Monarch for his boat trip to England. The British passenger ship appointments were very nice, even after the ship's conversion to a troop ship. Three officers shared a small stateroom with two beds, and had to rotate their sleeping schedule en route. The large ship, with excellent but crowded accommodations for the officers, headed for Glasgow, Scotland, plowing through the North Atlantic—changing courses every two minutes in order to avoid the Nazi "wolf pack" submarines.

Once in port, they immediately boarded the train for central England, near Oxford. This proved to be a dangerous location in England, because it was northwest of London in direct flight with the "buzz bombs" launched from northern Germany and Holland. The Germans loaded them with a quantity of fuel that would normally be expended over London but erratic fuel consumption and headwinds were variables affecting their accuracy. The bombs were not strategically targeted, but were of the "to whom it may concern" variety, meant to demoralize English citizenry by their random and violent damage. Because the Germans were not accurate in measuring the quantity of rocket fuel or familiar with the changing wind conditions, the rockets occasionally overshot London, damaging the countryside in and around Oxford.

The crew was ultimately stationed at Rougham Airfield near Bury St. Edmunds, a small community not without historical precedence. The famous and historic Magna Carta, which in June 1215 established a charter of liberties and privileges for citizens, was signed at Runnymede; the King (at the insistence of local Barons) affixed his seal to the Magna Carta in Bury St. Edmunds while in transit to Runnymede, assuring the Barons he would not recant his commitment.

Stafford and his crew were assigned to the Eighth Air Force, 4th Bomb Wing, 94th Bomb Group, first with the 331st Squadron and later with the 333d Squadron as a lead crew. Lt. Halm flew two missions as co-pilot with another crew to get the feel of combat flying, prior to leading his own crew into action. Several training flights prepared the men to work together as a team. They usually flew to adjoining airfields to pick up spare parts, and occasionally returned with their bays loaded with several cases of scotch for the Officer's Club and Enlisted Man's Club. Hence, the flights were sometimes called "liquor runs."

The crew appreciated their new B-17 Flying Fortress which was named *Gremlin's Hotel* and it served them well for eight missions until they became a "premier crew," after which they were

*The view from the tail gunner's position of a B-17.*

assigned a different aircraft. The B-17 had a reputation for having stability during flight and sturdy construction able to take combat abuse; it was also known for being easier to fly than the B-24 Liberator Bomber. The B-24, specially designed as a cargo ship, had greater bomb capacity, faster speed, and greater range; however, it lacked the solid construction of the Flying Fortress, and required constant flight attention because its narrow wing was less stabile in horizontal flight. Naturally, there was friendly conflict between the crews of the two major bombers, but you flew the plane you were assigned to fly—with no questions asked.

Once the breakout at St. Lo by ground troops occurred, the missions of the heavy bombers took on a new role—mainly bombing targets within Germany. After July 1, 1944, a majority of the tonnage directed toward Germany aimed at knocking out the production of jet fighters, which with some improvement could have dominated the airspace. It was common for bombing missions early in the campaign to be attacked by hundreds of Me-109s and FW-190s—inflicting tremendous losses of planes and crews. It was not uncommon for a bomber group to lose over half of their airplanes on a difficult mission. With the addition of long-range P-51 D fighters, bombers were escorted well into Germany and back, providing protection from marauding interceptor fighters.

When Lt. Halm and his crew first began to fly missions, air superiority had not been achieved, and there were significant aircraft losses. As the months progressed, escort fighters accompanied the bombers further and further into Germany. Stafford saw bombers go down, but their squadron was usually fortunate to remain intact.

Although changes in tactics and resources kept the Luftwaffe from sending up fighters, the Germans never ran out of anti-aircraft shells. They would disperse their anti-aircraft guns in a wide circle around the suspected target. When the bombers arrived at the Initial Point (IP) and started their bombing run, the Germans would send up a "box" of shrapnel that bombers would have to penetrate; because bombers could not use evasive action, they literally waded through the flying metal, until they could release their own packages of destruction. Although some bombers took direct hits from the cannon, most of the damage came from shards of coarse metal coming from all directions. The exposure for aircraft damage and personal injury continued without interruption until the end of the conflict. Although rarely expressed, these risks weighed heavily on the young men's minds because of their random nature and potentially severe damage.

The assembly point was where the bombers gathered to assume their position in the squadron formation. It took place over their airfield with planes flying a fixed pattern until they assembled. The planes would form their patterns at 10,000 or 15,000 feet, then climb to 25,000 feet when they entered enemy territory. With over 150 airfields in the area there would be many, many planes in the air at one time. Taking off with heavy loads of bombs from the several airfields required some time to gain altitude, as well as time to find your slot in the formation. The cloudy conditions prevalent in the area contributed to the confusion—but assemble they did, in formations of several hundred aircraft. A favorite route toward target was over the Frisian Islands, off the coast of Holland. There seemed to be a corridor without anti-aircraft or fighters—a sort of safe area. From the corridor they could disperse, turning toward their targets in Germany.

If the targets were socked in by weather, other targets of opportunity would be sought. It was better to leave a few "gift packages" or "calling cards" at alternate targets rather than return with a full load of bombs to dump in the North Sea. The development of radar meant you could see your target through the clouds, and missions could attack the main objective. Even with the most accurate of bombsights, bombing from five miles up could not guarantee hitting the target.

The Allies, after attempting many combinations of bombing patterns, developed a bombing technique for maximum damage during this phase of the war. The large formations carried a variety of types and sizes of bombs for a variety of effects. The lead airplane would drop its bombs as it approached the target. Other group bombers, who released when they saw bombs falling from the lead airplane, would release their bombs with the greatest number of airplanes over the target. Planes near the rear of the formation would drop incendiary bombs to start fires in the resulting debris, while the last airplanes would drop anti-personnel bombs in an attempt to keep away the persons trying to put out the fires. When General Sherman said that "war...is all hell," he was unaware of death raining from the skies. But he was still right.

Lt. Halm's crew, with Stafford as co-pilot, received a good deal of recognition because of the maturity and flying proficiency of Lt. Halm and the skills of the navigator, bombardier, and other officers. Operations' personnel positioned each formation in the best offensive lineup they could, much like a football coach. Lt. Halm's crew moved up rapidly from "tail-end Charlie," to lead a three-plane flight, to deputy lead of the squadron (taking over in case of damage to the lead plane), to lead plane of their squadron, then to lead plane of their bomb group (thirty to forty planes). Finally, they were fortunate to be the lead crew on a major 800 aircraft Eighth Air Force effort over Germany.

The prestige of being a lead crew had several benefits: they didn't have to fly combat as often, and they were given the best airplanes and equipment. The greatest benefit was they flew five fewer missions to meet their requirement. Instead of thirty-five missions, thirty was the requirement for completing a tour of duty.

Stafford had flown as co-pilot on his early missions, and on occasion, Lt. Halm let Stafford fly as pilot. Stafford had passed his training as pilot, but to assume that role in combat would mean a tour of thirty-five missions. The prestige of being a lead crew with the benefit of five fewer missions had greater appeal for Stafford.

The lead plane designation created a special problem for Stafford. As "group lead plane," the co-pilot's chair was often filled by an Air Force colonel or general who had charge of the mission. This meant the existing co-pilot (Stafford) became the formation control officer, riding in the tail gunner's cramped compartment, serving as a machine gunner, and performing additional responsibilities. Unfortunately, the "fish-tailing" action at the tail of the airplane reawakened Stafford's propensity toward motion sickness.

At his rear perch, Stafford had specific duties. To assemble the group of thirty-some aircraft following takeoff, the Formation Control Officer let out a colored magnesium flare on a long leash and ignited it with a jerk. The planes in the air over radio "bunchers" (signals) homed in on their lead plane by its proper altitude, location, and the colored flare. The group maintained radio silence so the enemy would not know the size of the offensive force. However, on the plane's intercom Stafford could suggest to Lt. Halm that he veer one way or another to facilitate the Flying Fortresses in their group seeking the proper assembly formations. Stafford communicated with the General in the co-pilot's seat via intercom, keeping him abreast of the formation's appearance, enemy aircraft activity (if any), and damage from anti-aircraft fire in the rear echelons.

After the mission, Stafford turned in his report rating the flying skills of the group's pilots. He rated the pilots who were following on their ability to maintain flying formation. He rated the tightness of the formation. He assessed the accordion-effect of squadrons dropping back and speeding up that might create a ragged formation. He reported the effectiveness of turns and formation realignment to the pilot and group commander as it might reflect on the mission's effectiveness in hitting the target.

Stafford's relocation to the tail position was not without responsibility. However, he still investigated how he might be relieved of his assignment because of motion sickness, but received no encouragement. The options were not favorable, and he decided to accept the circumstances.

Lead crews flew less often and received three-day passes instead of two-day passes. Stafford took advantage of every opportunity to visit London. As a shy and somewhat timid young man, he visited the historic sights, went to plays, took tours, and visited Parliament. His letters home reflect his interest in journalism, filled with activities of a cultural nature rather than hanging out in the pubs and dance halls. He used this opportunity to expand his education and expose himself to British culture. He wrote home frequently, and is known to have written six to eight letters to various friends at one sitting.

After every three-day pass to London, he returned to his base and climbed into his aluminum chariot "to walk on shrapnel."

Formation flying was practiced constantly—and with good cause. Flying lead in a group effort, a turn of ninety degrees (or any turn) meant a major transition of the airplanes following; the planes on the inside of the turn had to slow down, while the outside planes had to speed up. With a full load of bombs and ammunition, the response time was longer for speed changes and the potential for contact with other planes increased. Flying through clouds

*Lt. Robert W. Stafford at Rougham Air Field near Bury St. Edmunds, England*

meant loss of visual contact and "blind flying procedures" would be implemented. Wing planes might fly at forty-five degrees to the lead plane for a short distance, or climb or drop five hundred feet until they could rejoin. There were procedures for many eventualities, but they did not always work. With three squadrons in tow, thirty-six to forty airplanes in a formation could create pure chaos—particularly if formation discipline was not practiced. It is a marvel that more mid-air collisions did not occur.

Once air superiority was achieved by the Allies, missions were often flown with over 500 bombers intent on decimating the German production capability. Bombing airfields, rail yards, factories, bridges, refineries, and anti-aircraft sites would invariably produce some civilian casualties, which the Germans used for propaganda purposes. However, the propaganda machine failed to mention the damage inflicted by the Germans on the civilian population of England with V-2 rockets launched without specific targets in indiscriminate and barbaric destruction. The English people acknowledged this random devastation, kept their "stiff upper lip," and went about their business to end the conflagration and achieve unconditional surrender.

# STAFFORD
# CHAPTER THREE

As the war progressed, missions included more aircraft, and targets were more diversified. Fewer Luftwaffe fighter planes were dispatched to meet the incoming bombers, but occasionally a good number of them appeared to inflict as much damage as one or two passes would permit. Fighters usually attacked out of the sun, or the clouds, and usually on the nose of the first aircraft. The side gunners could not shoot forward, the navigator and bombardier were busy with their activities, and often the lead bombers were vulnerable to surprise. The belly gunner and top turret gunner could respond, but their turrets could not swing fast enough. Sometimes the Germans would repair downed P-47 fighters or a B-17 Bomber, and try to slip them into formation posing as a ship from another squadron. The intruders would give the altitude of the approaching Allies, then slip out of formation to avoid being hit by their own anti-aircraft barrage.

In the latter stages of the war in Europe, the Germans introduced their jet fighter. Developed in 1936, the High Command wasted several years attempting to develop the fighter as a bomber to deliver the bomb tonnage to force England's surrender. The early jets burned fuel in great quantity, and their range was limited. Had the High Command utilized their speed and maneuverability early in the war, the outcome could have been substantially altered. The Me-262 and Me-163 caused considerable excitement and damage when first introduced. They were much faster than our P-51s, and special formations and tactics had to be developed to overcome their superior performance capability. From his observation point in the tail gunner's position, Stafford watched several confrontations when six or eight P-51s spread out in a horizontal line behind the faster moving jet, and when the jet made a turn, as it eventually did, the Mustangs were able to cut it off and get their kill. Fortunately for the Allies, the remaining German pilots were young and inexperienced, which proved costly to their cause.

Bomber pilots had to deal constantly with the weather of the North Atlantic and the North Sea. The high moisture content of the air could potentially cause ice to form on the wings, and integral de-icing equipment had not yet been developed. The moisture content also caused condensation trails that were visible for miles, and aided the enemy in detecting incoming aircraft. Some clever German pilots would make a pass from the front, then fly through the formation and hide in the contrails. Tail gunners found that an occasional volley into contrails would flush out a German fighter.

The Allies' targets were usually over Germany and surrounding countries. Some targets, such as refineries and factories, were bombed several times. In one instance the Germans cleverly built a factory of sticks and canvas some distance from the real camouflaged location. Several missions damaged the fake factory, and when reconnaissance planes took pictures of the damage, the fake factory had already been rebuilt, ready for another deception. The Allies finally realized their error and obliterated the main factory.

## LT. ROBERT W. STAFFORD'S MISSIONS:

**Qualified for Instrument Card in accordance with AAF REG 50-3 dated January 6, 1943.**
**Passed: Instrument check March 2, 1944.**
**Successfully completed training and rated pilot March 12, 1944.**
**Total Hours: 242:55**

**Aug 6, 1944: AAF STA 468 (331st Squadron, 94th Bomb Group)**

**Mission 1:** 14 Aug 44. Mannheim Germany. First Mission: 26 Aircraft (A/C), 25 Bombed (Bd). Celebrated first mission without incident. Excellent weather. No flak.

**Mission 2:** 15 Aug 44. Handorf, A/F Germany. 30 A/C, 30 Bd. Flak intense, accurate and frightening. Got lost in clouds, ordered 180 degree turn to keep from flying into planes. Increased airspeed due to frozen indicator. Windows iced up; could have been a disaster. Coolness under extreme conditions duly noted.

**Mission 3:** 16 Aug 44. Rositz, Germany. 18 A/C, 12 Bd. Intense flak. Four bombers in other groups were observed exploding over Leipzig.

**Mission 4:** 24 Aug 44. Ruhland, Germany. 26 A/C, 24 Bd. Enemy fighters en route. Intense flak. One B-17 lost an engine; was shielded by friendly fighters.

**Mission 5:** 25 Aug 44. Rechlin, Germany. 26 A/C, 25 Bd. Arrived 19 minutes early; fighter escort appeared at appointed time. Intense flak. Damage heavy. Two planes from another group lost. No parachutes seen.

**Mission 6:** 26 Aug 44. Brest Tactical Target, France. 31 A/C, 0 Bd. Heavy flak and fighters on way. Poor weather (rain, haze, fog) over target. Returned with bombs not armed.

**Mission 7:** 27 Aug 44. Mainz-Northwest, Germany (Berlin) (alternate target) (94th Bomb Groups 200th mission). 35 A/C, 0 Bd. Flew new airplane. Deteriorating conditions, clouds built up. 180-degree turn ordered. Pitot tube iced up causing dive and 240 mph air speed. Corrected by applying pitot tube heat.

**Mission 8:** 01 Sept 44. Mainz, Germany (Tank manufacturing plant and flying bomb assembly plant). 38 A/C, 0 Bd. Clouds built up faster than aircraft could climb. Selected to be a "Lead Crew," assigned to 333d Squadron. Next two weeks spent flying every day, training as lead crew.

**Mission 9:** 26 Sept 44. Bremen, Germany (Submarine pens). 38 A/C, 35 Bd. Lt. Andrew Murphy joined crew as radar navigator operating a Pathfinder "Mickey" cloud-piercing radar set.

*Note: On September 27, 1944, Luftwaffe fighters pounced on a B-24 Liberator bomber formation near Kassel shooting down twenty-five aircraft. The 94th had bombed Kassel five days earlier without incident. On October 7, the 94th Group, without Halm's crew, was hit by forty or fifty fighters on a mission to bomb Bohlen, Germany, with eight bombers lost. Gunners claimed two to seven German fighters destroyed or damaged.*

**Mission 10:** 12 Oct 44. Bremen, Germany (Submarine pens). 30 A/C, 29 Bd. Moderate but accurate flak. Other units joined the 94th on the mission.

**Mission 11:** 19 Oct 44. Mannheim, Germany. 22 A/C, 19 Bd. Halm's crew led 4th Combat Wing "B" Group with two operations officers on mission. 2d Lead Crew assignment. Climbed to 29,000 feet due to clouds. Bombed secondary target due to weather. Moderate flak. Observed a fortress in a rear group spinning out of control.

**Mission 12:** 30 Oct 44. Merseburg, Germany (Synthetic Oil factory). 39 A/C, 0 Bd. Mission aborted due to weather; high clouds to 30,000 feet and enemy fighter contrails. Heavy flak and fighters on the way. Poor formation flying conditions and complaints from the rear echelons.

**Mission 13:** 02 Nov 44. Hamburg, Germany. 32 A/C, 30 Bd. Lots of flak, inflicting considerable aircraft damage. Halm's right wing (plane) was hit, fell back with two engines out. Tried to get to English coast, but no further word. Probably ditched at sea.

**Mission 14:** 06 Nov 44. Duisburg, Germany (RR marshalling yards). 29 A/C, 26 Bd. No Commander, so Stafford flew co-pilot. Briefing revealed up to 500 guns in target area. Flak was heavy, but not accurate. Bomb run flown in an arc to confuse radar. One plane aborted, collision loosened bomb racks, bombs rolling around. Plane returned and landed safely. 94th lost 3 bombers in preceding three days.

**Mission 15:** 09 Nov 44. Mainz, Germany (Saarbrucken was target, Mainz the alternate). 35 A/C, 0 Bd. Heavy flak and fighters on the way. Weather severe. The Pathfinder "Mickey" set failed on the lead aircraft and Halm's crew moved in to lead the Eighth Air Force. Command scrubbed mission, all planes returned.

**Mission 16:** 10 Nov 44. Wiesbaden, Germany. 38 A/C, 36 Bd. Assembly problems and weather en route caused problems. Flak was intense and accurate. Four planes damaged by flak, knocked out of the formation. Two airmen killed in action.

**Mission 17:** 21 Nov 44. Wetzlar, Germany. 34 A/C, 30 Bd. Flak encountered several times en route. Two planes aborted when hit by flak. One plane hit by flak, dropped bombs and returned. One B-17 and P-51 collided and both planes were lost.

**Mission 18:** 25 Nov 44. Merseburg, Germany (Synthetic oil refinery). 39 A/C, 32 Bd. Weather problems during assembly; clouds to 20,000 feet. Heavy flak did damage to most of the planes.

*Note: On November 30, 1944, the Eighth Air Force lost twenty-nine Fortresses. None of the 94th Bomb Group planes were downed during combat, but two of the 94th B-17s collided on final approach, and were observed by Lt. Halm and Stafford.*

**Mission 19:** 04 Dec 44. Mainz, Germany (Tank mfg. and flying bomb assembly). 38 A/C, 38 Bd. Winter weather worst on record. Heavy snow, ice, fog and low clouds made for risky conditions. Formation conflict today when an abrupt turn caused a low squadron to slide out of place and lose contact with the 94th lead; they bombed alternate target. Flak moderate but accurate. Losses due to weather exceeded losses to enemy action.

**Mission 20:** 15 Dec 44. Hanover, Germany. 37 A/C, 37 Bd. Weather worse than forecast. Diverted to secondary target. Meager flak. Two enemy jet aircraft sighted.

**Mission 21:** 27 Dec 44. Fulda, Germany. 36 A/C, 27 Bd. 94th led 4th Combat Wing. Big push to support ground forces during "Battle of the Bulge." Very cold, ran out of de-icer. Nine (planes) held back. Picked up 12 stragglers over England and five more near Belgium's coast. Bombed assigned target with good results.

**Mission 22:** 20 Jan 45. Hohenbudberg, Germany. 13 A/C, 7 Bd. Heavy snow, had jeep drive down runway to show location. Full power take off, but wheels hit top wire of fence. Plane No. 2 made it. Plane No. 3 hit fence and crashed, killing all on board. Stafford as Formation Control Officer attracted 11 more aircraft. Equipment malfunction and confusion over target. Seven aircraft bombed erroneously, others returned with bombs unarmed.

**Mission 23:** 06 Feb 45. Chemnitz, Germany. 38 A/C, 38 Bd. Weather and clouds worse than forecast; long mission with strong winds. Climbs and descents en route used up fuel supply. Alternate target bombed through overcast. Head winds on return held ground speed as low as 60 mph. Halm's plane hit by flak causing some fuel loss. Six bombers landed at former Luftwaffe base near battle lines at Valenciennes, France. Ate at soup kitchen with ground troops from the "Bulge." Negotiated for additional gas. On return to Rougham Field, maintenance discovered flak damage to main wing spar should have grounded plane in France. At Valenciennes, Stafford picked up altimeter from downed Canadian glider as a reminder of the mission. (Altimeter still in his possession.)

**Mission 24:** 16 Feb 45. Hamm, Germany. 35 A/C, 25 Bd. Moderate flak; good bomb score through broken clouds. One B-17 observed exploding at target area; no chutes. Another plane crippled.

**Mission 25:** 20 Feb 45. Nurnberg, Germany. 35 A/C, 35 Bd. Bad weather; low visibility frustrated the assembly. 94th became separated from Group over the English Channel but tacked onto another group to complete the mission. Traffic jam over target. Two B-17s observed in trouble; another floating in channel on way back.

**Mission 26:** 24 Feb 45. Bremen, Germany (Transportation hub). 38 A/C, 38 Bd. 1,150 plane raid. Marginal weather; bombed secondary target through overcast. Flak was accurate, the tracking barrage type. Lost two planes near target, but one turned up later in Belgium. Nine airmen MIA.

*Feb 28th.* Checked out as first pilot by Maj. Beuford C Bevins

**Mission 27:** 04 Mar 45. Ingolstadt, Germany. 36 A/C, 33 Bd. Hit secondary target through irregular cloud layers. Bombers showed contrails. Good Pathfinder run. Fighter escort all the way.

**Mission 28:** 15 Mar 45. Oranienburg, Germany. 38 A/C, 38 Bd. Crew led 94th with Lt. Col. Witham as Command Pilot. Heavy accurate flak for 30 minutes over target area. Aircraft in group ahead exploded. 94th plane hit badly; two engines smoking; four parachutes at 15,000 feet. Completed 94th Bomb Group's 300th mission.

**Mission 29:** 17 Mar 45. Ruhland, Germany. 39 A/C, 37 Bd. Led 94th Group. Extensive flak; most aircraft suffered some damage but all returned. In formation ahead two planes collided, breaking one in two. Saw crewman slide down deck into space without a parachute.

**Mission 30:** 24 Mar 45. Varrelbusch, Germany. 38 A/C, 38 Bd. Part of 1747 bombers and 800 Fighters in the attack force. Enemy jets sighted. Halm's crew completes 30 missions.

**Stafford completed 30 operational missions in ETO with a total of 241:05 hours.**

An English family named Hall lived next to the base. Their eleven-year-old son used to visit the base, and became friends with a number of the base personnel. They learned his father could develop film, so soldiers started sending their film home with young Cliff Hall, who would return the developed film. The pictures were of airplanes, accidents, personnel, and the usual soldier-away-from-home fare. The family was probably checked out to be certain they were not a nest of Nazi spies. By developing the photos, the family did the soldiers a great service. If taken into town, the film was subject to censorship, and sometimes half of the pictures were not returned. After the war, they learned the Hall family kept a duplicate copy of all the pictures they had processed, which proved to be a great resource for all the books and documents published after the war.

Lt. Halm's crew was extremely fortunate. They finished their tour intact, with no losses, and only one person injured. Waist gunner Bill Waite had taken a flak wound in the knee and received a Purple Heart. During their tour of duty the fighter response was intermittent, but the anti-aircraft fire never subsided. The greatest danger was from flying formation in inclement weather, and although collisions occurred in other squadrons of the 94th Bomb Group, the 333d was spared losses from collision.

November and December of 1944 produced some of the most severe weather in England and Northern Europe in a decade. Heavy snow, strong winds, and boiling clouds were commonplace and the cause of many fatal accidents.

In November, Lt. Halm and Stafford were hitchhiking on a main road running through the airfield, watching bombers return from the day's mission. They noticed two bombers on their final approach about to converge. A red flare from the control tower warned that the landing should be aborted. The lower plane climbed, its propellers hitting the plane above and both planes crashed, catching fire. When Lt. Halm and Bob arrived, it was too late to save the men still trapped in the airplane. The single survivor was a tail gunner. It was a very sobering experience, and especially sad because both planes were so close to getting home without incident.

Celebrating the 200th mission of the 94th Bomb Group created quite a stir. A very large celebration took place with a banquet, speakers, Glen Miller's orchestra led by Ray McKinley, and 700 young ladies brought in for the dance. Dinah Shore was the featured singer, with several other performers. Stafford and the crew had been on the base for only two weeks, but took part in the festivities. Stafford went to bed around midnight, and about 2:30 A.M. was awakened by Radioman Jarvis. Jarvis' marital status was in question, and he proceeded for an hour or so to "cry on Stafford's shoulder." It seems he had gone through a divorce, which he could deal with, but was totally offended that his former wife had the audacity to then marry the *pilot of a B-24 Liberator Bomber!*

Lt. Andrew Murphy had lost his crew and was assigned to Halm's crew as a radar-navigator. Murphy had been in England a few months, and when he was introduced to his new crew thought, "My God, I'm being assigned to a crew of kids." However, they had just been made lead crew, and he gained a new respect for them. They trained every day, perfecting technique, checking complex navigation equipment, and dropping dummy bombs on missions lasting seven to eight hours.

On one of their regular combat missions, the squadron diverted from their main target to another "target of opportunity," which happened to be the major Ludendorf Bridge at Remagen, Germany. Fortunately, it was not their most accurate mission. A short time later the bridge became the Allies first major entry into Germany, when a small contingent of German troops were unsuccessful in blowing up the bridge as American troops arrived. General Patton and the 9th Armored Division managed to get over 10,000 troops and tanks over the Rhine before the bridge collapsed from overloading.

The January 28 mission to Hohenbudberg, Germany, became a memorable mission. There was fresh snow on the ground, and without snow removal equipment, the pilots had to take off through the snow. The runway could not be identified, so a jeep drove down the center, to make tracks so the planes could follow. Lt. Halm's lead crew was first to take off in the early morning, their B-17 lumbered down the short runway, loaded to capacity with bombs. Since frost coated their wings, they caught the top wire fence at the end of the runway—but managed to stay aloft. The second plane managed to clear the fence. The third plane in the formation clipped the fence wire and plowed into the ground, breaking up in flames and losing all hands. The runways were changed after some delay, and the remaining planes took off, joining another bomber group. By that time, Lt. Halm's plane was at 15,000 feet, with one plane following. The control officer directed them to set off flares, hoping to attract a few stragglers and get the mission to nine airplanes of combat strength. Lt. Halm and Stafford did manage to attract additional planes, joined another bomb group, and continued on their mission. At the appropriate time the formation peeled off, striking the target assigned to the 94th Bomb Group. The 94th got credit for their mission that day when only two bombers from Rougham proceeded to the target and successfully left their calling card.

Fighter response was intermittent, and unpredictable. Frequently, Me-262 jet fighters would fly just out of reach of the bombers, not attacking. Just when the bombers felt secure, they would be surprised. On December 27, the Allies were warned that there might be a high concentration of German fighters en route. The 94th Bomb Group was spared, but the 100th Bomb Group of B-24s bombing Kassell, Germany, was attacked by over 100 Luftwaffe fighters with twenty-five Allied bombers shot out of the skies.

There were some interesting statistics compiled by the 94th Bomb Group:
- They flew 325 missions.
- They flew 68,153 combat hours.
- They used 8,500,000 gallons of fuel.
- They expended 2,661,100 rounds of ammunition.
- They lost 180 planes through all causes.
- They had 2,004 personnel killed in action, wounded, taken prisoner, or missing.
- They dropped 19,151 tons of bombs.

The introduction to *The Eighth Air Force Album*, a collection of pictures from that period in time, includes the following statement written by Lt. Col. John Woolnough (ret.) that bears repeating:

*"Most of us had an awful time in England. Sore throats and one cold after another. Never warm enough, food fit for Germans, fog, lumpy-damp beds and warm beer. You had to stand up on the trains or ride your bike if you wanted a little freedom. If that wasn't enough, the money system was a crime, there wasn't food in the restaurants, the*

pubs ran out of grog before you could get to the bar and you needed ration stamps to buy anything. Top that off with the fact that we had to get up at all hours to fight a horrible war every few days and you can see that England was not a lot of fun.

"All that has changed in retrospect. We see that period now as the most remarkable time in our lives. Most of us have not since been challenged like we were then. Many of us cannot remember more exciting times. We lived through an experience unique in the history of aerial warfare. We were part of the greatest air force ever assembled by any country. We fought in a cruel environment, under conditions that were next to impossible. We were part of history. At that time we thought it would never end—now we wonder if it really happened."

When their missions were completed, (now) Capt. Halm summed up his combat experiences:

"As a young man without any family ties, I had few responsibilities during my combat tour. To me the war was in a sense a great adventure. While I was scared to death at times, there was always a good feeling of challenge. I had a fatalistic attitude that I presume everyone had to have in some manner, but I also felt a certain immortality that said, 'It can't happen to me.' I must point out that this was not any kind of brave act on my part, but an attitude that helped me endure the strain of combat. Since the war I have often revealed my old feelings when people refer to the fearless fighters for freedom. I don't believe that this idealistic attitude was important to me. I believe that young men of every generation have felt the need of a challenge. I have often thought of this as I watch young men challenging authority and the establishment, and then progress toward more responsible views. I have thought that, in spite of the horrors of World War II, perhaps our enemy provided a means of venting our frustrations and emotions toward the cause of war, rather than fighting the inherited authority and social restrictions of our time."

It is easy to see why Frank Halm was chief pilot for a lead crew, and why he was a respected leader in the bomb group. Frank Halm and Bob Stafford have remained in touch and are close friends today.

For his efforts in the Eighth Air Force, Lt. Robert Stafford received:
- ✈ The Distinguished Flying Cross
- ✈ The Air Medal with four Oak Leaf Clusters
- ✈ The European Theater of Operations Medal
- ✈ The World War II Medal
- ✈ The National Defense Medal
- ✈ The Air Force Reserve Medal (received later)

Lt. Robert Stafford completed his missions March 25, 1945, and returned to the United States on leave soon after that date. He was at his parent's home on May 6, 1945, when Victory in Europe (V-E Day) was proclaimed. Lt. Robert Stafford had played his role in the destruction of the German industrial machine, which led to final victory.

# STAFFORD
# CHAPTER FOUR

**EXCERPTS FROM LETTERS HOME**

Stafford was a rather shy young man, probably more intellectual than athletic. He wrote numerous letters home containing great detail about his daily activities. The majority of the letters were six to eight pages long, hand lettered in a quiet, personal style. He responded to all mail, and some evenings would write five to eight letters at a time. Letters were written home every week, with V-mail letters in between to answer letters received. His parents saved all his letters. They are fascinating reading, as they chronicle Stafford's first arrival and captures his experience and growth to maturity as his tour of duty progressed.

His letters included small sketches of his corner bunk layout in his Quonset hut. He acknowledged receipt of his parents' letters as well as letters from friends back home. He always described the contents of the packages he received. At the conclusion of his letters, he would request items needed, and always asked for popcorn seeds.

When first in England, the crew's major activity was playing bridge, and Stafford would recount bridge hands and successful bids, as well as play. He later took advantage of his proximity to London and visited the city frequently. Rather than hang out in the Officer's Club, he would take tours, see stage shows, and go to movies or special events that he shared vividly with his parents.

Although all of Stafford's letters deserve some mention, selected excerpts give an indication of the young man's experiences living in England, growing up, and bombing the enemy.

**Friday Sept 1, 1944, 2016 [hours]**
*Dear Folks*
New developments—Our crew is to be a lead crew. We had our last mission now for some time. It was my eighth. We will be transferred to the 333d Sqdn.
The lead crews are the group leaders. We had progressed from a wing position to an element lead position and today we were picked for training as a lead crew by the 333d.

*The ramifications are many. It is a good break for Frank (First Pilot Frank Halm)—he should eventually make Capt out of it, as should Atwood and possibly Joe....As for me—I'm the oddball. It is supposed to be a break and all, but I am hardly sure of it. The Co-pilot rides as tail gunner and keeps tabs on the formation. He keeps the command pilot and pilot informed on everything in the formation and keeps the Sqdn leaders in position for good bombing and a good defense against fighters. The person doing this should be a pilot and an officer so the co-pilot ends up here.*

*Well you know that I've never been overwhelmingly in favor of flying and I didn't want co-pilot and I do not want to ride as a tail-gunner. It is just getting to be a question of how much I'm going to do or take to continue flying...*

*There are advantages. A lead crew (distinguished by a blue felt patch with a gold border worn behind the wings) gets the best of everything. They get the best planes, Motors Etc. In the 333d you get 3 day passes instead of 2 day. You don't fly nearly as often so it takes longer to get your missions in, but you don't have to have as many missions to complete a tour.*

*That's the dope. Were in the 333d Sqdn. We'll have to change quarters, just as I got everything fixed up so swell here.*

**September 16, 1944, Saturday 1710**
*Dear Folks*

*...Two enclosures: A picture of Frank, a navigator and I taken in front of Big Ben and the Houses of Parliament, just to the left of Westminster Abbey. That windswept skeptic on the left is me. The program from our 200th mission celebration held last night. We had a swell banquet with steak and ice cream and then went to a program in one of the hangars. The decorations were really good. The stage was beautiful and by the entertainers own admission, the best in the ETO. Glen Miller's band was led by Ray McKinley. Maj. Miller was planning a trip to the continent. Dinah Shore sang about ten request numbers and was very good. There were comedians, magicians, speeches and all. I had lent my hat to the magician for his act and when I went to get it after the show he said it was in Dinah Shore's dressing room. Well, Dinah Shore misunderstood my intentions, she thought I wanted her autograph. So I had to get an MP to get my hat for me...*

**Sept 25, 1944, 1710**
*Dear Folks*

...Well the general outlook is about the same on most everything around here. The politics concerning the crew and my position are rather obscure and most anything might happen....I have refused to fly in the tail position using airsickness as an excuse and am working with about 3 flight surgeons and others on the dial. I rather imagine I'll end up as a co-pilot on another crew....We are still training daily and will be at it for a little while yet...

**Oct 5, 1944, 2243**
*Dear Folks*

...I worked on my bicycle yesterday and put on a new back fender and fixed it up in general.

I popped corn tonight for about an hour and a half while listening to the World Series. I popped about 8 batches using butter and a lard can. Atwood, Frank and some of the others all enjoyed it. I better put in a request here for some more when you can get around to sending it.

I have my air medal in a nice case now and will send it some time this month. It is the medal with a lapel button et al...

**Oct 10, 1944, 1630**
*Dear Folks*

...There isn't any thing new in my case and I haven't flown tail since my last mission so maybe that is why I am more content....I have had a chance to do quite a little flying and shoot landings which is more to my liking. Frank and I will shoot landings tomorrow if nothing interferes...

**Oct 30, 1944,**
*Dear Folks*

...Saw Ted Heggen tonight at chow, but didn't get a chance to talk to him. He ought to finish up pretty soon...am listening to the Navy Notre Dame football game—Navy 32-ND 13...[Ted was an Ames boy flying B-17s out of the same base as Bob. Ted would return to become CEO of James Thompson and Sons Const Co of Ames.]

**November 12, 1944, Sunday 2010**
*Dear Folks*

...On missions, my latest score is the same recorded in the V-mail of a few days ago—16; my 16th was also Ted Heggen's 34th....

I'm getting used to my riding in the tail, but it doesn't make me like it. Of course the only sensible thing to do is do as you are told and I found out that sensible or not, it is the only thing I can do…If we have a rough day, Col Dougher (the C.O.) comes out and meets our plane and gets my full report first hand. As group lead I have to take care of my own formation as well as the other two squadrons.

I got some papers the other day certifying my rank as 2nd Lt as of Sept 22 by order of Gen. James Doolittle. Am waiting for the results of the ISC—Nebr game…

Personnel at Headquarters said the promotion was overdue and while the Order could not be backdated, they had a little leeway assigning a new officer serial number. The number assigned was easy to remember O-886600.

**Wednesday Nov 22, 1944**
*Dear Folks*
Packages coming in in big bunches. The S&S (Stars and Stripes, the Allies newspaper) tells us that there will be an average of 12 packages per person, 61,000,000 for 5,000,000 overseas (Army). Two packages today for me. One from Feldman's—a large can of popcorn (the perfect gift). One from Jake's with more popcorn and potato chips, the first I've eaten in six months….

…Now we lead the group which is a good job. 39 planes follow us and we take the shortest route which is nicer when riding in the tail. I've gotten sick several times, but just keep going. You get a swell view in the tail. As a group lead there is a lot more to keep me busy. Before we were a squadron with 13 planes. Now I am formation control officer for the lead squadron plus the whole formation of the hi and low sqdns, all three of which make a group. Then I help the Navigator (who has the hardest job in the group lead) get us in proper wing formation with 3 to 5 other groups I can see about 3/4th of the sky which is the best vision in the plane…

**Dec 5, 1944**
*Dear Folks*
…Listened to "Duffy's Tavern" one of my favorites…Off to operations at 1300. Yep we have to fly as usual. We are to drop 10 high altitude blues (100 lb practice bombs) and check the mickey.

While cycling to the drying room, I passed Ted Heggen. He said that he might be able to leave this pm so I told him what to tell you and that he shouldn't tell you where this base is even if you asked…

Another mission—19 now. Clipping enclosed.

Clipping: Stars and Stripes (no date)

**1,200 HEAVIES HIT NAZI RAILS**

Approximately 1,200 Fortresses and Liberators of the Eighth Air Force escorted by about 1,000 Mustangs and Thunderbolts of the Eighth and Lightnings of the Ninth, yesterday hammered rail yards and industrial objectives in the Reich.

The heavies struck at Kassel, Mainz, Giessen, Soest, and Bebra and elsewhere in western Germany.

Also in daylight yesterday RAF Lancasters continued the offensive against the railways of the Ruhr district with a concentrated assault on Oberhausen.

"German targets are due for the greatest weight of bombardment they have ever received, and winter weather will not protect them" Lt Gen Ira C. Eaker, Mediterranean Allied Air Forces chief, said, predicting the success of the new cloud-bombing techniques.

He described Ploesti as "the bloodiest air battlefield of the war," where U.S. losses were 350 bombers and more than 1,400 fliers. But, he said, **"It was worth it."** [Emphasis by author]

Eaker said a Rumanian official had told him that when Polesti attacks started the Germans were getting 26,000 tons of petroleum products daily from there, and when the attacks ended production had been cut to 3,505 tons daily.


**December 10 1944, Sunday 1435**
*Dear Folks*

*...This is a nice Sunday afternoon. The welcome pit-er-pat of tiny rain drops sounds on the roof ending our unseasonal drought of thirty-six hours.*

*....A lead crew does 30 mission now; subject to change. That's for officers. Our enlisted men will get along with less. Wing crews do 35 missions...I will be checked out as a first pilot when we get time, but are too busy now. It makes little difference and is only for the record, for I often fly the whole thing as 1st pilot with Frank as my co-pilot...If I were to get a new crew, we would have to train for a month and then I'd have to do 35 missions—there is no percentage in that...*

December 17, 1944, Sunday 2250
Dear Folks
   ...Your x-mas package with the Crisco and popcorn seeds arrived today, most welcome...
   No, the California X-mas package was from a girl I've never seen. I haven't had a chance to meet any English girls worth meeting. At least the type of girl that can be easily dated on casual acquaintance and about the only type an Army man meets, don't seem to appeal to me. While I would try to be democratic and say there was but one economic class in England, which there isn't—there are 4. I cannot help but notice the different levels of education which parallel the economic class distinction. A small minority of English girls go to high school, and a College girl is very rare. English girls are very much different than American girls. In general good conversationalists with little originality, heavily influenced by others. They don't seem to have any character that they can call their own. I would like to meet someone who might be representative of English debutants, even if only for drawing a psychological opinion. My moral code doesn't fit in well with the common run of Limey Lassie. So much for tonight's commentary—.

   Stafford's father, Clay, was an active Member of the Ames Rotary Club and encouraged Stafford to contact a local Rotary Club and express his interest in attending a meeting. The following two letters were received by Clay Stafford from Douglas Martin of District Thirteen, Rotary International of Great Britain and Ireland.

**Mr. Clay Stafford, Esq**          22nd December 1944

Dear Rotarian Stafford
   You will be delighted to learn that I received a call from your son Robert yesterday. He was very well indeed and had come to London on leave and was fortunate enough to have with him all the crew of his particular bomber. He tells me he has made 20 sorties over the Continent and has not so many more to make before being relieved of such duties,
   He expressed a desire to visit a Rotary Club and it was my pleasure to arrange for him to go to the Rotary Club of Battersea which is one of the 72 Rotary Clubs in greater London. There are about twenty that meet on Mondays, a similar number on Tuesdays and Wednesdays and a lesser number on Thursdays and Fridays, and it happens I have many friends at Battersea who I am sure would give him a warm welcome.

It is good to have these contacts, they all help to further our 4th Object. We do hope your son will be kept safe and well and before long will be on his way home again.
      Yours Sincerely     Douglas Martin

P.S. (handwritten) Strange to think at any moment day or night- even as I write this I may be blown to bits by a rocket bomb— without 1/2 seconds warning.


**Mr. Clay Stafford Esq.**           **28th December, 1944**

*Dear Rotarian Stafford*

Further my letter to you a few days ago I have received a letter from Bob this morning which speaks for itself and I quote below:

"I wish to express my thanks to you and the London Rotary Clubs for making it possible for me to attend one of your Luncheons. I enjoyed very much the visit to your office and the Rotary Meeting on Friday Noon in the Ardington Rooms. The members were most cordial and are planning to make it possible to stay with one of them for a few days during a rest leave in early January. My father will be very pleased to learn of your hospitality. Thank You. Sincerely..."

I am delighted to think of the reception he received and his kind thought in letting me know about it. In spite of five and a half years of the terrible strain of war – of living on an unsinkable aircraft carrier as this island has been described, we nevertheless wish to do our best to carry out the tradition of English hospitality.
      Sincerely     Douglas


**January 8, 1945, Monday 2200**
*Dear Folks*

...At the moment I am in a reflective mood having spent the day in London by myself. There are many instances and events which occur that I check mentally to mention when writing to you but a lot of them are lost before I get the pen and paper. Someday at home I'll remember the events and they'll make interesting conversation.

That "someday at home" brings to mind a funny philosophy. It is natural that I should think pro and con on the subject "of getting home sometime." Anybody in combat would, at least subconsciously, think of his 'chances.' Well, don't get me wrong. When I'm on a mission in the densest flak, I don't worry about being hit. That is something I can't conceive. But what I'm leading up to—I hope I don't break any censorship regulations here—the fact that when I hear a rocket bomb explode, and I will if it is within 20 miles, I realize a funny feeling. And what I am getting at is a repetition of the many tributes paid to the people of London who have gone thru the blitz, the buzz bombs, and are enduring the rocket bomb. I'll tell you about three instances today...Last time I was in London around X-mas I didn't hear one in the 3 days spent here. But you will know that there were at least 3 today—by the following.

I was touring the Houses of Parliament when one fell making a loud noise, which doesn't mean that it was necessarily close. The guard remarked, "They were busy again today!" Another fell during the show just after one of the actresses had cupped her hand to her ear and said, "Listen!" That really brought us a laugh.

And another time, everyone heard it but a deaf man would have noticed nothing. It's easy for me to be nonchalant but I really admire the Londoners who remain so after enduring so much....

**March 5, 1945, Monday 2104**
*Dear Folks*
I have 27 in now. I did my last mission with another crew....Our next mission will be a wing lead which is the next larger unit above a group and is composed of about four groups usually. Our last mission will be a division lead which is the highest. On the last mission I was on we led our division of several hundred ships.

...The other day we were flying at 18,000ft over an east coast city when we saw the vapor trail that a rocket leaves going straight up from the Dutch coast.

Another war reminder caused a little excitement here the other night. It seems a small force of German 2-engine planes were over dropping bombs and then they came down to strafe. I had gone to sleep early and was awaken by the warnings over our P A system. I was flabbergasted to say the least when a diving plane started blazing away with his 20 mm cannon close by. He just helped the farmers with their spring plowing tho. There was not much of a system to their attack. They just shot at random and any lights that might be showing. It was the first time piloted planes had made an attack of any size in 9 months...

**March 12, 1945, Monday 2138**
*Dear Folks*
   ...I left the base early Thursday morning and caught the 0943 train for London...Along the way I ran into Capt Kennedy, the Sqdn

bombardier and he and I got a room at the Reindeer Club in London. We lined up tickets for a play that night, and operetta the next. That night we ate dinner at the Grosvenor House and ran into Atwood who is also staying at the Reindeer Club. Ken and I saw the play "the Years Between," by Daphne Du Maurier and was very good as usual. The next day we ate lunch at the 'Junior Officers Mess' and then I went to the show "Keys of the Kingdom." We ate a nice rabbit dinner and saw the operetta "Gay Rosalinda" at night. The Operetta was based on Johan Strauss and was very entertaining.

Saturday...We went to the Gainsborough Motion Picture Studios which Atwood had arranged for us to go thru. We received a hearty greeting from a member of the publicity department and he took us on to several sets, including two on which they were shooting pictures...

We went back to Grosvenor House and I went to the show "Meet Me in St. Louis" and afterward wandered among the crowds in Picadilly.

Sunday morning Atwood and I went to church in Westminister Abbey. It is the service of the Church of England. While I was tentatively listening to the sermon, I estimated the center ceiling to be as high as a six-story building....

**WESTERN UNION  Mar 26 [sent 1945 Mar 27 PM 1 30]**
Mr Clay Stafford Box 626 Ames [Iowa]

HAPPY BIRTHDAY DAD  MISSIONS COMPLETED  BE HOME AS SOON AS POSSIBLE LOVE = ROBERT W STAFFORD

# STAFFORD
# CHAPTER FIVE

As was customary, Bob had enlisted "for the duration of the war." After his home leave, Bob reported to March Field, California. The general assumption was that pilots would be reassigned to the Pacific Theater of Operations. However, Bob was assigned to San Marcos Army Air Field in Texas where he flew training missions for cadets studying to become navigators. The military pipeline was becoming flooded with returnees from the European Theater. Bob had acquired enough points to meet the necessary number for separation from service, so he exercised that option and returned to Iowa, arriving July 4, 1945.

The war in the Pacific was progressing with heavy losses of life. Over 100,000 civilians died in the Philippines before the Americans reclaimed Manila in March 1945. Over 6000 American soldiers died and 19,000 were wounded on Iwo Jima, with 22,000 Japanese deaths. In April, the Okinawa invasion saw 110,000 Japanese killed, with 12,000 Allied soldiers dead and 37,000 wounded. It was apparent the war in the Pacific would get more costly in terms of human life.

Then, on August 6, 1945, Col. Paul Tibbets and his crew made the memorable flight to Hiroshima, Japan, to deliver "Little Boy." Three days later "Fat Man" was dropped on Nagasaki. Unconditional surrender (V-J Day) was accepted on August 14, 1945, and the final terms were signed aboard the *U.S. Battleship Missouri* on September 16, 1945.

Unknown to Bob, while he was attending Iowa State College prior his to entry to into the Air Corps, a process for purifying uranium was underway in a small wooden building next to the Dairy Industry Building. This modest temporary building, named "Little Ankeny," had no outward signs of security, but unknown to the students and faculty, was under a twenty-four hour watch. The system for processing uranium would ultimately furnish over 2,000,000 pounds for the effort that produced the atomic bomb.

Bob returned to Iowa State College in the fall quarter of 1945. Since many service men were returning, housing was a serious problem. Bob had pledged Beta Theta Pi fraternity when first attending Iowa State College, but the chapter house was full of students and returning veterans, so he lived at home. That fall, he was in charge of building the fraternity homecoming display. He received a good deal of satisfaction when it won first place in the homecoming competition. After completing his sophomore year, he transferred to Northwestern University in Evanston, Illinois, where in 1948 he received a bachelor of arts in business administration.

Earlier in 1948, the U.S. Army Air Corps was being divided between the Army and the new U.S. Air Force. Bob chose the Air Force Reserve, maintaining his status during the "Cold War" as an Air Force Reservist while attending Northwestern University; he was attached to a unit located at Chicago's O'Hare Field.

Every summer after high school, except for during the war years, Bob and his classmate Roscoe Earl Feldman had spent summers in Estes, Colorado, working at the Cheley, Colorado, Boys and Girls Camp. It was a popular summertime job for young high school and college students. While substantially less hazardous than herding B-17s over Germany, there was a similar exhilaration in climbing the highest peaks in Rocky Mountain National Park.

One day, Bob caught a glimpse of a Girls Camp counselor wearing a University of Iowa (U of I) sweatshirt. She noted his Iowa State tee shirt. Since U of I and ISC are traditional rivals, their acknowledgement of each other was decidedly cool—on the surface.

The counselor, Virginia Rosenberg, had a transportation problem. Ginny was a member of Alpha Delta Pi Sorority, which was holding its national convention at the Stanley Hotel in Estes Park about five miles away. The president of the U of I chapter of Alpha Delta Pi was Anne Gilman from Ames, a close high school friend of Bob's. Ginny let Bob know that his friend was in Estes Park, and could she please ride with him if he went to visit her? It seems that Bob owned a 1935 Ford which was one of the few autos belonging to a camp staff person in post-war 1946. Bob got permission from the camp leader, a date was arranged, and it was the start of a lifelong friendship—and marriage.

The next summer, Bob and Ginny (now engaged) returned to the Cheley Camps as hiking counselors. It was amazing how often Ginny's girls would be on a peak around noon to find Bob and his boys arriving at the same location via a different route.

Virginia's mother passed away when she was nine years old. Ginny was taken in and raised in Burlington, Iowa, by a loving and caring aunt and uncle. She was very active on the debate team at Burlington, and spent a good deal of time preparing and excelling in that activity. The Rotary Club of Burlington had started a youth

*Robert Stafford and Virginia Rosenberg on their wedding day August 29, 1948.*

club called "The Spider Web," which was available to all high school kids, and was attended by both parochial and public school members; it was quite active and continued for twenty-seven years before it was finally closed for lack of participation. This was Ginny's second major activity—hanging out there with her friends.

Ginny's successes in high school won her a debate scholarship to the University of Iowa, in Iowa City, which enabled her to continue her education. She continued to earn honors in debate, and was elected to the Phi Beta Kappa scholastic honorary. During her sophomore year, she was asked to join the Alpha Delta Pi social sorority, where she made many lifelong friends. Later, Ginny served six years as national president of the sorority.

Ginny was selected to become a counselor at the Cheley Camps in Estes Park, Colorado, where she enjoyed working with junior high and senior high students and met the young business student from Ames who was attending Northwestern University.

Ginny was not particularly impressed that Bob was a war hero. In fact, he never mentioned it. But, their relationship flourished and they decided to marry when Bob graduated from Northwestern.

On August 29, 1948, Bob and Ginny were married in Trinity Lutheran Church in Burlington. Marjory Ingvold, a fellow camp counselor, was maid of honor, and Bob's brother Dick was the best man.

Their honeymoon took them downriver to Nauvoo, Illinois, and then on to Chicago where they—and their 1935 Chevy coupe—boarded a boat and toured the Great Lakes, with side trips to Quebec, Canada, and Niagara Falls.

After graduating from Northwestern University, Bob accepted a position in Des Moines with Central Life Assurance Company, where he worked from the fall 1948 until February 1951. Having joined the Iowa Air National Guard, it was only natural that he was recalled into service at the outbreak of the Korean conflict. Bob and five other young executives from Central Life were recalled, creating some difficulties for the insurance company. Bob had become good friends with his immediate superior, John Hawkinson, Financial Vice President, who understood investing and spent time with Bob—who was eager to learn. They maintained a close relationship long after Bob left the firm, with John being a tremendous influence in Bob's life.

In March 1951, Bob's air guard unit, the 132d Fighter Wing, was sent to Bangor, Maine, with Bob as Finance Officer. Six months later, he was selected to attend Accounting and Disbursing Officers School at Fort Benjamin Harrison Air Force Base in Indianapolis, Indiana. He left Virginia, who had started work on a graduate degree, with a two-year-old child, Marcia—and a sled for transportation. He was gone for three months. While at school at Indiana, he learned the Air Reserve in Columbus, Indiana, was eager to have more pilots, and they quickly checked out this former multi-engine pilot. He flew AT-6s and C-47s on weekends, and graduated from the school with a bonus—his flying status was restored. Bob returned to Bangor when he completed training to see if Ginny was still pulling the sled.

Bob and Ginny developed a great affection for the citizens of Maine. The locals were a very thrifty lot (a real virtue in the eyes of any Finance Officer), and spoke a most unusual language. The midwesterners' favorite Maine expression was the word "ayuh" which roughly translated to "okay." The locals were also thrifty in the rental ads, such as "Rent with flush, call XXX-XXXX." The midwesterners were equally amused by the opening day of salmon-fishing season. By tradition, the first fish caught was always presented to the Governor, and fishermen lined both sides of the Penobscot River below the dam at Bangor on April 15, bumping elbows, tangling lines, and hoping to make that presentation.

However, by now the streams were so polluted from logging and industrial wastes, it took several days before the first salmon was caught.

In the spring of 1952, the 132d Fighter Wing moved to Alexandria, Louisiana. Alexandria proved to be an interesting assignment.

Alexandria was not only a military field, but also a municipal airport. Having been promoted to Captain, Stafford was the Finance Officer with two qualified deputies. Later, a letter arrived addressed to the Commander, 6th Liaison Squadron. The Wing Adjutant, unable to find an appropriate command to accept the letter, opened it himself and read that it was an activation order for the new 6th Liaison Squadron. Because Captain Stafford was a pilot on flying status, and because the Finance Office had three officers with a table of organization for only two, he was given the dubious honor of organizing the 6th Liaison Squadron, which he did on Special Order No.1. On Special Order No. 2 he named himself Commander.

With no aircraft and no airmen, Stafford assumed that nothing much would become of the 6th Liaison Squadron, so he continued as Finance Officer. Shortly thereafter, a teletype informed him that a new L-20 DeHaviland Beaver aircraft would arrive the next day from its factory in Canada, and—as the Commander—he should accept it. He did, leaving it tied down on the apron.

A few days later, another teletype and another airplane. This time, the pilot who ferried the aircraft from Canada was a commercial pilot, who had several hours of layover before returning by commercial flight. Stafford contacted the commercial pilot, who gave him a one and one-half hour instruction in the L-20 before catching his plane for the return trip.

The fighter command was ordered to provide logistical and personnel support for the new squadron, and Stafford left the Finance Office to organize his headquarters staff and ground staff. Initially, they housed in tents, but Stafford finally found something more permanent.

The Base Operations Officer, a Colonel, stopped by to indicate he would like a ride in the new L-20. Stafford advised him that he was limited in flying time in the new plane, but the Colonel was not deterred, and became Stafford's first passenger.

In the months that followed, Stafford found a dozen pilots on the base in desk jobs who enjoyed flying the six passenger 450 horsepower Beaver. Because of its advanced omni-navigational equipment and cruising speed of 127 miles per hour, flying the plane was a welcome change from shuffling papers.

The 6th Liaison Squadron ended up serving the local population in a number of ways. No rain had fallen in Louisiana for over a hundred days, and the skies were dark from the smoke of forest fires. The fires were started by disgruntled Cajuns who objected to the government policy of planting indigenous pine trees on Federal land; they much preferred oaks and pecans that were the staple diet of the Cajun hogs. Stafford and his "desk pilots" flew many missions with local firefighter spotters helping to control the numerous brush fires. Stafford also piloted radio broadcasters with national hook-ups who were reporting on this back-country war, which ended as soon as the seasonal rains returned.

Another time, they flew a young lady who had contracted polio to a hospital in New Orleans for treatment.

The base's C-47 used by the 132d Fighter Wing football team was down with a maintenance problem and was unavailable for one of their crucial games with Eglin Air Force Base in Florida. The 6th Liaison group was called upon to transport the team—six planes, five players each. The trip down was late in the afternoon, landing after dark. The return trip also involved flying at night. Few of the desk pilots were checked out for night flying. So, on the flight to Eglin, Air Force Base, Stafford conducted a night flying training exercise—flaps down, wheels down, landing lights on, etc.—over the radio. At both of the destinations, Bob circled the field talking to each pilot on his final approach. The mission was completed without a hitch, but Stafford cannot recall whether their team won the game.

With his twenty-one month tour of duty soon to be completed, Stafford was exploring his options. His replacement as Liaison Squadron Commander had already taken over, and Stafford was filling in as Air Base Adjutant—a position that required a Top Secret clearance. He had received an employment offer from the hometown bank of which his father was the president, but the proposed salary was about one-half of that of an Air Force Captain on flying status. The security clearance investigator was certain that Stafford was returning to civilian life; Stafford, with strong support from his wife, considered the salary differential and re-enlisted for a new twenty-one month tour.

From Alexandria, Louisiana, Stafford was transferred to Godman Air Force Base, at Fort Knox, Kentucky, with instructions to decommission the base—keeping the airfield open as long as possible. His credentials as Finance Officer on flying status were essential to the assignment because the Base Commander was the only other remaining officer who was a pilot. The books were closed

*Members of the Comptroller's office, 132d Air Defense wing, Iowa Air National Guard: Captain Jim Weinman, Finance Office; Lt. Franklin Peterson, Statistical Services Officer; Lt. William Lyons, Management Analysis Officer; Captain Robert Stafford, Comptroller).*

on Godman Air Force Base at the end of 1953. Fort Knox is the location of the U.S. Gold Bullion Depository, and while performing his duties, he and Ginny managed to take a trip through the vaults. He found the tour most interesting—as would most Financial Officers.

Stafford's next assignment was as Deputy Comptroller, Ninth Air Force at Pope Air Force Base in Fort Bragg, North Carolina. Major Woods, the Comptroller, was an officer he had worked with in Bangor, Maine. When the base Finance Officer died suddenly, Stafford assumed that position once more.

In 1954, Bob returned to the Ames Trust and Savings Bank in Ames, Iowa, where he had worked while in high school. He continued as a member of the Iowa Air National Guard until 1966. He served as finance officer and, later, comptroller of the 132d Fighter Wing out of Des Moines—a well-respected fighter group. Bob enjoyed his military association with the Guard, traveling to twenty-one states, and making numerous friends—some of who are still his closest friends today. Bob retired as a Colonel in the Iowa Air National Guard.

On January 1, 1968, Bob became President of the bank (now known as First National Bank in Ames), showing good leadership during its growth and expansion. At that time, deposits totaled $16,433,000. On March 29, 1971, they opened the doors to their new facility at Fifth and Burnett streets in Ames. Numerous new facilities were added, including the state's first "grocery store bank," several branch banks, and additions to the main bank building. In 1993 when Stafford turned over the presidency to Daniel Krieger, the deposits totaled $116,000,000. Banks in four neighboring communities are affiliated with the Ames National Corporation. Bob is chairman of the bank holding company's Board of Directors, which has assets of over $600 million. Bob continued as CEO until his retirement; he still maintains an office at the North Grand Branch of First National Bank in Ames and can be found there every banking day.

Ginny and Bob had four children; Marcia Marie was born in Des Moines on July 2, 1949, Craig William was born in Alexandria on November 17, 1952, Brian James was born in Fort Knox on December 13, 1953, and Maren Jo was born in Ames on May 7, 1957. The children have enjoyed personal success, and as of this writing, Bob and Ginny are proud grandparents of ten grandchildren and one great-granddaughter.

The 94th Bomb Group Memorial Association was organized in 1975 with Colonel Frank Halm as its first president. The group held biennial reunions at various U.S. locations through October 2000, with attendance among the largest single bomb group gathering in the U.S. Air Force. Post-reunion tours took many of the members back to Bury St. Edmunds and Rougham Field. Colonel Halm was also editor of the group's newspaper, *The Nostalgic Notes*. While the 94th Bomb Group Memorial Association has disbanded, another generation has taken over under the name of the 94th Bomb Group Auxiliary Association and a reunion was held in Omaha, Nebraska, in October, 2002. In England, a very active Rougham Tower Association also preserves the memory and publicizes the exploits of the 94th.

Bob and Ginny returned to England for a reunion of the 94th Bomb Group, and also have attended most of the reunions in the United States.

Although Stafford learned to fly under adverse conditions (preparing for war) for a task most uncivil (killing the enemy), he loved the sensation of being airborne. The opportunity to soar through the air, penetrate the clouds, and view the world from above, created an excitement he has never lost. Even the missions, other than the exposure to deadly flak and frenetic fighters, were

*The crew at the 1985 reunion: Andrew Murphy, radar officer; Frank Halm, pilot; Robert Stafford, co-pilot; Robert Atwood, bombardier; Joe Pettigrew, navigator.*

an esthetic experience. Perhaps the regimen of preparing to fly enhanced the euphoria of freedom of movement through space. The act of guiding a vehicle above the debris of gravity and experiencing the sensation of airborne flight will always delight and excite Bob Stafford.

On Friday, July 3, 1992, the Bury Free Press printed a special edition, entitled "Wings Over Here," to celebrate the fiftieth year of American troops arriving in England. A segment entitled, "Friendly Invasion," deserves our attention:

```
"AND SO they arrived, the young men from over
there. The date was 1942, and they came in their
thousands—nonchalant, confident, and eager to fight.
Some were returning to the land of their ancestors
and many were never to see their American homeland
again.
    Fifty years on we pay tribute to those who joined
the crew of what became known as the "unsinkable
aircraft carrier"—East Anglia. Their planes droned
ceaselessly into the local skies as day in and out
they pounded enemy targets.
    A thousand bombers were often to be seen in the
skies at a time. On occasions there were as many as
3,000 aircraft in tightly packed formations heading
from East Anglia towards enemy lines.
```

A total of 150 air bases dominated the regional countryside, about 30 of them were in Suffolk and 37 in Norfolk.

The arrival of the US Army Air Forces proved a devastating blow to the Germans. East Anglia became home to squadrons of Flying Fortresses and Liberators, aircraft which required crews of nine or ten, plus a huge army of ground crew to keep them airborne.

The cost in terms of human sacrifice can be counted on the headstones at the American Cemetery at Cambridge.

In all some 28,000 men died in missions from East Anglia, a further 18,000 became prisoners and about 9,000 were reported missing.

In the early days of their arrival airmen only had a three to one chance of completing the 25 missions required before they were sent home.

The Friendly GI invasion of our own shores helped to turn the tide of a conflict that had already been raging for rising three years. It also changed a way of life.

It is difficult today to imagine East Anglia as it was then. The pace of life was governed by the speed of the plow, as it had been for generations.

The young arrivals from the New World shared none of our inhibitions. They came from a world of technology that seemed light years away from our own. We may have spoken the same language and shared a common enemy—that was about all.

The Americans became our friends—and were ever in our thoughts as their bombers so often limped home on a wing and a prayer."

# BOOK TWO

# PHILLIPS

*Capt. Rollen Phillips*

*B-24 Pilot*

*Fifteenth Air Force*

*49th Wing*

*461st Bomb Group*

*765th Squadron*

*"I had several near-misses,
but many 'lucky' things happened to me."*

*—Phillips*

# PHILLIPS
# CHAPTER ONE

Rollen Phillips was at home in Nevada, Iowa, on December 7, 1941. At twenty-two years of age, his life would change significantly, but he does not remember any special response to the events of that day. The nation was starting to recover from the Great Depression, which had severely affected the Phillips family. Perhaps it was just another obstacle to getting back on their feet.

Wendell Phillips was married to Grace Arnett in December 1916, during the Great War; they settled on a farm near Marathon, Iowa. Wendell and Grace spent the "roaring twenties" trying to get their feet on the ground by farming in the area. Their only child, Rollen, arrived June 10, 1919, born in the farmhouse near Marathon. The family worked hard to make a livelihood in the rural community, but never seemed to get ahead.

The stock market crash in October 1929 affected banking nationwide and caused a massive rearrangement of agricultural ownership. The Phillips family became a victim of this unparalleled tragedy in America. It meant that Wendell would be a laborer or tenant farmer for the rest of his life.

The Phillips name was English in origin, but Rollen's grandfather was born in Canada, and there is no record as to how the family came to the United States. Rollen's grandmother's heritage was traced back to Wales, but again the progression of the family lineage is not recorded.

Wendell Phillips found employment as a mason's tender, and moved his family to Nevada, Iowa. Carrying bricks and concrete block, mixing mortar, and setting up scaffolding was physically demanding, but he was fortunate to have an income to provide for his family. Many families had no such opportunity. The next decade would produce a mindset of hopelessness, benign acceptance, and loss of self-worth.

Wendell Phillips worked hard as a laborer, in order to keep his employment intact. However, in 1931 he had an appendicitis attack that put him in the hospital for two weeks, after which he needed another month to recover. When he returned to work, he was devastated to learn he had been replaced.

A neighbor who lived next door in Nevada owned a farm in Story County and decided to give up farming, so he offered to rent his farm to the Phillips family. The farm was next to the Shipley Township School north of Nevada, which was handy for Rollen to attend. The family acquired a cow and a few chickens, started a garden, and could once again feed themselves—even though cash flow was low. They managed to scrape by, as most Americans did, during this period. During the severe winter of 1936, the Phillips ran out of coal for heating their house, and Wendell approached the farm owner for an advance of cash to purchase some coal. The owner said, "Wendell, I have only ten dollars, and I will give you five." Somehow, they survived the bitter cold and continued on the farm.

Rollen worked diligently on the farm while attending Shipley School, graduating from high school in the spring of 1937. He managed to find work assisting local farmers as a hired hand. His hard work and dependability assured his being needed as the seasonal work on the farms demanded.

One evening, he received a phone call from a friend in the Methodist Youth Fellowship (MYF) asking him to join in a youth activity that night. This was a period before television, when young people generated their own entertainment. It seems the MYF was having a "scavenger hunt" where young people would pair up to find an odd assortment of items assigned to them—some rare, most ridiculous. Rollen agreed to attend, and was paired with a young lady, Betty Russell, and they proceeded to race around town collecting their list of items. They don't remember winning any prizes. Their biggest find was each other.

After that evening they dated regularly, spending a lot of time roller skating under the big tent at the Story County Fairgrounds to the "Skater's Waltz," and participating in other MYF activities.

Betty's parents were farmers in Talmage, Iowa, near Creston, in Union County. Betty was born in the farmhouse, and was delivered by a doctor who neglected to file a birth certificate for several weeks. After the family pestered him enough, the doctor finally filed the certificate, but it wasn't until sixty years later that Betty realized she missed the opportunity to become a much younger woman, had vanity prevailed.

When the draft started, Rollen enrolled (as all young men had to do), and he received a draft number that indicated he would not be called immediately. However, after December 7, 1941, Rollen gave some consideration to enlisting.

Christmas 1941 was special at Betty's parents' house. With the impending conflict, everyone was apprehensive about what the future would hold. Betty and Rollen were going steady, but all future plans were on hold. For Christmas, Betty had splurged and purchased a very nice wristwatch for Rollen. Rollen had given Betty a large, beautifully wrapped package, and when she opened it, she was dismayed to find a box of miniature chocolates. It was difficult for her to hide her disappointment, but Rollen mentioned that she might look at the second layer of chocolates. She lifted the top layer, to find an engagement ring inserted in the center chocolate. Christmas 1941 exceeded her every expectation.

Rollen Phillips had never been in an airplane. He had seen them putt-putt overhead while working in the field, but he had never seen one up-close. He had seen pictures of military airplanes in the newspapers, but never the real thing. He decided he wanted to become a pilot—at least it *seemed* like a good idea.

Pilot training required a four-year college degree, which was later changed to two years in college. The demand for pilots was so great that they instituted further change so a person passing an examination would qualify. Rollen decided he wanted to learn to fly, acquired some books, and studied independently to get the background basics in mathematics, geometry, and some trigonometry. He traveled to Fort Des Moines for the examination, and passed "with flying colors."

He enlisted on April 4, 1942, but was not immediately inducted. The Air Force policy was that air cadets were not accepted if they were married. Rollen and Betty were quite serious about their relationship, and decided that they would wed after Rollen got his wings. In August, he received his orders to report to Kelley Field, Texas.

Rollen would later state about his service experience, " I had several near misses, but many lucky things happened to me."

*Cadet Phillips next to a Fairchild PT-19 during Primary Training at Uvalde, Texas.*

# PHILLIPS
# CHAPTER TWO

The several training sequences in the Air Force occurred in nine-week sessions. Pre-flight was the induction into service when you learned to march, salute, make beds, and learn about military conduct. You also got into physical shape through rigorous training, obstacle courses, and moving about the base in double-time. Rollen's nine-week session was shortened to four and one-half weeks. Lucky!

From there they went to Uvalde, Texas, for primary training, and the first opportunity to fly. They were flying Fairchild PT-19s. Normally, they flew with one civilian instructor, but Rollen had three instructors during his stay, one of whom was Bill Lounsbury from Colo, Iowa. Lounsbury lived only seven miles from Nevada, but Rollen had not met him before service. Mornings were spent in classroom instruction, and afternoons were spent in a cockpit learning to fly. On one training flight making turns, the flight instructor put Phillips on a course and said to take the plane down. Rollen noticed they were heading downwind, so he circled the field and landed upwind. The instructor jumped out of the plane and said, "Take her up." Rollen later said, "I took off, returned, and survived."

While at Uvalde, Rollen accumulated a number of "gigs" for minor indiscretions during training. The penalty was to "walk the calieche," or blacktop, for an hour carrying a duffel bag full of blankets. It seemed easy enough, but Rollen found out that a duffel bag full of blankets can sure get heavy. He did not have another "gig."

The next station was at Randolph Field, Texas, which had two sets of runways and could fly BT-13s on one runway, and BT-14s on the other runway. Both planes had 450 horsepower and were more of a challenge than the PT-19 with its 175 horsepower engine. Phillips was assigned to fly a BT-14 with a closed cockpit, and he adjusted to it quite naturally.

During Rollen's nine-week training session, Betty, and Rollen's father, Wendell, decided to catch a train down to Randolph for a visit. Betty was not about to lose her Iowa boy to a Texas "darlin'." They arrived a day early without a hotel reservation for the first night and started looking for a hotel. They ended up walking well into the Mexican section of town, which was unnerving and a bit scary for "simple Iowa farm folk." When they managed to find a hotel and check in, Wendell told Betty to put a chair up to the doorknob so no one could break in. Wendell hid his wallet under a pillow so it would be safe from robbers. In reality, they were probably safer there than in a highly transient facility close to the base.

Basic Training included dropping in over power lines, night flying, and instrument flying. At night in Texas, a haze or cloud would form about six feet off the ground every night and was often mistaken for the ground by incoming pilots. This miscalculation probably explained the number of aircraft with a cracked center section on the wheel supports.

Night flying proved to be interesting. One night while flying in formation, the lead ship's lights went off, and Rollen reacted by backing off the throttle just a bit, so as not to overtake the plane ahead. When the lights reappeared, he was in perfect position.

Flying under a hood, the instructor would give directions for the student to follow, and rate the student on his ability to follow instructions. The instructor said, "Go to 300 feet, bearing 160, rate of climb 300 feet per minute, level off and turn forty-five degrees, cruising speed of 160, back off a bit, right, right, left, hold it." Rollen took off the hood to discover they were flying in formation with other planes.

They moved to Ellington Field, outside Houston, Texas, for Advanced Training. At that location, instructors would determine if the cadets would become fighter or bomber pilots. Apparently, Phillips was destined not to be a fighter pilot, as he was assigned to fly a BT-10 twin-engine trainer. The plane was sensitive to handle because of the tail wheel. If the plane turned too abruptly, it would immediately go into "ground loops," spinning in uncontrolled circles in one spot. Night flying cross-country was performed in an AT-6 with 650 horsepower, which gave the pilots experience with a more powerful engine. Gunnery training took place flying over Matagordo Island, shooting at ground targets with machine guns that fired through the propellers.

As graduation neared, Rollen made arrangements for Betty's arrival and a wedding. He had made friends with Lt. Frank Sergeant from New Hampshire who had similar plans, and they agreed to be witnesses for each other's wedding. Betty and Rollen had no trepidations about the possibility that Betty could become a widow because of the exposure of his aircraft to the German

*Second Lieutenant Rollen Phillips and Betty Russell were married April 22, 1943, outside Ellington field, near Houston, Texas.*

Luftwaffe. Their decision was made on the basis that "things would work out."

On April 22, 1943, Class 43-D graduated at 9:00 A.M. Rollen Phillips received his wings and a temporary commission in the Army of the United States as Second Lieutenant, with his bride-to-be pinning on his wings and bars. That evening, both couples were married in a local church by the church's minister. The ceremony had no special adornment and no one in attendance other than an organist—who was practicing Easter music at full vibrato. It is a casual observation that such simple ceremonies almost guarantee a marriage that will last for over fifty years!

Six members of the graduating class did not get furloughs, but were immediately shipped to a new duty station at Moses Lake, Washington. Phillips was one of those selected—assigned to the base about one hundred miles from Spokane.

Betty and Rollen grabbed their suitcases and immediately boarded a train for Spokane. They had to ride a packed chair car aboard a train that did not have an extra seat or a dining car. The first three days of their honeymoon was spent riding a crowded chair car on a slow-moving train and dining on apples and Ritz crackers obtained from the Red Cross in railroad stations along the way.

Betty and three other wives found housing in Spokane, while their husbands rode the bus a hundred miles to the base. Moses Lake was not prepared for the new arrivals, so the husbands made numerous trips back and forth.

A number of new B-17s finally arrived at the base, and Phillips was assigned as a co-pilot to a new crew, complete with navigator, bombardier, pilot, and gunners. Mornings were spent in the classroom, and afternoons were spent flying. Formation flying and dropping dummy bombs were the main emphases. Saturdays, they received shots, and went to the gunnery range. They were required to run through an obstacle course on their way to the range, and one day they ran for a quarter-mile wearing gas masks. There was a link trainer at the base, and the pilots also spent time brushing up on their flying skills.

Once again, their group was placed in an accelerated program, so the nine weeks were cut short. Six co-pilots were selected to become first pilots, and Phillips was fortunate enough to be selected. (Lucky again?) They moved to Geiger Air Force Base outside Spokane for another nine-week training session. They concentrated on flying formations, high altitude flying, and practicing bombing.

When training was complete, they were to go to Pendleton, Oregon, to pick up a new B-17. They were loaded aboard a six-by-six truck for the long drive to Pendleton, sitting on wooden slats that were most uncomfortable. Phillips apparently bruised a bone in his bottom, and visited the hospital in Pendleton to have it looked at. Close inspection discovered a cyst close to the tailbone, and Phillips was given the option to live with it being uncomfortable, or to have it removed. Phillips chose to have it removed, and was sent back to Spokane to the Army hospital. It turned out that the cyst was a prenatal condition that had grown to the size of an index finger; the removal kept Phillips in the hospital for six weeks.

Phillips's B-17 crew acquired a new pilot in his absence. They picked up their new airplane, went overseas, and were assigned as a replacement crew in the Eighth Air Force in England. While on the seventh mission over southern France, their formation was attacked by German fighters. The plane took a direct hit in the bomb bay, and the plane exploded with no survivors. Again, Phillips's temporary setback was fortuitous.

When Phillips was released from the hospital he was reassigned to Peterson Field in Colorado Springs, Colorado, to be a part of the 484th Bomb Group flying B-24s. After being checked out in the B-24, Phillips was assigned to be pilot and was given a new crew. His co-pilot resented Phillips's advancement, since he felt he should have been promoted to that position—but he ultimately accepted his role and became a valuable part of the team.

The B-24 was developed just prior to America's entry into the war. It was developed by Consolidated Aircraft to increase bomb capacity and speed over the other airplanes in service at the time. The plane's gross weight of 64,500 pounds could carry 6000 pounds of bombs as well as 6000 pounds of ammunition for defense against enemy fighters. The plane was 67 feet long with a wingspan of 110 feet. The four huge Pratt and Whitney 1200 horsepower engines were capable of attaining 290 miles per hour, and when fully loaded would cruise at around 200 miles per hour. The B-24 was the only airplane that served in every theater of military operation during WWII.

The B-24 was a totally different airplane from the B-17. It was faster, had more carrying capacity, and had a special wing design that gave it more lift. However, the special wing design caused the plane to be less stable in horizontal flight, and it had to be adjusted in flight constantly. The wing tips might vary as much as six feet from ground to flight; the weight of the engines and a full load of gas would cause the wings to droop while on the ground, but when airborne they would slope upward. If they started going different directions, the pilots really got worried.

One of the most important objectives in four-engine flying was coordinating engine speed—having the propellers rotating at the same speed. Rollen learned that use of the controls, dials, and visual observation kept the plane performing smoothly and efficiently. Having been trained in a B-17 probably made him more aware of the subtleties of four-engine flight. Any flying differences between the B-17 and the B-24 were overcome, and training continued for overseas assignment. As to which was the best airplane? You flew the one they gave you!

The group was temporarily moved to Harvard, Nebraska, and Phillips was put in charge of the troop trains en route. A few of the enlisted men found the box lunches before they were to be handed out and ate their share. In Denver several men slipped off the train to find a liquor store, and still managed to find Harvard, Nebraska,

*Rollen and Betty just prior to his going overseas.*

on their own. Several other minor skirmishes convinced Phillips that he was not cut out to be a "train commander."

Betty and a few other wives dutifully followed through all the Air Force Base changes, finding housing in apartments, or renting houses on a short-term basis. Each community near the bases recognized the circumstances surrounding the young couples' transient needs, and there always seemed to be something available. It may not have been the most desirable housing, but the wives learned to accept what was available in order to spend a few precious moments with their loved ones.

That time of year Harvard, Nebraska, was cold and desolate, which created problems with oil lines on the airplanes, as well as other minor problems. The bomb group flew from Harvard to El Paso, Texas, for a brief time for additional training, and was finally sent to Lincoln, Nebraska, a staging area for going overseas. At Lincoln, Phillips, as pilot, had to sign for his aircraft to the tune of

*Lt. Phillips and his crew as they prepared to leave for North Africa.*

$240,000. This was the customary practice for equipment located within the continental limits of the United States. Phillips decided that if he lost his airplane he would have to become a general in order to pay for it. At the military service pay scale in those days, he would have to be a general for a long, long time!

The day finally arrived that Betty had dreaded. Betty and Rollen both knew that someday they would have to say their goodbyes when the overseas assignment came. It would be extremely difficult for both of them. Betty was particularly fearful, but was consoled when a young nineteen-year-old navigator named Grayson put his arm around her and said, "Now Betty, don't you worry. We'll take good care of your guy."

Grayson ended up having four sons—all of whom attended the Air Force Academy.

From Lincoln the crew flew to West Palm Beach, Florida. At ten o'clock the next night they were given an envelope and a compass heading, climbed aboard a plane full of gas, and took off following the heading. After flying one hour as instructed, they opened the envelope and learned their destination was Tunis, North Africa.

The first stop was the Isle of Trinidad. The next morning they flew over the mouth of the Amazon (it was *huge*!) on their way to Belem, Brazil, on the east coast. They spent the night in tents that were mounted on concrete slabs thirty inches above level land. It seems that during a heavy rain, this barely kept the tents above water.

From Belem they proceeded to Foraleza, Brazil, also on the east coast, and then onto Dakar, Senegal.

A large gas tank had been installed in the bomb bay to extend their flight time, and was used first before switching over to the wing tanks. The crew sat huddled behind the gas tanks with some comfort since the temperature was not too cold. It seems that 9000 feet was the best altitude for conserving gas and airplane performance. There seemed to be a permanent front of clouds on the horizon, and they ran into rain and storms intermittently.

From Dakar they flew up the west side of the Atlas Mountains to Marrakush, Morocco, in the Sahara Desert. Daily temperatures were well over 100 degrees, but at night the sand released the heat and the temperatures plummeted. Sleeping in a "tent city" on cots proved to be a chilling experience. Each cot had five blankets, and the proper mixture of blankets above and below would determine if you froze from the bottom up, or the top down. The secret was finding the best "wrap" to even out the layers and still be able to get out of them in the morning.

From Marrakush they flew to an air base near Tunis where they laid over for a few days. The crew decided to visit Tunis, and particularly the Casbah, whose intrigue and mystique appealed to the young airmen. The streets were narrow and crowded with cloth-covered stands piled high with goods. The odors, the local dress, and the items for sale were most interesting, but they were warned to be out of the Casbah by 5:00 P.M., because servicemen were not safe after that. So much for the romance of the Casbah.

The local toilets were a revelation to the Iowa boy. A simple six-inch diameter hole in a concrete slab over a sunken container—with no privacy—was not as elegant as an Iowa outdoor privy, even one with loose hinges.

During the eight days they were in Tunis they noticed an enormous pile of war material fifty or sixty feet high just outside the base. One day, several of the crew decided to investigate the pile, and when they were about twenty-five feet up the side had several rifle shots zing past. They were informed the pile of material was off limits to everyone. Their curiosity was not rewarded. The ultimate disposition of the contents of the hill of material made them even more curious.

Flying over the Sahara Phillips experienced a rare occurrence, a phenomenon called "St. Elmo's Fire." This unusual occurrence was described by the French-North African pilot Antoine De Saint-Exupery in his book *Wind, Sand, and Stars*. Phillips noted this phenomenon on his number-one propeller—the tips exhibited a condition like sparklers, or a phosphorescent glow. Some believed

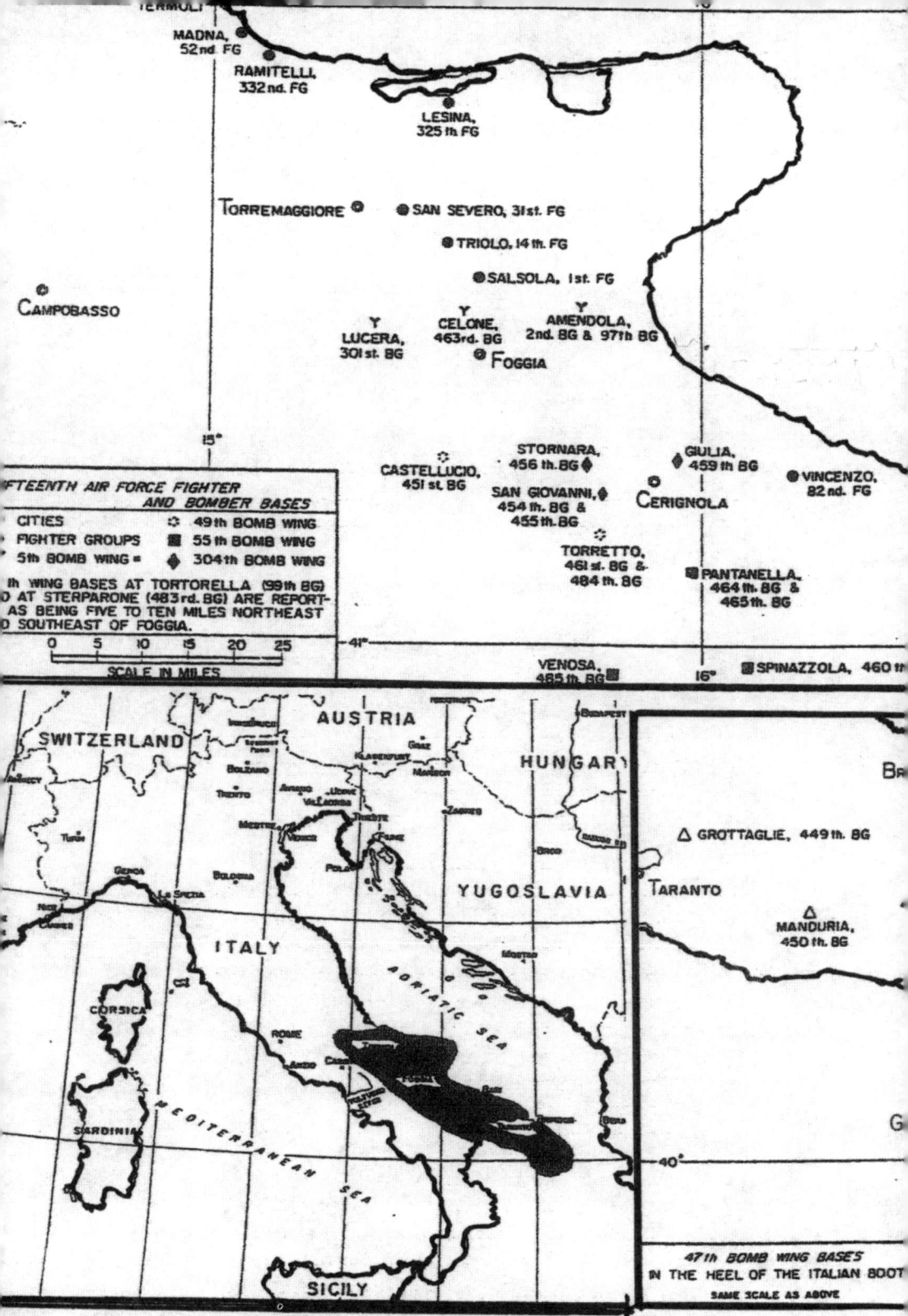

Map of the airfields on the west coast of Italy.
Ground troops had retaken the southern half of Italy.

PHILLIPS | 73

*Living quarters in Camp. Notice the side flaps are extended over makeshift walls to increase the size of the tent floor area.*

it was due to static electricity, but why was it on one propeller and not the others? The "fire" was sometimes seen at sea, but was a more common occurrence when flying over the desert.

The next stop was Sicily, and then on to Torretto Field in central Italy near Foggia. It was an airfield captured by the Allies in early 1944, with two runways serving two bomb groups. The 484th Bomb Group used one runway, and the 461st used the other.

Phillips and his crew were assigned to the Fifteenth Air Force, 49th wing, and the 461st Bomb Group.

Initially, Phillips flew as a co-pilot on three missions to get the feel of combat and to experience the variety of problems that must be addressed during a mission. Early in the war, the Germans sent up fighters to attack prior to the drop area, then tried to hit stragglers on the way home. As the Germans ran low on gasoline, the fighter attacks were less frequent, but any bombing mission might be hit by a gaggle of fighters trying to disrupt the Allies in their bombing efforts.

Once in rotation, crews flew every few days. Crew members were often rotated or substituted due to injury or fatigue, but Phillips's crew managed to remain intact during its tour of duty. The operations staff had a difficult time, since they did not always know how many crews or planes would be available. Some targets would be more costly than others, and operations had to select the right experience for a difficult mission, knowing there would be casualties.

And of course, there was always the anti-aircraft fire. The Germans never ran out of anti-aircraft shells, and were most effective in placement of artillery and altitude bursts to do the most damage. Pilots talked about being able "to walk on flak," and being able to "dig foxholes in it." New crews knew little about what they were getting into, but somehow it all worked out for Phillips's crew.

The Norden Bombsight was supposed to be the best bombsight in the world, but its accuracy was suspect because of the variables superimposed on it. When flying in formation, the lead navigator set the course, and other navigators spent their time double-checking the flight path and keeping watch as gunners. The bombardiers followed the lead bombardier. The scariest part of the mission was when the pilot told the bombardier, "It's all yours." At that point, the bombsight took over flying the airplane, and would hold position, altitude, glide, and tell them when to open bomb bay doors to release the bombs. The other bombers would then release on the sight of bombs falling, hoping to saturate the target area. On one mission the report was, "Missed the bridge again." Or as Phillips said, "Sometimes we hit the target, and sometimes scored a hit on a donkey in a field."

Score was kept by the number of hits within a 1000-foot-radius.

Cloud cover was always a problem, sometimes affecting bombing runs as well as affecting the flying personnel. A mission over Verragia was very misty, and cloud cover was so heavy one could not see the plane on his wing. Phillips suddenly became disoriented and experienced vertigo, thinking he was flying sideways. He asked the co-pilot to take over while he tried to gain control of his faculties. It was a terrible feeling not to be in proper orientation. After a minute or so there was a break in the clouds, so Phillips could see the ground and he immediately regained a sense of stability.

Staying healthy was most important. All the crew—and especially the pilots—made a conscious effort to avoid catching colds, which caused ear problems affecting balance and stability, especially when airborne. Since missions were flown at 20,000 to 25,000 feet, oxygen masks were worn, and if you had ear problems, you did not fly. The temperature varied with the seasons—with it being beastly cold at minus forty degrees in the winter at 25,000 feet, to damn cold during the summer. It was usually cold enough to chill down a couple of beers secretly stowed aboard. Crews made it a point to not eat gaseous foods because at 25,000 feet the air pressure is quite different from sea level, and the stomach would bloat with some pain involved.

Crew responsibility was critical, with each person held accountable for their area of expertise. Phillips had great respect for the crew engineer, whose responsibilities included handling communication, the radio compartment, and the gas controls—adjusting the tanks for uniform consumption, thus making the plane easier to handle. He also knew how things worked and was a problem solver en route to the target.

There were instances when the Germans would send up a lone fighter plane to radio the bombing-run altitude, so anti-aircraft could set their fuses at the correct level to inflict as much damage as possible. Other times, Germans repaired a B-17 that would float into a mission—acting as a stray or lost plane to give location and altitude. They would then drift away as they neared the fire zones. In other instances, the Germans learned the radio frequency in use that day, and successfully helped disabled planes to land, only for the pilot to discover he had landed at a German airport.

Phillips's crew had trained for several months, flown halfway around the world, and were now assigned a unit, a field, and had a job to do. They were a part of a bigger team, and were ready to help that team damage as much of the Third Reich's industrial capacity and ability to wage a brutal war as they could. These young men had a $260,000 flying machine that could carry 6000 pounds of bombs of all sizes, shapes, and descriptions, and could deliver them deep into German territory. They were ready for their opportunity.

# PHILLIPS
# CHAPTER THREE

Records for bomber group missions were kept in numerical sequence. The missions pilots flew varied from day to day and were governed by what planes and crewmen were available, as well as the difficulty of recent targets. The listing of Phillips's missions below are for his sequence only. Once the missions started, Phillips flew with his original crew. Some crews would experience injuries or sickness and the roster would be filled with airmen as they were needed. The men manning the machine guns were rotated more frequently than the pilots, navigators, and bombardiers. As pilot, Phillips flew three missions as a co-pilot to gain combat experience before assuming command of his own plane. When missions began, Phillips was fortunate enough to be located in the interior of formations, rather than in outer "Tail-End Charlies" who had greater exposure to fighter attack.

The crew had arrived in the 461st Bomb Group in early April. They flew their first mission April 17, 1944. Phillips's first mission was actually the 461st Bomb Group's fourteenth mission.

**Mission 1:** 17 Apr 44. Target: Belgrade Zemun Airdrome, Yugoslavia. Target was obscured, no bombs dropped.

**Mission 2:** 24 Apr 44. Target: Chitila Marshalling Yard, Bucharest, Romania. The third trip to Chitila. Bomb rack malfunction on lead plane caused bombers to overshoot their target. Of 25 fighters seen, several encountered, one destroyed, one damaged.

**Mission 3:** 30 Apr 44. Target: Alessandria Marshalling Yard, Italy. Clear skies. Only 17 percent of bombs hit targets.

**Mission 4:** 1 May 44. Target: La Spezia Harbor, Italy. Heavily overcast. Formation split, one cluster bombing La Spezia, others hit eight alternate targets in northern Italy.

**Mission 5:** 6 May 44. Target: Pitesti Marshalling Yard, Romania. The axis of attack was down the track line rather than across the RR lines. Missed original aiming point, but eliminated 5,500 feet of track.

**Mission 6:** 10 May 44. Target: Wiener Neustadt, Nord Airdrome. Rough Weather. Hit hard at Initial Point by fighters; approach into strong headwind kept formation in flak for eleven minutes. Destroyed seven enemy planes, seven probables, three damaged. One bomber lost, 26 damaged, one ball turret gunner killed. Phillips's plane had minor damage.

**Mission 7:** 13 May 44. Target: Imola Marshalling Yard, Italy. Target assigned was Marshalling Yard at Faenza. From Initial Point (IP) wrong target selected at Imola. 28 percent of bombs hit within 1000 feet of aiming point. No aircraft seen.

**Mission 8:** 17 May 44. Target: Poroto Ferrajo Steel Mill and Harbor (Elba Island). Good weather, good bombing. Score 29 percent within 1000 ft.

**Mission 9:** 23 May 44. Target: Subiaco Road Junction, Italy. Tactical mission in support of ground forces in Italy that were pushing the enemy northward. Ground maps used as target charts. Flying over mountainous area, although 8/10 undercast. 67 Percent within center of impact.

**Mission 10:** 25 May 44. Target: Carnoules Marshalling Yard, France. Now bombing in France. 35 Percent within target area and roundhouse.

**Mission 11:** 27 May 44. Target: Salon De Provence Airdrome, France. Extremely heavy flak at coast. Airdrome housed a nest of Ju-88 that raided shipping in Mediterranean. Score 24 percent. One plane lost, heading north into France.

**Mission 12:** 29 May 44. Target: Wiener Neustadt Werke 1, Austria. Flak intense and accurate. 461st arrived at target first; had to change course since another bomb group was dropping on top of them. Crews were enthusiastic about coverage given by our fighter escort.

**Mission 13:** 31 May 44. Target: Concordia Vega Oil Refinery, Polesti, Romania. Enemy added smoke screen to fighter and flak concentrations. Score 27 percent on mission. One plane lost, one made it to Island of Vis, where crew bailed out. All missed the island and are presumed lost. Commendation from Commanding Officer.

**Mission 14:** 2 June 44. Target: Szlnok Marshalling Yard, Hungary. Good weather; little flak. No enemy fighters.

**Mission 15:** 5 June 44. Target: Fornovo di Taro RR Bridge, Italy. On this mission Lt. Col. [XXX] took his turn at missing the bridge. Target obscured by clouds, missed by 1000 ft.

**Mission 16:** 7 June 44. Target: Antheor Railroad Viaduct, France. High overcast made it necessary to drop bombs from 18,000 feet. Using 1000 lb. bombs, score of 49 percent with several direct hits on the viaduct. All planes returned but 18 damaged, and six combat crew wounded.

**Mission 17:** 11 June 44. Target: Giurgiu Oil Storage, Romania. Group score of 44 percent. No flak, but 18 enemy fighters. Six enemy destroyed, four probably destroyed, and one damaged. Two bombers lost, one man injured.

**Mission 18:** 13 June 44. Target: Porto Marghera Aluminum Plant and Storage, Italy. Many complications. The lead plane aborted, and deputy lead navigator missed orientation. Eleven planes aborted, and deputy chose alternate target at Marghera instead of Neuauging Aircraft Factory, the original target. Aluminum factory destroyed, but AF refused to score mission.

**Mission 19:** 23 June 44. Target: Giurgiu Oil Storage, Romania. Second trip to oil storage area using 1000 lb. bombs instead of 250 lb. Flak intense and accurate with 29 planes damaged but none lost. Two men injured. 68 Percent within 1000 feet of impact point.

**Mission 20:** 25 June 44. Target: Avignon East Marshalling Yard, France. A diversion from oil storage targets. Good weather, no fighters or flak. 26 Percent of bombs on target.

**Mission 21:** 26 June 44. Target: Korneuburg Refineries, Austria. Refinery in open country covered by smoke from explosions of first two groups in the wing. Most bombs missed target area. One plane left at Initial Point and disappeared. Received commendation from General Spaatz.

**Mission 22:** 30 June 44. Target: Blechammer south Synthetic Oil Plant, Germany. Very bad weather, completely undercast. Intense, heavy flak and effective smoke screens. Bombing done visually with unobserved results.

**Mission 23:** 3 July 44. Target: Bucharest Mogasaia Oil Storage, Romania. Target obscured with cloud cover, some planes bombed alternate target. One plane lost due to mechanical failure.

**Mission 24:** 6 July 44. Target: Aviano Oil Storage, Italy. Target only 600 feet square, bombed with fair results of 48 percent. One plane had completed fifty missions out of 56 the Bomb Group had flown.

**Mission 25:** 8 July 44. Target: Korneuburg Oil Refinery, Austria. Weather excellent; lots of fighters and damage by flak. 52 Percent success within 1000 feet of impact point.

**Mission 26 :** 22 July 44. Target: Romana Americana Oil Refinery, Ploesti, Romania. Still rough. Despite numerous attempts to bomb Ploesti, it is still difficult. Planes dropped bombs early. Two hundred eighty Heavy anti-aircraft guns kept planes from target. A number of planes lost over target and landing at home. A wheatfield fire close to home base obscured field; a bomb dump was put on fire. Some planes ran out of gas and crashed, and others set down at alternate airfield.

*Note: The sixty-ninth mission of the 461st Bomb Group (July 25, 1944) deserves special mention, even though Phillips did not fly on it, as it points out the hazards the young men faced. The target was the Herman Goering Tank Works, Linz, Austria. Just as the twenty-one airplanes opened their bomb bay doors for their final run, they were attacked by twenty-five twin-engine and 125 single-engine enemy airplanes. Since the new crews did not have their belly turrets dropped into position, the Germans attacked from below, firing rockets into the bomb bays. Fighters continued the attack, and eleven bombers were knocked down "as parachutes, tracers, rockets, enemy fighters, and exploding bombers filled the air with confusion." In addition, four other bombers were lost for other reasons. The nose gunner on one of the crews counted thirty-two parachutes in the air at one time. The last flight in the Allied formation had a field day shooting at planes that were attacking the lead formation, and claimed fourteen enemy aircraft destroyed, six probable, and three damaged. The final count, when all Allied planes had returned, was thirty-one German aircraft destroyed, nineteen probable, and nine damaged. Of the fifteen Allied planes lost and the 113 officers and men who went down, seven officers and nine enlisted men were on their fiftieth mission.*

**Mission 27:** 28 July 44. Target: Phlorina, Greece. The marshalling yard and RR yard were hit with a good pattern of bombs. A ground report later indicated the railroad station was badly damaged, and casualties to the Germans were 250 killed and 750 wounded while they were waiting to board the train.

**Mission 28:** 3 Aug 44. Target: Zahuradfabrik Aircragt Factory, Friedrichshafen, Germany. The primary target was the Raderasch Chemical Works, but because of the nine-tenths cloud cover over the target area an alternate target was hit. Many bombs fell short into the water. One plane was lost.

**Mission 29:** 10 Aug 44. Target: Ploesti Xenia Oil Refinery, Romania. Back to Ploesti with about the same results. Smoke screens and black clouds from burning oil obscured the target. Thirteen planes returned with holes in them.

**Mission 30:** 14 Aug 44. Target: Genoa Gun Positions near Frejus, France. A tactical mission against coastal guns; scored 64.5 percent. Conditions ideal. Crews speculate about preparing for southern invasion on coast of France.

**Missions 31, 32:** 15 Aug 44. Target: Frejus Beach, France. Support for today's invasion of southern France. Intent was to destroy beach defenses, isolate battlefield by bombing rail and road bridges, block defiles and rail lines towards the Alps, and drop propaganda leaflets to convince enemy troops to surrender. Dropped 100 lb. general-purpose bombs. Staff officers were allowed to participate to experience what happens during missions. All crews returned to the base without incident.

**Mission 33:** 22 Aug 44. Target: Lobau Underground Oil Storage, Vienna, Austria. The group bombed through heavy smoke from fires, but had several direct hits. The bombers had a long running fight with 34 fighters, 11 of which were destroyed. Sixteen of the bombers were damaged by intense anti-aircraft fire. One bomber had a fuel leak and went down over Yugoslavia.

**Mission 34:** 27 Aug 44. Target: Venzone Viaduct, Italy. Registered a score of 73.9 percent.

**Mission 35:** 1 Sept 44. Target: Ferrara Railroad Bridge, Italy. Failed to destroy bridge. Seven planes became separated from formation and bombed bridge at Boari Pisani, Italy.

**Mission 36:** 2 Sept 44. Target: Mitrovica Railroad Bridge, Yugoslavia. Scored 57.3 percent with concentrated pattern on west approach to bridge, and six direct hits on the tracks.

**Mission 37:** 3 Sept 44. Target: Smederovo Ferry Slip, Yugoslavia. The highest score ever on a mission—92.2 percent within 1000 feet of the target.

After completing their missions, several local flights were made while they tested radar effectiveness for equipment soon to be installed in the bombers. Phillips's tour was April 1944 through September 1944, throughout the summer months. Living in tents was inconvenient, but far more livable than coping with the winter weather. Pilots who flew during winter faced a totally different set of circumstances; during winter, weather was more volatile and unpredictable, clothing more cumbersome, and plane and crew performance dramatically changed. Another example of Phillips's luck?

Because Phillips flew thirteen missions that were considered double missions, his last mission was number thirty-seven. Several of those missions were over oil fields and oil processing plants; although they did not destroy them, they did enough damage to seriously curtail production, which ultimately kept the German fighting machine from continuing the war.

# PHILLIPS
# CHAPTER FOUR

The airbase at Cerignola, near Foggia, had limited facilities. The airmen lived in tents housing eight to ten men, with wooden floors elevated off the ground a few inches. The men slept on steel cots and lived out of footlockers and duffel bags. Bathing involved a metal helmet filled with warm water. Toilet facilities consisted of an oversized outdoor "privy." The best description of living conditions was that they were relatively crude.

For heating the tents a maintenance crew devised a fifty-five-gallon metal drum laid sidewise, with a number of holes in the top. A copper tube ran from the container to a five-gallon container of aviation gasoline, dripping a steady stream of liquid into the "heater." Amazingly enough, it was quite a successful heating apparatus, even though one or two tents were incinerated every year.

The regular routine for a mission was to get up at 3:30 A.M., do the usual chores, and eat a breakfast of powdered eggs, bacon, toast, and coffee. They would don their flying clothes, grab their parachutes and other equipment, and head for the briefing room. Seating was on planks, and all maps were covered and window curtains drawn until the briefing started. They would be on the flight line for takeoff by 7:00 A.M. Maintenance and armament would have the planes repaired, adjustments made, and ammunition and bombs in place.

One day during the briefing there was a huge explosion that blew out the high windows in the briefing room. The group thought they had been bombed, but an auxiliary power unit about a mile away had caught on fire—spreading to a plane fully loaded with bombs and ammunition. The result of the explosion was a hole nine feet deep and 120 feet in diameter; while there was nothing left of the airplane, one of the engines flew some distance hitting another bomber and doing enough damage to put it out of commission. The squadron performed their next mission with two less airplanes.

Airplane crews were rotated after their missions were completed. However, the maintenance men, armorers, and base staff served until the war was over. The permanent crew saw many plane crews come and go, enduring the camp conditions, weather, and working conditions far longer than the pilots. They were very knowledgeable on how to repair an airplane and keep it airborne, and were also extremely inventive in solving not only airplane conversion, but coping with day-to-day living. After every mission, the machine guns were broken down, cleaned, oiled, and reinstalled for the next mission. Engines were serviced and tuned to peak performance. The maintenance crews had a great sense of dedication in recognizing their responsibility to assure that the aircrews would not be placed in jeopardy due to equipment failure. The men aloft truly appreciated the efforts of the men on the ground.

The maintenance crews, because of their long residency, also knew where the "action" was in every small surrounding community.

Phillips and some friends were watching bombers returning from a mission on one of their days off. Most planes were not shot up and were returning in good shape. One plane had the landing gear down—but not locked—and when it landed, the gear folded and the plane began to ground loop, breaking into two pieces. There was no fire, and the crew survived, but this had a very sobering effect on Phillips, and the image remained with him for a long time.

On every mission, Phillips carried a map printed on a piece of parachute silk that could easily be tucked away in a pocket; in case they were downed, he had a reference map that might suggest an escape route. Fortunately, it was never put to use, but it is an interesting memento still in his possession.

Some missions were "milk runs," with no fighter interceptors and little or no flak. On one such run Phillips and crew returned, and when they inspected their airplane discovered an eighteen-inch hole in their vertical stabilizer. Members of the crew were not aware of being hit or damaged, and the plane had continued to function with no discernable problem. Another example of "Phillips's luck?"

After one raid on Ploesti, they were returning to their field when they were notified that a grass fire was obscuring the landing site, and they diverted to another field to put down until the fire was under control. Subsequently, when the plane failed to start, the crew had to be trucked back to their base for the debriefing. A maintenance crew was sent over to inspect the plane and determine what was wrong, and discovered that a steel shard of flak had penetrated the aluminum skin, severing connections to an electrical bus bar about 1/4 inch by 14 inches in size. It was located in a conduit, or gutter, next to the cockpit. Apparently, it did not affect the ignition during flight, as the plane had magnetos that generated power for the flight, but it did affect the electrical transfer for starting the engines. Had it influenced flight, they would have gone down over enemy territory. Had it not hit the bus bar, or been one inch higher or lower, it would have gone waist-high through the nose compartment. "Phillips's luck," again?

Crew responsibility was very important, and Phillips's had great respect for the engineer during flights. The engineer was responsible for manning the top turret, controlling gas flow to balance the tanks for uniform consumption and level flight, and a myriad of other things. He knew how "things" worked and was a problem solver en route to the target.

The design of the B-24 put the bombardier and navigator in the front turret in cramped quarters, working around the bombsight. They were trained to handle a machine gun, since defense of the plane was necessary even when they were performing their primary duties. The bombardier usually dropped his bombs when the lead plane dropped, so he was not as intensely involved in his craft, unless they became separated from the main group. The navigator also followed the lead plane, but often found the squadron separated, and his responsibility was to get the team home. Planes were modified to meet the German defenses, and when the Luftwaffe learned that a frontal attack was the most effective, a two-gun turret was adapted up front.

Shell casings flew out of the turrets, but the casings from the side gunners remained in the plane. There were instances when expelled shell casings would hit the top turret of a trailing plane, breaking the 5/8-inch plastic, causing intense discomfort in the negative-forty-degree temperature—adding an immeasurable wind chill due to the 180 mile per hour speed. The crews soon learned that "little things" could create undue discomfort—or even complete disaster.

Formation flying was always a challenge because formations were both lateral and staggered. This gave better coverage from attacking fighters, as well as protection from "drifting." Usually, there were three planes flying in a staggered cluster, parallel to each other, with the other planes in a diamond pattern. The outside plane, or "Tail-End Charlie" was the one most picked on by enemy fighters, and the loss ratio was very high. On one mission, flying an interior position, Phillips's plane observed a bomber next to them "burning like a torch," and experienced the futility of knowing that there was absolutely nothing they could do about it. On another mission, three planes collided while approaching the Initial Point and went down with all hands lost.

The B-24 was an airplane that had no forgiveness. You had to fly it all the time. When establishing altitude, you went to the altitude plus three hundred feet, and then coasted into position. The pilot was kept busy all the time. The rest of the crew was watching for the enemy while the pilot was busy keeping the plane up, on line, in formation, and on target. Fortunately, for all their exposure and difficult missions, Phillips's crew managed to avoid being seriously hit and no crew members were wounded or lost.

Free time was limited. However, during one lull in their schedule after twenty-five missions, Phillips and other members of his crew and squadron were bussed to Naples, and then traveled by boat to the Isle of Capri. It was time for rest and relaxation (R&R), and the soldiers slept between sheets for the first time in over four months. They were impressed with the history of the Isle. One of the Roman emperors had a sumptuous residence on the island, and enjoyed numerous female visitors. When the Emperor tired of their companionship, he would throw them off the high cliffs into the Mediterranean. The young officers realized the guide could have manufactured all kinds of stories, and they probably would have believed them.

The vacationers also visited the "Azure Cave," went on a Red Cross tour of Naples, and toured the ruins of Pompeii at the foot of Mt. Vesuvius.

In August, Phillips took a three-day pass to Rome. He visited the ruins of the Coliseum, ruins of the Forum, and visited St. Peters Basilica at the Vatican. They were fortunate to be in the Basilica when Pope Pius XII was holding an audience. Staying in an uptown hotel and eating in an elegant Italian restaurant with strolling violinists was equally impressive to an Iowa Protestant boy.

Phillips had flown a plane to Rome, and the return trip to the base prompted a number of enlisted men to try to hitchhike back with him. He put a few aboard his plane, and when they crawled into the tail section of the tricycle, landing-gear airplane, the tail was soon resting on the ground. They redistributed the bodies, which solved that particular problem. Rules were broken when every man aboard the plane did not have a parachute. However, they arrived safely back at the base and no one was the wiser.

When it was finally time to return to the United States, Phillips had been promoted to the rank of captain. At any rank, going home was delicious anticipation.

# PHILLIPS
# CHAPTER FIVE

Captain Rollen Phillips's tour was finally completed, and he proceeded via land to Naples where he spent seven days in processing. He boarded a Navy transport, the General Thomas Mann, for a return trip across the beautiful blue Mediterranean through Gibraltar—heading across the Atlantic Ocean for Newport News, Virginia. Still wary of submarine action, the ship changed course every twenty seconds. Living below the waterline did not appeal to Rollen, and like many others, he became quite seasick. The first day out, the ship's gun crew test-fired its five-inch gun that just happened to be located directly above Rollen's compartment. It not only rattled the entire ship, but it scared the hell out of everybody below deck—thinking they had been torpedoed.

The men were fed twice daily aboard ship, but this did not help Rollen, who was used to regular meals and a contented stomach. His companions told him he had a weak stomach, but when he leaned over the rail, he could project his stomach's contents as far as anyone on board. The saving grace for Rollen was a box of Baby Ruth candy bars and lots of bunk-time. He managed to survive the seasickness, but he never did adapt to bathing and shaving in cold seawater.

When they finally docked and disembarked in Newport News, one of the airmen crew members went to the post exchange (PX) and said, "I want two quarts of milk!" When the milk arrived he proceeded to empty each bottle in a long, continuous gulp.

From Virginia they traveled to Jefferson Barracks, Missouri, in a chair car train with every seat full. When passing through Indiana, the train pulled off on a siding while a train next to them slowly chugged past, carrying German prisoners of war to a camp. It was noted that the German prisoners were traveling in sleeping compartments. A young lieutenant on Rollen's train returning from the infantry war in Germany saw the prisoners in the comfortable sleeping cars, and World War III almost erupted on a rail siding in the small Indiana town.

From Jefferson Barracks, Rollen caught a ride to Iowa, and arrived in Nevada about 6:00 A.M., catching Betty still in bed. He tiptoed upstairs and surprised her—much to Betty's chagrin. She has never forgiven him for not warning her of his return, since she wanted "to be prettied up and dressed in her best" for his welcome home. The officer and gentleman maintained then, and to this day, that Betty looked "just wonderful."

While her husband was overseas, Betty worked in Nevada in a "dime store" for eight dollars a week. She rented a small room in a private home. She took a second job taking tickets in the local theater—working the first shift and avoiding late hours because she had to get up to go to her other job. She later worked for Doan Agricultural Services and for a Doctor of Osteopathy. She moved in with two girls in a small apartment for companionship. The girls talked about being war widows at an early age, sharing letters, fears, and aspirations. Betty always wanted to be a nurse but never had the opportunity. She wanted a family, but did not want to be pregnant while Rollen was overseas—she wanted to start the family when he returned. She wrote letters to him regularly, and treasured the ones she received from her pilot. Rollen's return erased the gray shadows of uncertainty and filled her life with sunshine.

After a thirty-day leave, Rollen received orders to report to Miami Beach and, after eight days, reported to Liberal, Kansas, as a B-24 flight instructor.

After a brief assignment in Smyrna, Tennessee, at instructor's school, he then went back to Liberal as an operations officer. The good news was Betty could join him there. He was Operations Officer in Liberal until he was reassigned as Operations Officer in Hondo, Texas, where he also taught Chinese cadets to fly.

Housing for Betty and Rollen was not readily available in Liberal. The town was small, with only one hotel, which was less than desirable housing. Betty went door to door, knocking on every door frame to see if there was a room to rent, or if they knew of one. Betty arrived at the home of a minister, and indicted how desperate she was for a room. The minister indicated he and his wife would talk it over, and she should come back. On return, the minister asked if Betty or Rollen smoked or drank; they reassured the minister they did not. The minister and his wife had three bedrooms, one already rented out to a service couple. The couple's small child was in the second bedroom, and the third was the minister's bedroom. After thinking it over, they rented their own bedroom to Rollen and Betty, and moved to the basement where they converted an unused coal room into a bedroom. Betty and Rollen were most thankful for the minister's generosity and consideration for the two service couples.

One weekend while the minister was away, the Phillips were visited by a cousin with his wife and child. The cousin had just returned from a prisoner of war camp, and it was their first opportunity to get together. Victory in Japan had just been announced, and they celebrated by buying a big watermelon and being "relieved and jubilant." During the weekend, the group visited the city park in Liberal. The Base Commander, a lieutenant colonel, had been sitting at an adjoining table and was about to leave, so he brought over half of a watermelon for the group to share. Rollen (who was in uniform) acknowledged the gift, but did not stand according to military protocol. As the commander left, he admonished Rollen, saying, "Since you did not stand when I came over, I expect you to eat the watermelon standing at attention," and marched away.

Obtaining housing for the Phillips was one thing—coping with everyday living, doing laundry, finding meals, dealing with rationing stamps, and finding gas for travel was of constant concern. Many military wives sacrificed more to be with their spouses in military towns than one can imagine. In many ways, military wives deserved a medal for their perseverance, faith, and love.

The war in Japan was still in progress when Rollen arrived in Liberal, Kansas, and since his enlistment was for the "duration plus six months," he assumed he would be sent to the Pacific Theater. However, he had accumulated so many activity points toward discharge they decided to terminate his enlistment. They shipped him back to Jefferson Barracks, Missouri, for processing, and on April 19, 1946, he separated from service.

Rollen had graduated from high school in 1937, and had a strong desire to continue his education. His wanted to enter Iowa State College (now University) in the new program in Aeronautical Engineering. He was concerned about continuing his education since he had been out of school for nine years. Shy of meeting the mathematics entrance requirement, he purchased a math book, studied hard, and passed an examination for entry in the fall quarter of 1946.

Betty and Rollen also started their family. Their first child, Sharon, was born on April 23, 1946, just four days after Rollen's separation from service. Their second child, Linda, was born May 3, 1948. Their third daughter, Rhonda, was born April 21, 1951. Their son, Richard, was born on October 15, 1956, and suffered the calamity of being under the critical eye of three older sisters (and having only one bathroom in the house)!

Rollen attended Iowa State College for three years, commuting from Nevada, living on the GI Bill, and doing whatever additional work he could find with the brief time available. He had a wife, two or three children, and a full academic load that included calculus, engineering physics, chemistry, and theoretical and applied mechanics.

The college prided itself on two courses that "separated the men from the boys." They were considered the "weeding out" classes that gave the college its "tough" reputation. Freshman Chemistry and Theoretical and Applied Mechanics (T&AM) filled that role. Both courses required mental discipline and extreme application of all of one's faculties to survive the courses. The T&AM faculty took great pride in its reputation—for the courses' degrees of difficulty, and for demanding a semester's coursework in a quarter's time period. At one time, courses in the humanities were required to take T&AM as proof of mental discipline. It was the course that "did in" many a student. It contributed significantly to ending Rollen's educational dream.

With the loss of the GI Bill and a family to feed, Rollen looked at other options. He had taken part-time employment at the Iowa State Press, but now he took a full-time job as a pressman in order to support his family. He entered wholeheartedly into his new position, working with the huge presses. His sense of responsibility, knowledge of mechanical operation, and ability to adapt to changing processes and techniques, made him a valuable employee. He could tune the four-color presses just as he had tuned the four huge 1200 horsepower engines on his B-24 for a smoother flight. The Iowa State Press published the most books in the state, and was one of only two university presses in the United States. He was a dedicated employee for thirty-five years, retiring in 1984.

When the Korean Conflict erupted, Rollen received a form required by the military for consideration for recall to service, but because of his family situation he was not recalled. One fellow in Nevada was recalled and offered to rent his home to the Phillips while he was away. The Phillips moved into their new quarters, but a short time thereafter the renter left service early and returned—leaving the Phillips without a home. They contacted a local Ames realtor who found them a small house, that they could purchase—if they used all of their resources. It was a modest two bedroom home on Stafford Street that has been their home ever since.

Of course, raising three daughters in a one-bathroom home was not without some conflict. Rollen, having been an only child, now had difficulty coping with the frantic family interaction. But, like his military experience, "we hoped for the best and we survived."

In 1957, Rollen joined the Masonic Lodge. After four years, he became Secretary of the Lodge. Three years later, he entered the line of officers, and after working his way through several chairs, was elected Grand Master of Arcadia Lodge No.249 in 1967. Also, he learned the Ritual of the Three Degrees, took an exam from the Grand Lodge, and was appointed a Masonic Instructor for three years, advancing to the title of District Lecturer. He was appointed the Grand Master's Representative for one year for the district, served as Instructor for the local Lodge, and is authorized to use that knowledge wherever necessary in this state. Rollen has derived a good deal of pride and satisfaction from his membership in the organization.

Betty went to work after she had raised the family, working part-time at a J.C. Penney retail store; she retired from there in 1985.

Since retiring, Rollen and Betty have traveled extensively, taking thirty-nine trips with tour groups. They have been all over the United States, on trips varying from three to thirty days. The most enjoyable was a trip to Nova Scotia and Prince Edward Isle. They have not taken any cruises—probably because of Rollen's experience crossing the Atlantic Ocean.

A recent bus tour took them to New York City. On September 9, 2001, they stood on the observation deck on tower two of the World Trade Center to view the Island of Manhattan and the Statue of Liberty. Two days later, the towers were destroyed by terrorists who crashed Boeing 747 passenger planes with full loads of gasoline into the ninety-eighth floor. Again, was it another Phillips near miss?

In early January 2002, Betty Russell Phillips celebrated her eightieth birthday with a reception at the First Methodist Church. On display were pictures of their four children, eight grandchildren, and six great-grandchildren, flowers, and several cakes; in attendance were numerous friends. Betty, in a pretty pale-green dress and lovely corsage, stole the show when she playfully put her arm around Rollen's neck and announced to the world, "Did you see the great prize I got at the MYF scavenger hunt?"

Randy Dunkin, one of daughter Rhonda's boys, completed his training as a helicopter pilot at Fort Rucker Military Base in Alabama; Randy asked Rollen to attend the graduation ceremonies. Randy had made a display case for Rollen's military decorations and memorabilia, and Rollen would certainly not miss

*Rollen and his grandson, Randy Duncan, who made a case for Rollen's medals.*

the opportunity to see his grandson's graduation. One of Rollen's proudest moments came when Randy approached him at the ceremony and asked him to pin his new pilot's wings onto his uniform.

After Rollen pinned the wings on Randy, the Fort Rucker Commanding Officer called Rollen forward, presented him with a medallion, and special mention was made of Capt. Rollen Phillips's wartime accomplishments:
- ↳ Thirty-eight missions over enemy territory with the Fifteenth Air Force.
- ↳ A Distinguished Unit Citation.
- ↳ The European Theater of Operations with three stars, and the Air Medal with three Oak Leaf Clusters.

The occasion was very special.

Like rollerskating on warm summer nights at the Nevada Fair Grounds, simple experiences become special memories with time.

*Rollen pinning wings on Randy Duncan at helicopter pilot graduation.*

# BOOK THREE

# HUSTON

*Lt. Dean Huston*

*P-51 Pilot*

*Eighth Air Force*

*352d Fighter Group*

*487th Squadron*

*"The maintenance and armament crews saw their team in combat for the first time, and cheered the dogfights as though they were attending a football game."*

*—Huston*

# HUSTON
# CHAPTER ONE

Doctor Anderson sat at his office desk looking out the window at the swirling snow. It would appear to be a slow day, since travel in rural Early would be curtailed by the mounting drifts. The snow had started the previous morning, depositing ten to twelve inches of the fine crystals; but, this afternoon the bitter northwest wind was sweeping across the prairies, reducing visibility and rearranging the snow into huge drifts. There was not much windbreak between Early, Iowa, and the North Pole.

"I'm sorry, Vaughn. There is absolutely no way I can get to your farm, even though it's only three-quarters of a mile away. Being on the highway doesn't make a damn bit of difference. I haven't seen a soul downtown since yesterday noon. It's bad out there. Doesn't Ruby know better than to have labor pains during a snowstorm?... Well, if you think you can make it in your bobsled, I'll be ready to go....Do you think Ruby can hold on that long?...OK, I'll be ready." He placed the phone on the hook, and prepared for the cold journey. As he pulled on his four-buckle overshoes, he mused out loud, "Well, if Ruby can hold on till we get there, she'll get herself a genuine 1923 Valentine's Day baby."

He started preparing his satchel, and waited for the bobsled to appear on Main Street.

There would be no church this morning since corn picking had to be completed. It was a relatively warm day, even though there was boot-deep snow on the ground. The neighbors worked as a harvesting team, and assembled a few one-row corn pickers to complete the process. Today, however, with that much snow, it would be a hand-picking day on the inside of the field, while mechanical pickers worked the edge rows.

Dean Huston had graduated from Early High School the spring of 1940. He wanted to continue on to college, but had to work at home for a year to earn school money. Dean was young. He had graduated at seventeen years of age, and he needed a year or two of seasoning before venturing off to college. He started Iowa State College (now University) in the fall of 1941, had completed his first quarter of college, and was home to help during harvest time. At that time at Iowa State College, the academic schedule allowed two extra weeks for students to help on the farm during harvest time.

Vaughn Huston, his father, could well use Dean's help with chores and grain farming. Farm life was in the phase of a major transition, with tractors becoming more affordable, and rural electrification adding to farming convenience. But farming was still labor intensive, with unrelenting daily chores. Every farm had cows, pigs, and chickens that needed attention daily.

The men stopped for the late afternoon ritual of coffee and a sandwich break. Dean's mother, Ruby, and sister, Mary Lou, had delivered hot coffee, ham sandwiches, and homemade cookies. It took several breaks a day to keep the energy level up, and the feet warm. They crawled into Vaughn's 1935 four-door Chevy, poured steaming coffee from the thermos, and held the ceramic mugs to warm their hands. They turned on the AM radio, hoping to catch H.V. Kaltenborne, the popular news commentator. Instead, they heard the first reports that the Japanese had bombed Pearl Harbor. They sat transfixed, listening through the static, as the sketchy reports indicated that America would soon be at war.

Although the military had studied Japanese military activities and suspected additional expansion throughout the western Pacific, central Iowa was totally unaware of the potential conflict. In Iowa, crops had to be harvested, and grain prices had to reflect a net gain in order to meet farm payments, buy new equipment, and meet the needs of preparing for next year's crop.

The determination and resolve of the American people would not be initiated until they recovered from the shock of being thrust into international conflict and the subsequent realization that American property had been destroyed.

The five men sat in the Chevy quietly sipping their coffee, staring through the cornfield, trying to make sense of it all. Vaughn Huston exhaled a deep breath, looked wisely at his young son who he knew would soon be going to war, and quietly muttered, "I'll be damned."

# HUSTON
# CHAPTER TWO

Vocational Agriculture held a special interest for Dean Huston. He grew up on the farm at a time when water was drawn from the ground with windmills, toilets were at least fifty feet from the house, and kerosene was the main lighting and heating source in the home. The progress from 1938 to 1940 indicated that Vocational Agriculture would measure and advance agricultural life, and there would be a future in teaching in that area.

Dean had enrolled at Iowa State College in fall 1941 at the age of 18. Attending college and working on the farm meant that he would have a military exemption for a short period of time, but ultimately he would be called into service. He was interested in aviation, and decided to join the Air Corps in February 1943. The Air Corps (which it was initially called) required four years of college, but later lowered the requirements to a minimum of two years of college before induction. This was later changed to passing a written examination and a physical.

Dean worked one summer while in college in the local lumberyard, a Payless Cashway that was headquartered in Iowa Falls, Iowa. Dean became quite close to the owner, Sanford Furrow. He encouraged Dean to return to Payless after the war to train and grow with the company. Dean could not promise anything since he was still interested in Vocational Agriculture. Payless would grow to become an enormously successful lumber company in the years following WWII.

Dean was finally inducted into military service in the fall of 1943, and he reported to Jefferson Barracks, Missouri, for preflight training. It was his second trip out of state, his first being a train ride to Chicago when he had accompanied his father and a load of cattle to the stockyards; he was nine years old at the time. They rode in the caboose, and the train stopped at every small town between Early and Chicago. The abrupt starting and stopping of the train banged the couplings between cars and it was a most uncomfortable, long trip.

From Jefferson Barracks he went to Morehead, Minnesota, for classroom work and a few hours of flight training. Flying out of a nearby Fargo, North Dakota, airfield created a good deal of excitement for the cadets because a squadron of B-25s were in training there, also.

*Huston sitting on the wing of the "Hawk-eye-oan" P-51 D in England.*

After training sessions at Santa Ana, California, they went to Thunderbird Air Force Base outside Phoenix, Arizona, where they flew Stearman primary trainers with large radial engines and fixed landing gear. The airplane was great at acrobatics, and this whetted Dean's appetite to fly fighters. From Phoenix the cadets went to Pecos, Texas, where they flew BT-13s with 450 horsepower engines. He was not fond of Pecos, being a typical Iowa boy, he wondered who would ever want to live in that God-forsaken desert.

The cadets then went to Luke Field, Phoenix, Arizona, where they flew the AT-6 closed-cockpit plane with an even larger radial engine. The performance characteristics of the AT-6 convinced him that he definitely did not want to be a bomber pilot.

Finally, at Luke Field in February 1944, one year after he had enlisted, he received his wings and his commission as Second Lieutenant. His wings were pinned on by one of the numerous young ladies who hung around the base, hoping to strike the fancy of a young pilot—*any* young pilot.

Although Huston was casually interested in these young damsels, he was more excited at being assigned to a base in Florida where he would learn to fly P-51s, the new North American Aviation fighter plane. After being trained and checked out in the first edition of the 850 horsepower P-51A fighter plane, he was then shipped back to Luke Field, Arizona, where he learned to fly the latest P-51 D.

The P-51D was bubble-domed, with a liquid-cooled sixteen cylinder Merlin Rolls Royce engine that was rated at 1650 horsepower—almost double that of the P-51A. It became the definitive classic fighter airplane of WWII, not only because of its extended range, firepower of six .50 caliber machine guns, maneuverability, and speed, but also because of its esthetics.

It was—simply put—a beautiful aircraft.

Time was spent at target practice, shooting at a canvas target towed by another airplane. Each pilot's cartridges carried a colored dye, and hits could be counted by counting the different color dye marks. Ground targets also used color dyes to indicate accuracy. This practice was great fun because no one was returning fire.

Completing training, Huston received his overseas orders. He traveled to Trenton, New Jersey, where he boarded the Queen Mary for a trip through the North Atlantic where they landed in Scotland. The Queen could outrun submarines, and changed courses every twenty seconds to make torpedo targeting more difficult. The crossing was without incident.

Huston would be a member of the Eighth Air Force in England. Assigned to the 352d Fighter Group, 487th Squadron, he was stationed in Bodney—about forty miles west of Norwich, close to East Wretham. It was a grass field, located near over 150 air bases in East Anglia; it housed B-17, B-26, and B-24 bomber and fighter groups.

The members of the 487th painted their P-51s a distinctive color and pattern. The propeller hub and nose cowling were painted a royal blue. The special paint job and their success in air sorties earned them the nickname "The Bluenosed Bastards of Bodney."

In addition, the pilots named their airplanes, and some of the graphics were quite elaborate. Other planes had simple lettering. There were no standards in expression of the names, but they were usually a reflection of the pilots' personalities or the graphic artists' abilities.

Huston was a member of one of the most successful fighter squadrons in the European Theater of Operations. The squadron boasted the two most accomplished American Aces in the war. Major George Preddy was credited with 32 planes destroyed, 5 strafed on the ground, and 26.83 planes shot down in aerial combat. Colonel (then Major) John C. Meyers was credited with 24.5 shot down and 13 destroyed on the ground, for a total of 37. Some of their exploits are legendary.

Major Preddy achieved particular acclaim for his exploits. Fighter pilots flew every day, but on one occasion the weather

*Members of the 352d Fighter Group: J.C. Meyer, James Mayden, Joe Mason, Wille Jackson, and George Preddy.*

reports indicated the next day's flights would be canceled. Preddy proceeded to the Officer's Club and imbibed a bit too much. He awoke the next morning with a monstrous hangover, only to learn that the mission was rescheduled, so he decided to "give it a bit of a go." He crawled into his airplane, only to throw up what was left of the previous night's ingestion. Escorting bombers over Germany, the squadron responded to a large number of German fighter planes attacking the group. During the engagement, Major Preddy proceeded to shoot down six enemy airplanes—the most ever by an American pilot in a single day.

On another mission, while escorting bombers, Major Preddy was attached to the 328th Fighter Group as part of the 20th Bomber Group's mission. Other fighter groups included the 352d, 357th, and 364th. That day, his fighter group shot down twenty-five enemy airplanes, with Major Preddy accounting for three of them. Twenty-five planes destroyed in one engagement was the highest number scored during WWII in the Eastern Theater of Operations.

During a mission on Christmas Day 1944, Major Preddy was flying over France, chasing a German Me-109 at the low altitude of 700 feet, when he was hit by friendly anti-aircraft fire. He managed to get his canopy off, but could not get out of the plane, and was killed on impact. Only one other aircraft in the 352d Fighter Group was recorded as shot down by friendly fire, and that was on January 1, 1945.

Lt. Col. Meyers became the commander of the 487th Fighter Squadron and led many successful missions. His flying days ended when he was injured in a car accident in late January 1945, but he continued in military service and had an illustrious career.

By the time Huston was assigned to the 487th, air superiority over Europe had essentially been achieved. Because of the range of the P-51 D, bombers could be escorted to Berlin and back with fighter cover. Consequently, the main activity of the 487th was escorting bombers and strafing. Since the fighters were substantially faster than the bombers, bombers would leave their bases before dawn, while the fighter pilots would have a leisurely breakfast, take off mid-morning, and overtake the bombers as they entered Germany.

Once Huston was added to the 487th, his role was to fly as wingman to a more experienced pilot. This meant seeing fighter action, but not being the active aggressor. Flying escort meant many routine flights, as the German response was substantially reduced. For instance, on December 6, 1944, they participated in the largest raid of the war. One thousand eight hundred eighty-four bombers escorted by 883 fighters dropped over 5000 tons of bombs on targets in central Germany. Unfortunately, the 352d Fighter Group was assigned the task of patrolling the Giesson area, and missed out on the fireworks entirely.

Huston named his blue-nosed airplane the "Hawk-eye-oan" after his home state. Unlike bomber pilots who were required to fly a number of missions, the fighter pilots were required to fly a number of hours to fulfill their military obligation. The number of hours varied with mission and task, but a total of 275 hours was the amount required for a tour of duty. Each pilot or airplane was assigned two ground crew men: a maintenance man who kept the plane in ship shape in both mechanical performance and body repair, and an armament specialist who made certain the machine guns were functional and fully loaded. After every mission, the armament specialist would break down each machine gun, clean and oil it, and prepare it for the next mission.

The machine guns could fire 3000 rounds per minute, which meant each gun would deliver fifty bullets in a one-second burst. With three guns mounted in each wing, a one second burst could deliver 300 small steel objects per second in the general vicinity of a target. The usual burst was a two-second burst. The machine guns were calibrated to converge at 1000 yards. The object was to aim where the enemy was *going to be*—flying at 350 miles per hour—rather than at where they were. The recoil from the six guns never affected the flight or speed of the airplane, which is quite remarkable. All shells were expended, which lightened the load of the plane in flight, aiding maneuverability.

Huston was ultimately credited with two planes shot from the air and one destroyed on the ground for three "kills."

Huston never liked strafing because of the unknown danger involved. Certain missions called for strafing enemy ground troops, vehicles, convoys, trains, or anything that was moving. In one recorded instance, a pilot was strafing a rail yard, chasing a train. While bearing down on the engine, the boiler blew up with the plane directly overhead, destroying the airplane and killing the pilot.

One of the biggest fears of fighter pilots were Allied anti-aircraft gun crews being unable to identify aircraft, and indiscriminately shooting at anything and everything in the air. At 300 miles per hour, distinguishing characteristics of fighter aircraft become a blur. It was also a problem for fighter pilots in the air, when immediate identification and reaction were necessary.

Fighter craft flew every day, which meant a few days off were often spent "sleeping in" rather than taking a three-day pass to London. When they did get to London, it was difficult to get a decent rest since the Germans were sending "buzz-bombs" (and later, V-2 rockets) into London on a regular basis. The constant drone of aircraft when sleeping on the base was more acceptable than the frequent explosions in London, which even at a distance seemed too close.

To a "green" farm boy from Iowa, traveling about London underground in a "tube" (subway) was as exciting as a roller coaster at a county fair. Striking up conversations with cabbies in their "lorries" proved to be an education in itself. Trips to London were infrequent, unless assigned to deliver personnel or equipment in a Norseman transport plane.

The one extravagance Huston permitted himself was to order a pair of genuine, custom-handcrafted flying boots made by a celebrated British leather craftsman. Huston, after much wrestling with Iowa frugality counting and recounting his resources, entered the well-established bootmaker's shop. In his first breath, he inhaled the accumulation of centuries of odors of leather craftsmanship. They did not ask his shoe size. They measured each foot separately—sole, toe, ankle, and leg (since these were calf-high boots)—with an aging, barely readable tape measure. After paying fifty or sixty American dollars—an extravagant sum—they informed Huston it would take six to eight weeks. With great anticipation, the day arrived when he could pick the boots up. They

*The P-51 D became the classic fighter plane of WWII.
(Photo courtesy of Robert H. Powell)*

fit perfectly, and were his pride and joy. The Iowa farm boy was finally a fighter jockey in classy English boots. Imagine how this would play in Early, Iowa!

When he returned to the U.S., he took them to a local shoe repair in Ames, Iowa, to have them half-soled. When he returned a week later to pick them up, they were missing. Gone! Stolen! Huston considers the theft an Anglo-American tragedy to this day.

Periodically, Huston was assigned to fly a C-64 Norden Norseman to London or another base for supplies or equipment. The C-64 was a lumbering airplane that became airborne at fifty-five miles per hour, had a top speed of seventy-five miles per hour and landed at fifty miles per hour. Flying it was a strange sensation after flying a P-51 at 375 miles per hour, "balls out."

*Huston at a group reunion with Art Helling, Huston's maintenance "crew" in England and Belgium.*

# HUSTON
## CHAPTER THREE

All pilots are required to keep a "Pilot's Log" where all flights are recorded for the time spent and specific exercises performed. Huston's logbook has many interesting entries that not only recorded what he was doing, but sometimes his mental attitude while doing it.

## FROM PILOT'S LOGBOOK

**13 Apr 44:** First flight in fighter plane. P-51A With V-1710 Allison engine. At Hillsboro's RTU

**26 May 44 to 6 June 44:** Dive bombed—practice 100 lbs. Skip bombed—practice 100 lbs. Gunnery 2558 rounds of .50 Cal, performed 10 housings, all practice.

**28 July 44:** Assigned P-51 1650 horsepower Merlin Rolls Royce Engine.

**29 Jul 6–Aug 44:** Local training flights.

**8 Aug 44:** P-51B-5 Combat to France. First Mission. Bomber escort.

**12 Aug 44:** P-51C-7 France. Another bomber escort (and a long one).

**13 Aug 44:** P-51C-7 River Seine—First Dive bomb (canal locks) and strafing run. (Transport on a road)

**15 Aug 44:** P-51B-10 Merseburg—Another bomber escort.

**24 Aug 44:** P-51B-7 Merseburg—Bomb escort—brought flight leader back.

**26 Aug 44:** P-51C-1 ?—Bomber escort.

**27 Aug 44:** P-51D-5 Combat—bomber escort—Brought flight leader back.

**30 Aug 44:** C-64A Norseman R-1340 P&W—Checked out in C-64.

**31 Aug 44:** P-51B-15 Local, familiarization with K-19 sight. Camera gunnery.

**1 Sep 44:** P-5—Ludwigshafen—Bomber escort—mission recalled, bad weather.

**3 Sept 44:** C-64 Norseman—Flew Doleac to London, returned to 479th. Flew Lt. Pickering to get his 51, returned to 479th to pick up two members, trip completed. Ran into rain.

**5 Sept 44:** P-51D—local—Test fired guns on new ship.

**5 Sept 44:** P-51D—local—same thing over again, flew formation with a B-24.

**8 Sept 44:** P-51-D—Combat German—Fighter sweep to strafe a couple of towns.

**9 Sept 44:** P51-D-10—Combat to Germany—Escort, strafed trains. Left magazine went out, first battle damage, flak hole in left wing.

**10 Sept 44:** P51B—Escort to Germany—First victory/one destroyed on the ground. Big day for 487th. Strafed aerodrome and claimed 21 planes to no losses. I GOT MY FIRST.

**14 Sept 44:** P-51B—Training flight with four ships.

**16 Sept 44:** C-64—Took Fowler to XXXX, Return.

**17 Sept 44:** P-51D—Had to land in France on British Field.

**18 Sept 44:** P-51D—Fighter sweep to Germany. Swept an area to cover supplies being flown in.

**19 Sept 44:** P-51—Local test hop. Crew chief asked me to test repaired carburetor. Went to 39,000 feet. Air so thin, thought I would stall out.

**20 Sept 44:** P-51D—Fighter sweep to Holland. Escorted supply carrier C-47's and paratroopers.

**22 Sept 44:** P-51D-10—Bomber escort to Kassel Germany. Uneventful escort.

**26 Sept 44:** P-51D-10—Bomber escort to Osnabruk, Germany, uneventful trip.

**27 Sept 44:** P-51B—Fighter sweep to Koblenz Germany. Heap big batch of FW-190's. Battle damage.

**28 Sept 44:** AT-6—Flew down to London get Lt Sears, who had just gotten back from bailing out in Belgium.

**29 Sept 44:** C-64A—Flew 5 to London, returned.

**30 Sept 44:** P-51B—Bomber escort to Handorf Germany. Rather uneventful. Had a hard time keeping clear of little friends.

**2 Oct 44:** P-51D—Bomber escort to Kassel, Germany. Uneventful. Escorted Schuh back to Bodney base.

**3 Oct 44:** P-51B—Test hop, local. Big practice dogfight with P-47's. More fun.

**7 Oct 44:** P-51B—Bomber escort to Ruhland, Germany. Bad day—head cold and was sick to stomach. Headache, too.

**9 Oct 44:** Spent time in Link trainer.

**13 Oct 44:** P-51B—Training flight, local.

**14 Oct 44:** P-51D-10—Bomber escort to Cologne, Germany. Milk run, lots of planes, all Allied.

**15 Oct 44:** P-51D-5—Bomber escort to Cologne, Germany. Ran short of gas, landed in France. Completed trip after refueling.

**16 Oct 44:** P-51D-5—Local training flight. Butler, Huston, Bateman & Landrum. Big rat race.

**17 Oct 44:** P-51D-5—Bomber escort to Cologne, Germany. Another milk run. Lotta Allied airplanes again.

**22 Oct 44:** P-51D-15—Bomber escort to Hanover, Germany. 10/10 coverage below all the way. Milk run.

**24 Oct 44:** P-51B—Fighter sweep to N.W. Hanover. Went to strafe but didn't—bad weather. Lost fellow '51 pilot Jack "Moose" Landrum KIA. Too bad!

**25 Oct 44:** P-51-D—Bomber escort to Hamburg, Germany. Uneventful escort. Taylor's last mission.

**26 Oct 44:** P-51D—Local flight, test fired guns. First flight in my brand new airplane.

**27 Oct 44:** P-51D-5—Local training flight. Second flight to 30,000ft to check hi-blower. A joy ride.

**29 Oct 44:** P-51D-10—Local training flight. Pretty much routine.

**31 Oct 44:** P-51D-10—Bomber escort to Mersburg, Germany. Huge show, but recalled because of weather.

**5 Nov 44:** P-51D-10—Bomber support to Frankfurt, Germany. Not much doing, a big rat race.

**6 Nov 44:** P-51D-10—Bomber escort to Hamburg, Germany. Same today, good weather over there.

**8 Nov 44:** C-64—Took armament men down there to see about K-14 site. Return.

**10 Nov 44:** P-51D-10—Bomber escort to Cologne, Germany. Blue flight on escort. Rest of squadron strafed.

**11 Nov 44:** P-51D-10—Local flight. Test hopped for prop oil leak. Ship AOK. Second flight. Tried out new K-14 sight on my ship.

**12 Nov 44:** P-51D-10—Local flight. Uneventful.

**21 Nov 44:** P-51D-10—Combat. Bodney to Brussels. To Merseburg, Germany. Had to bring Maj. Duncan back. Landed at Brussels. Same day, returned home.

**22 Nov 44:** P-51D-10 —Local. Had big dogfight with '51s "for fun."

**23 Nov 44:** P-51D-10 —Escort to Glsenkirchen, Germany. A Thanksgiving greeting to the Jerries.

**24 Nov 44:** P-51D-10 —Escort to Merseburg Germany. Flew with Col. Meyer's flight. Field was zero-zero, so landed at Horington. (364th).

**25 Nov 44:** P-51D-10—Returned from 364th.

**27 Nov 44:** P-51D-10—A BIG DAY. Got my first victory in air.

**2 Dec 44:** C-64A—London—Took Doc Dodson down to London. Gave James and my asst crew chief a ride, too. Returned.

**3 Dec 44:** P-51D-10—Local. Flew formation with P-47s, strafed field.

**4 Dec 44:** P-51D-10—Bomber escort to Soerst Germany. A long mission, lots of weather over there.

**5 Dec 44:** P-51D-10—Bomber escort to Berlin Germany. My first mission to Big B (Berlin). A milk run, though.

**5 Dec 44:** P-51D-10—Had to get one hour of night flying.

**6 Dec 44:** P-51D-10—Bomber escort to Merseburg, Germany. Flew Col Meyer's wing. A lone 109 seen.

**9 Dec 44:** P-51D-10—Bomber escort to Stuttgart, Germany. 486th shot down a Me-262 over there.

**10 Dec 44:** P-51D-10—Local. Test hopped for rough engine at full power.

**11 Dec 44:** P-51D-10—Bomber escort to Ludwigshafen, Germany. Uneventful mission, lots of bad weather.

**23 Dec 44:** P-51D-10—Antwerp. Headed for new base on continent, but had to land in Antwerp.

**24 Dec 44:** P-51D-10—from Antwerp to Y-29 at Asch, Belgium.

**26 Dec 44:** P-51D-10—Local. Test and practice flight.

**27 Dec 44:** P-51D-10—Local.

**31 Dec 44:** P-51D-10—Local.

**1 Jan 45:** P-51D-10—Got a 190 destroyed, but shot down by own flak.

**13 Jan 45:** P-51D—Another GCI but uneventful.

**20 Jan 45:** P-51D-10—First flight on new engine, but was a failure. Prop threw much oil.

**21 Jan 45:** Ground Control Intercept (GCI) again, same story uneventful.

**21 Jan 45:** P-51D-10—Test hopped for oil leak—same deal again.

**22 Jan 45:** G C I again. A milk run.

**22 Jan 45:** P-51D-10—Same oil leak again. Boy was I mad!!

**23 Jan 45:** P-51—Late afternoon patrol—called short on darkness.

**24 Jan 45:** Same as above

**25 Jan 45:** Same as above

**25 Jan 45:** P-51D-10—Finished fast timing ship. Gave the field a good buzz and O&P #2.

**27 Jan 45:** P51D-10—Y-29 to A 84—Flew over to new field in Major Halton's flight.

**1 Feb 45:** P51-D-10—"A" squadron, long trip. Flew element lead for Lt Schuh.

**3 Feb 45:** AT-6 —Flew Lt Heyer over to get his ship. Looked up Kennedy while there and had lunch with him. Flew back alone.

**6 Feb 45:** P-51D-10—Bomber escort to Central Germany.
Flew Major Halton's wing. Bad weather at target so they bombed opportunity targets.

**8 Feb 45:** P-51D-10—Bomber escort to Leipzig. Bombers recalled—we swept the Cologne area.

**10 Feb 45:** P-51D-10—Bomber Escort to Ruhr Valley. Led Schab's element. Uneventful mission.

**11 Feb 45:** P-51D-10—A-84 to Valeneinnes. Flew down to pick up PRU ships to escort them.

**11 Feb 45:** P-51D10—PRU escort to central Germany. Started out with a P-38 but the weather turned us back.

**16 Feb 45:** P-51D-10—Area patrol to Osnabruck area. Escorted Bakers 24's & t'was a dry run as usual.

**22 Feb 45:** P51D-10—Bomber escort to Staudel, Germany. Saw first jet. It was a Me-262. Came home with Red Dog. [The nickname of a pilot from Marshalltown, Iowa named Nutter]

**24 Feb 45:** P51D-10—Bomber escort to Hamburg, Germany. Flew #3 in Littge's flight. Had trouble with one drop tank.

**26 Feb 45:** P-51D-10—Bomber escort to Berlin. Got a little cloud flying. Was 10 /10 at target so could not see the city.

**28 Feb 45:** P-51D-10—Bomber escort to Ruhr Valley. Wood led squadron, Rigby was on my wing. Hawn's gyro went out.

**1 Mar 45:** P-51D-10—Bomber escort to Leipzig. Was yanked out of sack late. Flew Vickery's flight.

**5 Mar 45:** P-51D-10—Local test hop. Test hopped Waldron's ship. Reading flew with us.

**7 Mar 45:** P-51D-15—Local test hop. Tested Rigby's ship. Got in some instrument time.

**9 Mar 45:** P-51D-10—Area patrol over Frankfurt area. Ended up leading Yellow flight. Was leading the whole mission.

**10 Mar 45:** P-51D-10—Medium escort to Haiger Germany. Escorted A-26's. Tex Sears lead squadron.

**12 Mar 45:** P-51D-10—Bomber escort to Ruhr Area. Flew Maj. Halton's no.3. Rigby was my wing.

**13 Mar 45:** Training flight with Graves.

**21 Mar 45:** Test hopped a ship. Buzzed a "rest home". Pulled too much Hg.

**22 Mar 45:** P-51D-10—Bomber escort to Neinburg. Escorted 20 Lancasters. Don't believe they ever dropped bombs.

**24 Mar 45:** P-51D-10 —Fighter sweep in Dummer L. area. Helped cover the invasion of Germany—east Ruhr.

**25 Mar 45:** P-51D-10—Bomber escort to Lutzendorf. BAD DAY! Lost Roebuck off my wing to a Me-262.

**25 Mar 45:** P-51D-10—Escort again to east Bonn. Escorted B-26s uneventfully.

**26 Mar 45:** P-51D-10—Fighter sweep to Nurnberg Germany. Reached 270 [hrs] mark. Butler took picture of my take-off.

**3 Apr 45:** P51D-10—Local. Put in four hours to get flying pay for April.

**275.05 Hours: 352d Operations official time for Lt. Huston.**

Late in the war, pilots began seeing more and more German jet airplanes. Some of the encounters were disastrous, with the jets attacking out of the clouds and making a pass before any diversionary action could be initiated. Such was the occasion on the 25th of March when Huston was flying an escort mission to Lutzendorf, Germany. Huston was flying with his close friend Lt. Roebuck flying wing. A Me-262 suddenly descended on them, his twenty-millimeter cannon scoring a direct hit on Roebuck's plane, and damaging Huston's wing with numerous penetrations. Huston took off after him, but could not catch him. One of the tricks to fighting a jet was to follow it to the ground, where the jet's engines were not as effective, and where it often ran out of fuel. No such luck.

Huston's opinion about German aircraft was quite favorable. The Me-109 was an excellent airplane, developed well before the war started. However, as American technology improved, the P-51D proved to be a superior airplane. The major difference in air-to-air combat was the quality of the pilots. The Americans were better trained. The best German pilots were excellent, but there were very few left in the Luftwaffe. Superior Allied forces had taken their toll, and replacements were limited.

# HUSTON
# CHAPTER FOUR

On December 16, 1944, the ground war in Northern Europe changed dramatically. The German Army assembled a large land force of more than twenty divisions, and attacked the Allied lines in the Ardennes Forrest, near the city of Bastogne. The surprise attack caught the Allies completely off guard, and threatened to penetrate the Allied defenses and to throw their armies back to the beaches. The concentration of several Panzer Divisions attacking a weak point in the defensive line, as well as a violent winter storm that hit a few days later, portended disaster for the ground troops.

The weather was so severe that the air superiority enjoyed by the Americans came to a complete halt, and German tanks advanced with little resistance. Members of the 101st Airborne, 9th Armored Division, and other units were surrounded—but they battled on, holding their positions until reinforcements could arrive. This pivotal battle, the "Battle of the Bulge," has been well documented.

The Ninth Air Force Tactical Command (stationed in northern France), which had been supporting the ground force advances, also needed reinforcement. For this reason, the 352d Fighter Group in Bodney was reassigned to northern France to assist in turning back the enemy. After the Allies had successfully contained the German advance at Bastogne, the 352d Fighter Group was temporarily assigned to the Ninth Air Force, stationed at several locations in Northern Europe. The 487th was assigned to a captured airbase, Y-29, just outside Asch, Belgium, near Liege, sharing it with a wing of P-47 Thunderbolts.

Y-29 was one of sixteen or seventeen Allied air bases located in Northern Europe. Some bases were captured German airfields, while others were hastily improvised for all-weather flying. Each base was surrounded by Allied anti-aircraft artillery that served to discourage German strafing, which could destroy airplanes on the ground.

On December 23, the 352d Fighter Group packed and headed for Belgium. The weather at Y-29 was socked in, so they landed in Antwerp to spend the night. The following day, the weather cover permitted continuing to Base Y-29. It was close enough to the breakthrough at Bastogne to provide easy access for support, while being relatively secure from ground forces—but not from air attack. That same day a skeleton force of maintenance and armament crews arrived in C-47 cargo planes, and immediately set up shop—with limited facilities—to service the fighter planes.

As soon as the weather permitted, the 487th began flying local missions over the area. Their missions included escorting bombing runs, strafing railroad marshalling yards, parked aircraft, trains, and shooting at most anything else that moved.

The move to Y-29 was not without inconvenience for the pilots and crew members. The weather was much colder, and there was a good deal of snow on the ground. The men dug foxholes for safety during the isolated daily flyovers by Ju-88s, who occasionally dropped a few bombs to remind them they were unwelcome on the continent.

In Bodney, the airmen lived in Quonset huts, the half-round structures built for speed of erection and efficiency of exterior surface. They were small, so the stoves, although inefficient, heated them adequately. A separate building housed the latrines and showers. The building was heated, and hot water was readily available. The relocation introduced the aircrews to living in tents—French tents. The tents leaked and were drafty and cold because the stoves worked only half of the time. The latrine tent was unheated, and the water for showers was cold. It took several weeks to find a private residence large enough to accommodate the pilots, but one was found and appropriately commandeered, and was accessed by jeep.

The German High Command, in preparation for the breakout in the Ardennes, was also attempting to find a way to regain control of the air. During the month of December 1944 a large response force was assembled, in part by reducing the number of fighters attacking Allied bombing missions. They also increased airplane production and set about training pilots for a massive air assault. An interesting fact was that throughout the intense Allied bombing of the Rhineland late in the war, German aircraft production continued unabated until V-E day.

The High Command devised one last effort to severely cripple the Allied air war and prevent the incursion into their homeland. The Germans knew that the Americans were a predictable lot, and that New Year's Eve would be spent in drunken revelry; the Americans would be hung over and would sleep late on New Year's Day. It would be a perfect time to destroy their aircraft on the ground. The Germans planned a massive air attack called "Operation Bodenplatte."

*Briefing room map showing intended route for escorting bombers over Germany.*

The Germans arranged for 800 to 1000 aircraft to hit the sixteen or so air bases scattered in Northern Europe on New Year's Day in a grand effort to destroy aircraft and do irreparable damage to the Allied air effort. With Focke-Wulf 190s strafing the airfields and Me-109s flying cover, it could be a devastating blow to the Allied effort. At Y-29, forty-eight P-51 Mustangs were parked on one side of the field, and forty-plus P-47 Thunderbolts were parked on the opposite of the runway—with all planes dispersed non-uniformly around the countryside.

For the Allies, January 1, 1945, was just another day to do battle.

The 487th was scheduled to fly escort on a bombing mission over central Germany. On New Year's Eve, Lt. Col. Meyers, Squadron Leader of the 487th and Temporary Commanding Officer of the 352d Fighter Group, saw the operations report for the entire wing to fly escort. He immediately picked up the phone, contacting the Ninth Air Force Commanding General "Pete" Quesada, requesting that a squadron be kept behind for security measures. The Headquarters refused his request. However, Col. Meyers was adamant, and repeated his call several times. Finally, the fourth call got the desired results from General Quesada, and Col. Meyers immediately selected eleven persons in his squadron for a 5:30 A.M. wake-up call.

The officers were notified of their early morning responsibilities, and were told to get a good night's sleep since they would be up early. The 487th Squadron included Squadron Leader

Lt. Col. Bill Halton, Capt. Bill Wisner, Capt. Sanford Moats, Capt. Henry Stewart, Capt. Ray Littge, Lt. Alden Rigby, Capt. Nelson Jessup, Capt. Alex Sears, Lt. Dean Huston, Lt. Walker Diamond, and Lt. Col. John Meyers.

The next morning when the pilots piled out of their tent, the weather was foggy and overcast, with frost on the metal runway. While the pilots were having breakfast, the maintenance crews, who had been working all night, started the airplanes, double checked the armament, and topped off the extra gas tanks carried for escorting bombers. The P-51s burned a gallon of gas per minute, and with their tanks holding 360 gallons, their range was about six hours of flying time. When engaged in combat they would drop their auxiliary tanks for greater maneuverability.

That morning, the maintenance crew also prepared the other thirty-six aircraft with additional gas tanks for their escort assignment.

This fateful morning, the German "Operation Bodenplatte" was delayed due to the overcast conditions, but as the cover started to break up, the Luftwaffe was given the green light.

In Bodney the airfield was grass, so the planes would take off four-abreast. However, the steel fabricated runway at Y-29 permitted only two planes side by side. At mid-morning the weather was starting to break up. The twelve planes of the 487th taxied to the end of the runway, and Col. Meyers and his wingman advanced their throttles and raced down the runway. Looking ahead, they detected puffs of anti-aircraft fire above the trees. When they were about three feet off the ground, with wheels still down, the first two Focke-Wulf 180s dropped in over the trees. Spotting the big C-47s beside the runway, they veered to destroy them, crossing the takeoff path of Col. Meyers. Meyers gave them a short burst from his six .50 caliber machine guns, destroying one plane and damaging the other. He retracted his wheels and looked for more German planes.

As the remainder of the 487th squadron took to the air, they immediately started a one-on-one dogfight with the fifty or so German planes that were swarming the area. There was no opportunity to form teams—the usual fighter technique of an attacker with a wingman to protect the attacker. Each pilot was without a wingman, on his own ability, and each pilot rose to the occasion.

The aerial combat was intense, with most of it happening within one-half mile of the airfield, under 1000 feet, and within full view of the flight crews. The maintenance and armament crews saw their team in combat for the first time, and "cheered the dogfights as though they were attending a football game."

As the German airplanes continued to roar in, the maintenance personnel sought refuge, some hiding under fully-loaded gasoline tanker trucks. One airman found shelter in a bomb storage facility, not recognizing its inherent danger until the battle was over.

FW-190s had been assigned the task of strafing the field, while Me-109s supplied overhead air cover. Immediately, all were involved in the dogfight. Col. Meyers continued his attack, shooting down two more airplanes before running out of ammunition. He then spent half an hour avoiding contact with the enemy, not wanting to land for fear of being a sitting duck. At one point, two 109s found him, but when he feinted an attack, they sped off.

Other members of the squadron continued to do battle with great success.

Huston was finally airborne when, at about 350 feet, he found a 190 on the tail of Lt. Moats, who was attacking another 190. Huston called for Moats to turn left, and when he did, Huston climbed under the tail of the pursuing 190 and gave it a two-second burst. The aircraft took numerous hits—throwing off debris—and caught fire, and nosed into the ground. He immediately did a 180-degree turn and found he was on the tail of two 109s. He was about to give a short burst when he noted any overshoot would hit Allied planes on the ground, so he maneuvered to a new angle and was set to pull the trigger when his P-51 suddenly lurched.

Huston glanced at his instruments—his oil pressure was zero. Without oil, the 1650 horsepower Merlin Rolls Royce engine would either blow up or freeze. He had to make an immediate decision whether to try to save the airplane or bail out. At his altitude, the prospect of releasing the canopy, rolling over to bail out, and having the chute open in free fall was not a good one. His alignment, fortunately, was directly at the airfield, and he decided to try to land as best he could. He dropped the wheels and headed in. As expected, his engine froze as he touched the ground and he rolled in without power. He managed to keep rolling to get off the runway so other planes could land without hazard. He leapt out of the airplane and found a slight depression in which he could wait out the combat.

The air battle continued for another half an hour, at which time the Germans hastily retreated from the area.

The results of the battle over Y29 were astounding. Twenty-three German aircraft were destroyed by the twelve planes and were scattered around the nearby countryside still burning. Many more were damaged and were retiring from the fray.

Two American C-46s were damaged. Not one single fighter plane was lost, either in the air or on the ground. Several of the P-51s were damaged, but remained in flying condition. An hour later, the remainder of the 352d Fighter Group fulfilled their mission—escorting bombers over Germany.

Huston's "Hawk-eye-oan" was the only casualty. It had one small, half-inch hole in the engine cowling. They later learned the plane had been hit by one .50 caliber bullet fired by Allied anti-aircraft, and that bullet hit the oil pump dead-center. Huston had been shot down by friendly anti-aircraft fire. Up to that time, only two pilots in the 352d Wing had been shot down by friendly fire—Lt. Huston and Maj. Preddy.

Huston had survived, but missed a great opportunity to add to the number of airplanes destroyed.

Lt. Col. Meyer was credited with two planes down. Capts. Whisner and Moats got four planes apiece. Capt. Stewart and Lt. Rigby each claimed three planes, and Capt. Littge downed two planes. Col. Halton, Capt. Jessup, Capt. Sears, Lt. Diamond, and Lt. Huston each claimed one "kill."

"Operation Bodenplatte" turned into a disaster for the Luftwaffe. Of the eventual 600 to 800 airplanes that actually participated, the Germans lost 230 aircraft, including 30 of their most experienced pilots. They did manage to destroy, on other airfields, over 160 Allied airplanes. But their total loss of planes and pilots was a sound defeat for the Luftwaffe. Most of the German planes destroyed at other fields were brought down by anti-Aircraft fire.

The superior performance of the 487th on New Year's Day was one of the best examples of superior training, equipment, and determination. Later that day, General Carl Spatz, General Hoyt Vandenberg, and General Elwood "Pete" Quesada flew in to Y-28 to compliment the 487th for their outstanding performance. Their compliments were drowned out by the pilots and maintenance and armament personnel who had watched the action from the ground and continued to "cheer the pilots like they were at an Army-Notre Dame football game."

Lt. Huston's "Encounter Report" states:

"I was flying Yellow 4 and managed to join White 5, Lt Moats just after takeoff, even though the fight was already going on, almost at the edge of the field. I was about 300 yards astern and above Lt Moats when a FW 190 started to crawl up behind him. Lt Moats was already engaged with another ship and I told him to break left. He did and the 190 followed but not with enough lead. I broke down and under him coming up in a turn about 100 to 200 yards behind him, firing about a 2-3 sec burst. Hits were observed all over the wings and fuselage, with flames resulting immediately. He went into a dive from about 2000 ft (?) and crashed into the ground. I saw no chute.

I claim One (1) FW 190 Dest."

Signed: Lt. Dean Huston

The 2000-foot entry is suspect because Huston does not remember getting above 500 feet during his time in flight. Very few airplanes got above 1000 feet that day.

One Me-109 had crash-landed about a quarter-mile from the end of the runway and had not burned. Huston and two other pilots jumped into a jeep and drove out to inspect the enemy aircraft, because they had not seen one up close. As they approached the airplane, the German pilot was still in the cockpit, dead. Huston was dismayed to discover a fifteen- or sixteen-year-old fuzzy-faced lad, who had responded to his country's call for one last-ditch effort to end Allied air supremacy. This discovery of the young airman made a profound impact on Dean—and it still bothers him to this day. **He** was just a kid. He was *just* a kid. He was just a **kid**.

*Me-109 shot down over Asche, Belgium, during the "Legend of Y-29." It was piloted by the ill-fated teenager.
(Photo courtesy of Robert H. Powell)*

# HUSTON
# CHAPTER FIVE

With Huston's "Hawk-eye-oan" rendered "hors de combat," he immediately started pressing for the installation of a new engine, which was promptly attended to. The only damage to the exterior skin was one small half-inch hole in the cowling—much less damage than other airplanes engaged in the air battle had received. It took several weeks for the engine installation and for working out the bugs, as his logbook attests. With the new engine installed, Huston went on a test flight to fly it to maximum capacity, and took it up to 39,600 feet. Huston indicated the "stick got a little floppy at that height," and he was afraid of stalling out. After the repairs met his satisfaction, several missions were flown GCI (Ground Control Intercept) in response to suspected attacks by isolated German Aircraft. After the January 1 incident, a little more attention was paid to incoming foreign aircraft.

The January 1 incident raised a good number of "what if" questions:
- What if General Quesada had refused to allow one squadron to remain behind?
- What if the weather had broken and the Luftwaffe had arrived five minutes earlier?
- What if Lt. Col. Meyers was not taxiing down the runway as the Germans came over the trees?
- What if the entire squadron had not gotten airborne?
- What if Huston's plane had not been hit as he was about to fire a two-second burst?
- What if the bullet penetrating Huston's plane had been thirty-six inches to the rear?
- What if Huston's plane had not been aligned on the runway?
- What if the American pilots had not had superior training and experience?

In terms of crippling the U.S. fighter force and extending the conflict, five minutes made a substantial difference. In terms of shortening the war, the performance of the 487th Squadron made a substantial difference. The air battle became known as the "Legend of Y-29."

Huston completed his tour of duty on April 3, 1945, and his rotation to return to the United States began. Huston had flown a total of seventy-three missions, and received the Air Medal and the Distinguished Flying Cross. He destroyed a FW-190 and a Me-109 in the air, and a Ju-52 on the ground.

On April 13, the 352d Fighter Group returned to Bodney, England, to their old base. They continued to fly missions with replacements pouring in as the veteran pilots completed their tours of duty. The 352d continued to establish a stellar record in the defeat of the German Luftwaffe.

At the conclusion of the war in Europe, the 352d Fighter Group counted 519 German airplanes destroyed, with a loss of only 118 planes. It was the best performance by a fighter group in the European Theater of Operations.

The 352d Fighter Group's special efforts were rewarded with two Distinguished Unit Citations.

Lt. Huston was awarded the Air Medal with six Oak Leaf Clusters.

He also received the Distinguished Flying Cross (DFC). The DFC Citation read:

*"For extraordinary achievement in aerial flight over continental Europe on September 10, 1944, November 27, 1944 and January 1, 1945. On the first date, Lt. Huston, with his squadron, made a daring attack on an enemy airdrome. Exhibiting great skill and courage, he assisted in neutralizing a flak tower and three gun emplacements, and then strafed the field destroying one Ju52.*

*During the mission dispatched on Nov 27, the squadron encountered approximately thirty ME-109s, one of which was shot down by Huston. For the remainder of the operation he flew cover for his element leader while the leader attacked and destroyed seven locomotives.*

*On Jan 1, Huston was taking off from an advanced base on the continent when approximately fifty enemy fighters attacked. Although he was impeded by full fuel tanks, he unhesitatingly joined in the battle and was successful in destroying one aircraft. The expert airmanship, courage and zeal in combat displayed by Lt. Huston on these occasions reflect the highest credit upon himself and the Army Air Forces."*

The "Hawk-eye-oan" was reassigned to Lt. Myron Reynolds. On April 17, while escorting a group of bombers over Germany, the fighters broke off to strafe several airfields in the area. Lt.

Reynolds and the "Hawk-eye-oan" never returned, and was listed as missing in action.

Huston left England aboard a converted cruise ship, landing in the U.S. on April 23, 1945, the day President Roosevelt passed away. Huston arrived at his home in Early, Iowa, on May 6, for a well-deserved leave.

For his next assignment, he was ordered to report to the Redistribution Center at Santa Ana, California, on May 28.

The local newspaper carried an interesting account of what happened next:

*"Lt. Dean Huston, who recently spent a furlough at home after serving with a P-51 fighter group in England, has received an honorable discharge from the air corps. Upon completion of his furlough, Dean reported to the Air Forces redistribution center at Santa Ana CA, where he was informed that he was eligible for discharge and given one week to accept. Dean wrote home that it was the hardest decision he has ever been called upon to make. He conferred with several of his Air Force buddies and with chaplains, who convinced him that he should accept the discharge. Such discharges are given with the provision that the discharged may be recalled to duty at any time that he is needed and at the same rank when discharged. Dean is expected home next week."*

Dean returned to Early, Iowa, to a flurry of family gatherings, dinners, and celebrations.

The young man had left his community September 1943, and returned a hero in May 1945. For twenty months, he was fortunate to survive the opportunity of a lifetime—flying a beautiful aircraft in a deadly game.

A good deal of national news was breaking at this time; President Franklin Roosevelt passed away on April 23, 1945. The four-term President who had served through the depression, provided moral support and lend-lease to England and Russia, and envisioned our world political structure after the international conflict, did not live to see the unconditional surrender of Germany or Japan. Harry Truman, who was sworn in as our thirty-second President, attended to those details.

On May 14, President Truman entered the Oval Office, flanked by his cabinet, aides, and family. It was his sixty-first birthday, and he started to read a speech he had just delivered to 200 newsmen a few moments before. At 9:00 A.M. the radio broadcast began, and in a clear unemotional voice, he announced the victory in Europe. "The Allied Armies, through sacrifice and devotion, and with God's help..." The physical conflict in Europe had ended. A larger political conflict was about to begin.

In August the first atomic bomb was dropped, and soon after victory in the Pacific was achieved and celebrated.

In September of 1945, Dean joined the hundreds of returning veterans taking advantage of the GI Bill and reentered Iowa State College to complete his degree. He changed his major and received a Bachelor of Science in Agricultural Economics degree in the spring of 1948. After graduation he took a position at the Storm Lake DeKalb Seeds Plant, just a few miles from his hometown in Early, Iowa.

When the Korean conflict broke out in 1950, there was some concern that Dean would be recalled to service. He secretly relished the opportunity to fly a jet aircraft. By this time he was married, and fortunately the call to arms was not received. However, a close friend was recalled and retrained to fly jets. To Dean's dismay, the young man "bought the farm" in Korea.

# HUSTON
## CHAPTER SIX

The Memorial Union at Iowa State College (ISC) was a large, gray limestone Italiante-style building sitting majestically on a side hill, reflecting its imposing form in a small lake close by. Although large, it was delicate and formal in detailing. It was the center for socializing and alumni services on campus. Iowa State was not considered a "socializing campus," but plenty of hand-holding and nuzzling went on inside its cavernous spaces. It also provided part-time work for a number of Iowa farm boys and girls, which contributed significantly to their tuition costs.

The general manager of the Union was "a growed-up farm boy" who understood and liked his association with students. Don Stevens was a sandy-haired gentleman who enjoyed his role serving the ISC community. On one occasion, he ran into Dean Huston and without solicitation remarked, "You know, Dean, I know a young lady I think you should meet." To this day, we do not know if that was a legitimate service of the Memorial Union or not. Nor do we know the frequency of Stevens's casual observations.

Maybl Gertrude Olson was unusual in two ways: First, she was named after a close friend of her mother, thus the spelling of Maybl. Second, she was raised with indoor water, indoor plumbing, and indoor electricity—a rarity in those days.

Her father was a respected professor and the head of Engineering Drawing at ISC. Oscar (O.A.) and Goldie Olson lived in town, where Maybl and her older sister Louise attended Roosevelt Grade School, Junior High, and the new Ames High School at Fifth and Clark streets.

When she graduated from high school, she felt the need to attend a college away from home, and chose Grinnell College in Grinnell, Iowa—a scant eighty miles down the road. Grinnell College, with an enrollment of only 400 men and 400 women, was a well-respected academic institution. Maybl was interested in a teaching career. Since Grinnell focused on preparing students in the disciplines of science, medicine, law, and religion, Maybl decided to transfer to the National College of Education in Evanston, Illinois; this school had a national reputation for progressive teaching. Graduating in 1943, she accepted a position in Lakewood, Ohio, teaching second grade. Being on her own, several hundred miles from Ames, was a great learning experience. After teaching for two years she wanted a change of scenery, so she worked for two years for an internal and allergy specialist in Lakewood—particularly enjoying learning about the field of medicine.

Maybl's mother passed away while she was teaching in Lakewood, which was quite traumatic for her. While working in the doctor's office, she received word that her father was having a difficult time adjusting to widowhood, and she decided to return to Ames to look after him. She returned in November of 1947, not only to live with her father, but also to serve as a secretary for her father's side-business.

As a professor of Engineering Drawing, Mr. Olson had designed a lettering guide of machined, clear plastic that permitted adjusting guidelines for lettering. It was simple, sophisticated, and precise. It encouraged uniformity and consistency in lettering. It trained thousands of young engineers, architects, and draftsmen to letter better. It also meant that every young engineer, architect, and draftsman had to have an Ames Lettering Guide in their pencil box. O.A. Olson's Ames Lettering Guide is an "American classic" in drafting circles.

Professor Olson's close friend, Don Stevens, called him one day and casually noted, "By the way, O.A., I have a blind date for your daughter." Professor Olson was a kindly man, and received his close friend's comment with good grace. Dean had just graduated and was leaving for Early, but the blind date was set up for March 25, 1948. Their first date was to a movie in Boone, Iowa; after the movie, they stopped by a "road house" in Boone for a casual beer and a little dancing. At that time, the Dean of Students at ISC was a staunch Methodist, and the only two taverns in the city of Ames were confined to the east end of Main Street. The Dean of Students employed two "plainclothesmen" who regularly toured the taverns in Story County, routing out any students who might succumb to the evils of drink. At one time, women students had to be in their dormitories at 10:30 P.M., and the house proctor would check their breath when they came in to verify they had not consumed (gasp!) beer or alcohol. Detection or repeated infractions could result in a dressing down or dismissal from school. A small onion or Sen-Sen (a breath freshener) in a co-ed's purse was as necessary as lipstick.

Consequently, sensible adults quietly visited other communities to avoid any discovery or confrontation. This, of course, changed when enough returning servicemen—who had been exposed to the worst conditions of the war—expressed their

*Dean and Maybl Houston cutting the cake at their wedding on June 8, 1950.*

viewpoint loudly and vociferously. Change was slow, but the GI's mission, once again, was accomplished. For many years, the College tried to display to their rural constituency that Ames was "just like Grundy Center, with a college in it."

Dean and Maybl had a delightful evening, and Maybl admitted, "He made my heart flutter." However, since Dean had accepted a position with DeKalb, their relationship was occasional and carried on at some distance. Dean decided to enroll in graduate school at ISC and returned in the fall of 1949. Dean and Maybl started seeing each other on a regular basis, and on Valentine's Day (and Dean's birthday) 1950, Dean asked Maybl to marry him. They exchanged vows at Bethesda Lutheran Church on June 4, 1950.

Dean and Maybl lived with her father until Dean received his master's degree in Agricultural Economics. They then moved to West Union, Iowa, where Dean became a District Extension worker, replacing a close friend. After one year, Dean became an extension specialist for 158 farms in Muscatine, Iowa. They lived there for

*Dean flying his Mooney Mark 21 over Ames. It is definitely not a P-51 D.*

seven years, adding two brothers to David Merle, who had been born in West Union on August 4, 1952. George Anton was born May 14, 1954, and Steven Vaughn entered the world February 3, 1958.

As O. A. Olson aged, he realized he needed someone to assist him in his business operation, and talked to Dean and Maybl about returning to Ames. Dean purchased an interest in Olson Manufacturing in 1958, and returned to Ames where they purchased a lovely home where they still live today.

In 1961, they grew out of Olson's "basement operation" and erected a new manufacturing plant on the outskirts of town. Dean took a hint from the movie "The Graduate," and branched out in sheet plastic, developing new markets for the clear acrylic material. Dean may have also been subliminally excited by the clear plastic because that was the material used in the bubble canopy of his P-51 D. As their sons attended college, gaining degrees in business and industrial education, they were introduced to the plastics business—starting Central Iowa Plastics in Des Moines, Iowa, and later Arrowhead Plastics in Kansas City, Missouri. The Ames plant, Olson Manufacturing, was later incorporated into the Arrowhead operation. The most recent expansion is a new manufacturing and retail facility in Omaha, Nebraska.

What became of the Ames Lettering Guide? It is no longer hand-machined from sheet goods, but is now injection-molded, with great precision. And there are still 100,000 sold every year.

In order to continue his interest in flying and expanding the business, Dean joined four or five friends in purchasing a single-engine Mooney four-passenger aircraft. As Olson Manufacturing expanded to Des Moines and Kansas City, scheduling business trips became a problem, so in the mid 1970s Huston purchased a Mooney Mark 21 to use for his frequent business trips. Parenthetically, Huston contends that some scheduled flights for fishing trips were all business. He continued flying until 1994, when he reluctantly gave up flying and sold his airship.

Dean paid his civic rent by serving on the Ames City Council for eight years, from January 1972 until December 1979. Serving on a city council in a university community with "an educated constituency" is a unique challenge. The social upheaval of the times certainly contributed to the difficulty of walking the fine line between responsible community judgment and a somewhat frivolous and judgmental society.

Dean also was an active member of the Ames Rotary Club, where his record of over twenty-seven years of perfect attendance surpasses all other club members. It reflects a determined staying power—and an unnatural resistance to heartburn.

Dean returned to England for the 352d Fighter Group reunion in 1985 and enjoyed the company of many of his flying friends. Many members of the 487th Squadron were there, and the strong camaraderie continued. He also attended reunions in Oklahoma City, Oklahoma, and Texas in later years.

On the return flight from the English reunion aboard a British Airways Boeing 747, Dean expressed to the steward his interest in visiting the cockpit. The steward contacted the pilot, who immediately invited Dean to visit with him up front. The pilot, Tom Stainthorpe, spent several hours talking to Dean in the cockpit. Unsaid, of course, was Stainthorpe's appreciation for American participation in WWII and the sacrifices that were made by the Air Force in defending his home country. Any two pilots can find many topics of mutual interest, and when the flight was completed, Huston wrote a thank-you note for the courtesy extended. Stainthorpe responded, and a great friendship developed. On the next trip over, Tom welcomed Dean to his English home. They attended a soccer match and visited several traditional English pubs to capture the local flavor. Dean and Tom continue to communicate regularly.

The twenty-month sojourn that exposed a young Iowa farm boy to combat conditions high in the skies over Germany is not without some serious reflection. Maybl has stated many times, "I'm glad I did not know Dean then. I would have been so worried."

Dean was one of the lucky ones who could live his dream. He was a part of General Dwight Eisenhower's "great crusade." He

*Huston visiting with pilot Stainthorpe in the cockpit of a Boeing 747 on the way to a group Reunion in England. Stainthorpe and Huston remain good friends.*

learned to fly, and kept flying in perspective. He served in the same squadron with two of the greatest aces in WWII. He served in a unit that took great pride in its accomplishments. He survived seventy-three missions without physical harm. He participated in one of the pivotal air battles in the latter stages of the war.

He was the recipient of the Distinguished Unit Citation Medal, Eastern Theater of Operations Medal with three stars, the Air medal with Six Oak Leaf Clusters, and the Distinguished Flying Cross.

And he was privileged to fly one of the most beautiful aircraft ever built.

It was a fortuitous twenty-month sojourn that Dean Huston can reflect on with great humility and quiet satisfaction.

*Oil painting by Harley Copic of the P-51 D "Moonbeam McSwing" piloted by Wm. T. Whisner 352d Fighter Group, 487th Squadron. (Photo courtesy of Marvin Bradburn)*

# BOOK FOUR

# DANKBAR

*Lieutenant Roman Dankbar*

*B-24 Bombardier*

*Fifteenth Air Force*

*47th Wing*

*98th Bomb Group*

*344th Squadron*

---

*"Our crew bombed Ploesti twice,
but I do not know what the missions were titled.
But we were sure there."*

*—Dankbar*

# DANKBAR
# CHAPTER ONE

Ploesti.

It is a word that causes WWII airmen to squint their eyes and turn quiet. Even those airmen who never flew there know of the many sorties, sacrifices, and stories about trying to bomb it.

Ploesti, Romania, was the site of several refineries and synthetic oil plants that were the main source of oil and gas that lubricated the Nazi military machine. Romania was one of Hitler's first conquests, and their refining facilities were necessary for the continuation of expanding his empire. The Allies recognized the importance of its products and made numerous concerted attempts to damage the facilities there. Only a few attempts were moderately successful. The cost was high.

Roman Dankbar did not participate on the original raid on Polesti. However, the 47th Wing, 98th Bomb Group, 344th Squadron of the Fifteenth Air Force, which he later joined, was the lead group of the main thrust of the second bombing—and his unit carried this proud distinction.

The first raid on Ploesti took place on July 1, 1943, by elements of the Eighth Air Force in England. Most of the airplanes never made it to the target as they were met by intense anti-aircraft fire and hundreds of German fighter planes. There was over sixty-percent loss of aircraft, and little damage done to the refineries.

The story of the second raid on Ploesti is retold here in order for us to understand the magnitude of commitment by the young airmen in carrying out their assigned duties.

The Ninth Air Force, 98th and 376th Bomb Groups flying B-24s, was stationed in the Benghazi-Benina sector of Libya. Col. John Kane was the Group Commander of the 98th Bomb Group and was popularly known as "Killer Kane." Early in July, the two heavy-bomber groups were reinforced in North Africa with three bomb groups from England. When the Allies invaded Sicily on July 10, 1943, they bombed airfields, ports, and other strategic targets before and after the invasion. A few days later, on July 17, they bombed Naples, and on July 19, they bombed Rome for the first time. Further operations were suspended so they could prepare for the next campaign.

The bomb groups flew a series of practice flights, long distances, to practice low-level bombing on targets marked on the desert floor that resembled the layout of refineries in Ploesti. Formation flying at low levels exposed them to prop-wash, the air turbulence caused by flying too close together. They viewed movies of the Ploesti area taken by photo-reconnaissance that showed the variety of facilities: power stations, distillation plants, refineries, and storage facilities. Once at the site, the bomb groups would disperse to their assigned specific targets. If the lead navigator was off from the main alignment by 100 feet, the following groups would be off course, and miss their target. Precision flying at low altitudes was mandatory. The objects were precision bombing and surprise.

Planes were modified by adding three machine guns in the nose above the bombsight, tilted slightly down, and controlled by the pilot. A modified gunsight replaced the Norden bombsight for use in low-level bombing. Two 400-gallon gas tanks were anchored in the bomb bays to enhance the fuel supply, and the rear bomb bay held four 1000-pound bombs. Planes flying at the rear of the formations held six 500-pound bombs with forty-five-second delay fuses. Waist gunners had several boxes of small incendiary bombs to throw out of the waist windows to add to the enemy's problems of repair and fire control.

On August 1, 1943, five groups of liberators lifted off the tarmac in Benghazi. The long flight proceeded from Benghazi over the Mediterranean to Albania, over southern Yugoslavia and the northern tip of Bulgaria, to Ploesti, Romania. After releasing the bombs, the bombers would return to the nearest Allied air base. The flight was expected to take no less than fourteen hours.

They crossed the Mediterranean at 2000 feet and reaching landfall, climbed to 16,000 feet to clear the mountains. Running into cloud cover, part of the group chose to fly above the clouds, while the other part chose to fly just under the clouds to conserve fuel. This separation caused serious problems, which ultimately were the demise of the mission. Since radio silence was mandatory, they could not communicate their locations. The airplanes above the clouds—aided by a change in the wind direction—were well ahead of the second group by a full sixty miles, and the single attacking force became two distinct forces. Instead of bombing simultaneously, there would be a time separation between strikes, enabling the Germans to adjust their guns for the second wave.

Col. Kane called for his groups to circle once, in order to tighten up the formation, since they had drifted apart going over the mountains. They approached their first Initial Point (IP), Pitesti, at

500 feet, and turned toward their second IP, Targoviste, on time and on target. As they turned to their third IP, they could see columns of smoke and flames rising ahead at Ploesti. The lead had separated from the group, instead waiting for the remainder of the group to catch up, and had made their run, dropped their bombs, and set the stage for a suicide-run by the remaining airplanes.

The second wave did not alter their course. They gritted their teeth and followed Col. Kane into the maelstrom.

As the bombardier took over aligning the airplane, the ground erupted with every caliber of weapon the Germans had available. Passing over the Phoenix Orion refinery, a storage tank exploded and the lid, 100 feet in diameter, flew through the formation like a frisbee. Col. Kane took his group on their bombing run at well under 250 feet, releasing their bombs on target. Every manned machine gun aboard the bombers returned fire at gun emplacements, and shot at anything that moved. A number of planes flew through flames rising from the ground, and many of the group did not make it through the run. Those that did had engines knocked out and severe damage to their planes.

Beyond Ploesti, the crippled airplanes joined one another, and the few undamaged planes flew close by for protection. The damaged planes could make only 135 miles per hour ground speed. Because of the crippled planes, Col. Kane asked the navigator to find the nearest Allied base. He ordered the planes lightened to conserve fuel, and machine guns, oxygen bottles, and all extraneous items were cast overboard.

Remnants of the 98th Bomb Group managed to take a direct course to Cyprus Island, violating Turkish Neutrality in doing so. One plane lost power and had to ditch at sea just off the Turkish coast. All personnel were lost.

Several of the damaged planes survived landing, but were damaged beyond repair and were abandoned. Their crews ultimately returned to their base in Benghazi.

The success of the bombing raid is suspect, because the refining capacity was partially reduced when facilities were only partially destroyed. The cost of the raid was expensive in planes and human lives when the 98th Bomb Group alone lost over sixty percent of its planes.

The 98th Bomb Group was originally at Hergla, Tunisia, in North Africa with the Ninth Air Force. When they moved to Brindazi, Italy, they were attached to the Fifteenth Air Force. Because of their North African connection, the bomb group was nicknamed the "Pyramiders."

The 98th Bomb Group later moved to Lecce, Italy, on January 17, 1944, which is where the crew that included bombardier Lt. Roman Dankbar joined the "Pyramiders."

# DANKBAR
## CHAPTER TWO

There are many sleepy small towns in the state of Iowa. Most of the small towns have origins resulting from railroad traffic in Iowa. Early trains needed lots of water for their boilers because the efficiency of engines was not the best. Every seven miles the train would stop to fill the water tank, which produced steam for the next seven miles. As a result, the "boiler factor" or the "railroad factor" established community patterns in rural Iowa. Railroad speculators would sell this area to an eastern investor, who would plat a town and commence to sell city lots.

As the steam boilers improved they required stopping every fourteen miles, then forty miles, and then greater distances before the introduction of the diesel engine into railroading. The towns fourteen miles apart flourished, then faded, when businesses moved to the towns that were forty miles apart. The smaller towns just sort of survived by serving the farming operations surrounding these communities. If there was no rail line present, a small community might focus on a local business, school, or church.

Haverhill, Iowa, a few miles south of Marshalltown, was on the Milwaukee Railroad main line and serviced the large Catholic population in the area. German Catholic farmers had emigrated during the late 1860's to avoid the constant small wars that plagued Europe at that time. Haverhill attracted German families that had settled in Luxembourg, Iowa, and Galena, Illinois, and most were of the second-generation variety.

Roman was born August 28, 1922, the youngest child of the twelve children of Henry and Elizabeth (Pille) Dankbar. Henry farmed 240 acres, two-and-a-half-miles from the bustling town of 144 people. It was a productive farm, and there were plenty of cows, pigs, and chickens as well as an oversized garden to feed a large family. They had outdoor plumbing, drew water from a deep well with a windmill, and lived without electricity. The family extravagance was to allow the children to study by Coleman gas lanterns, which were much more efficient and brighter than the smelly kerosene lamps. In 1936, Rural Electrification brought electricity to the farm and the first building wired was the barn, in order to install a brand new electric milking machine.

*Cadet Dankbar in his bombardier graduating class.*

The family consisted of five boys and seven girls. By the time Roman arrived, several sisters were working in Marshalltown and one brother was married. Being the youngest had its advantages, but getting out of work was not one of them. From his earliest years he was given chores on the farm, and he held a job while attending college.

In good Catholic tradition, Roman attended grade school at St. Joseph's parochial school in Haverhill, where the teaching nun had him sit in the front row because of his size. Several students in the class, held back from the previous year, emphasized the contrast in size. He then attended high school in Laurel, Iowa, graduating at seventeen years of age. In the fall of 1940, he began studies in Civil Engineering at Iowa State College.

Roman had to register for the draft when he turned eighteen, but instead, he enlisted in the Army Air Corps with the promise that he could complete his college education before reporting for service. However, as the mobilization of armed services changed, the demands changed, and Roman received orders to report in February, 1943. His desire to become a pilot was short lived, when he learned that that particular cadet class was full, so he opted to become a bombardier.

*Second Lt. Dankbar in his new uniform on his way overseas.*

Roman followed the familiar path to Jefferson Barracks, Missouri, then to Moorhead, Minnesota, for six weeks. At Moorhead, he took college classes, and spent ten hours learning to fly a Piper Cub. From there he went to Santa Ana, California, for pre-flight, and finally to Albuquerque, New Mexico, for bombardier training. Training lasted two months and consisted of flying in AT-11s and dropping dummy bombs from 10,000 feet. There was some radar training, but most was bombardier training. After AT-11s, they flew in B-24s—dropping bombs from 28,000 feet and were rated for hitting a 1000-foot diameter circle.

He received his bombardier wings and his commission as a Second Lieutenant in Albuquerque in April 1944, in Class 44-6. His wings and bars were pinned on by his commanding officer.

Dankbar next flew to Mountain Home, Idaho, where he met his new crew. August in Idaho was colder than usual, but it was still poor preparation for the exposure they would have during the winter months in Italy. The crew was transported to Lincoln, Nebraska, where they all admired their bright, shiny, new B-24. Lt. John Jamison, the pilot who just happened to be from Wisconsin, named the plane the "Badger Beauty." The co-pilot was Lt. Ralph Johnson from Chicago and the navigator was Norman Whalen, who was on his second tour of duty of fifty missions.

*Bombardier Dankbar, front low left, with his crew and B-24 bomber.*

From Lincoln, Nebraska, the new plane flew to Greiner Field, Connecticut, and the next day flew to Gander Field, Newfoundland. From there, they found the Azore Islands in the Atlantic, then flew on to Tunis, North Africa. From Tunis, they flew to Lecce, Italy, and were assigned to the Fifteenth Air Force, 47th Wing, 98th Bomb Group and 344th Squadron. The Crew had become "Pyramiders."

Pride in the "Pyramiders" was reinforced by navigator Norman Whalen, who was the lead on Col. Kanes's plane on the first bombing of Ploesti by the 98th. He recounted dropping their load of bombs on the McKee distillation plant of the Astra-Romana refinery at Ploesti at forty-three feet. They later learned they had completely demolished it.

They were in Lecce only three days when the pilot and navigator were assigned to another crew for two missions to get the feel of combat and what their responsibilities would be when en route. In order to add firepower to the front of the aircraft, a turret was placed in the nose of the plane, making the nose quite crowded. The gunner was inside the turret, the bombardier kneeled over the bombsight, and the navigator stood facing a small map table attached to the firewall in front of the pilot's compartment. Using the Norden bombsight became quite difficult when they were under attack, because the gunner and navigator were very active in the small space.

At Lecce, the crew moved into the city of tents and were not even acquainted with the base when they entered rotation and started flying missions. The four officers shared the four-person tent, with an oil heater whose inefficiency was exceeded only by heaters in a few other tents. Lt. Jamison was determined to have acceptable living accommodations, so he arranged for a wooden floor to be installed using packing crates scrounged from maintenance. He hired Italian laborers to erect a chimney to exhaust smoke well above the tent; the local workers would work hard all day for a pack of cigarettes—which had a good deal of trading value in town. A separate building held the toilet facilities, mess hall, and commanding officers' headquarters. There were no sidewalks, but there were gravel paths to keep soldiers out of the mud during the rainy season, which, incidentally, lasted all winter long. The paths were marginally successful.

The four officers slept on canvas folding cots, and lived out of their B-4 bag (a flexible canvas suitcase). Laundry was washed in any large can you could find, with soap purchased at the Post Exchange (if you were lucky), and clothes were dried on a line in the tent. Primitive, is the word.

Grumbling about accommodations kept their mind off the dangers to which they were exposed. Still, every day they bundled up in their flying suits and went to work destroying enemy facilities.

*Bombs exploding over Messina, some hitting the bay and some hitting the city.*

# DANKBAR
# CHAPTER THREE

Dankbar's missions started on September 24, 1944.

| | Date | Target | Flying Time |
|---|---|---|---|
| Mission 1: | 24 Sept 44 | Kalamaki | 6:10 |
| Mission 2: | 10 Oct 44 | Vicenza | 6:20 |
| Mission 3: | 12 Oct 44 | Borogini | 7:45 |
| Mission 4 & 5: | 13 Oct 44 | Vienna | 8:45 |
| Mission 6: | 14 Oct 44 | Maribor | 8:00 |
| Mission 6 & 8: | 17 Oct 44 | Vienna | 8:20 |
| Mission 9: | 23 Oct 44 | Ora. | 7:40 |
| Mission 10 & 11: | 06 Nov 44 | Vienna (Moosebier.) | 8:00 |
| Mission 12: | 07 Nov 44 | Avisio | 8:00 |
| Mission 13: | 15 Nov 44 | Innsbruck | 7:55 |
| Mission 14 & 15: | 17 Nov 44 | Vienna | 8:00 |
| Mission 16: | 18 Nov 44 | Aviano | 6:45 |
| Mission 17: | 21 Nov 44 | Zenica | 4:45 |
| Mission 18: | 22 Nov 44 | Ferrara | 6.20 |
| Mission 19: | 06 Dec 44 | Szombathely M/Y | 7:15 |
| Mission 20: | 16 Dec 44 | Innsbruck | 8:10 |
| Mission 21 & 22: | 18 Dec 44 | Florisdorf (Austria) | 7:45 |
| Mission 23 & 24: | 31 Jan 45 | Moosebier. (Austria) | 7:20 |
| Mission 25: | 01 Feb 45 | Moosebier. (Austria) | 8:00 |
| Mission 26 & 27: | 05 Feb 45 | Salzberg | 6:00 |
| Mission 28 & 29: | 14 Feb 45 | Moosebier. (Austria) | 8:10 |
| Mission 30 & 31: | 16 Feb 45 | Hall M/Y | 9:10 |
| Mission 32 & 33: | 19 Feb 45 | Vienna (Austria) | 8:15 |
| Mission 34: | 23 Feb 45 | Verona (N. Italy) | 8:15 |
| Mission 35 & 36: | 27 Feb 45 | Salzburg (Germ.) | 8:40 |
| Mission 37: | 28 Feb 45 | Isarco RR Bridge (N. Italy) | 7:40 |
| Mission 38 & 39: | 12 Mar 45 | Florisdorf (Austria) | 8:15 |
| Mission 40 & 41: | 13 Mar 45 | Regensburg (Germ.) | 8:55 |
| Mission 42: | 14 Mar 45 | Varazdin (Yugoslavia) | 6:55 |
| Mission 43 & 44: | 15 Mar 45 | Schwechat (Austria) | 7:20 |
| Mission 45 & 46: | 21 Mar 45 | Neuburg (Germ.) | 8:50 |
| Mission 47 & 48: | 23 Mar 45 | St. Vaientine (Aust.) | 8:35 |
| Mission 49 & 50: | 25 Mar 45 | Cheb-Obers. (Czech.) | 9:10 |

Sorties: 33        Missions: 50   Flying Time: 254:55 Hours

*Winter conditions at the city of tents, Toretta Field, near Foggia.*

# DANKBAR
## CHAPTER FOUR

Winter in Italy was unpredictable and very wet. The winter of 1944 was one of the most severe in Europe in many years, and the number of unusual weather fronts influenced the regular sorties over enemy territory. Missions flown in severely bad weather used radar to locate the targets, which assisted finding the targets but could not guarantee hitting them. Railroad marshalling yards were the chief targets because they distributed supplies to the German fighting men and women.

Unlike the Eighth Air Force, the Fifteenth Air Force used a squadron composed of seven airplanes, bomb groups consisting of four squadrons, and wings of three or four groups. Several bomb groups participated in a mission with each bomb group—and sometimes squadrons—assigned to a different target, dispersing once they arrived at the IP.

Once the crew arrived in Lecce, their shiny new plane was placed in a pool of airplanes used in combat. Assigned a plane from the pool, the crew found some adjustment was necessary since each plane had different handling characteristics. The maintenance crews worked overtime to keep the planes in top shape. Planes returning from missions were pretty well shot up, with engines needing repair or total replacement. Winter weather caused hydraulic lines and metal parts to perform in unusual ways. Adjustments were a constant factor in keeping the planes aloft. While in the air, damage to the hydraulic lines was a problem, but the planes had mechanical backup to drop the wheels, adjust the flaps, and keep other control items functioning.

On one mission flying in bad weather over northern Italy, Dankbar looked down through the nose plastic and discovered the plane below climbing under them, almost ready to touch them with their propellers. The pilot, after receiving the news, began an abrupt climb, putting the big four-engine bomber into a stall. At that moment, they ran into air turbulence from several airplanes ahead of them, which flipped the big bomber upside down. The pilot immediately performed a Split "S" maneuver to right the plane. During the plane's transition, some of the bombs fell out of the bomb rack with one 1000-pound bomb passing through the closed bomb bay door. Because the bomb bay doors were jammed,

Dankbar immediately cranked them open with the mechanical backup, releasing the remaining bombs. However, three bombs were still hung up. Treading carefully on the narrow four-inch walkway over the opening, Dankbar hand-released the remaining three bombs using a screwdriver to release the clips. He had the foresight to snap on a chest parachute before stepping into the bomb bay opening. The cold wind whipping through the airplane, or a sudden lurch could easily turn the bombardier into a "human bomb."

The pilot demanded to know what Dankbar had done, and he replied, "I took care of the problem!" This variance from specific procedures was dangerous, as any simple mistake might blow up the airplane. However, Roman's action of releasing the bombs was not reported to authorities by the pilot.

The plane returned to their home base, and the crew did not get credit for the mission. Instead of becoming a statistic, they were much relieved to be home—safe and sound.

It was not unusual for planes damaged on a mission to put down at an alternate field in order to make repairs before returning to their base. Dankbar's crew, during one sortie, had one engine damaged and one totally nonfunctional. They managed to land at an alternate field, boarded another airplane, and returned to Lecce.

Flak was a constant on every flight. The Germans never ran out of artillery shells and were efficient in directing their fire. Airmen knew the more important the target, the greater the concentration of anti-aircraft batteries. Winter weather usually produced heavy cloud cover, which meant that German fighters would be lurking nearby; it was much easier for them to dart in and out of the clouds to make a pass at bomber formations than it was in clear skies—and was not nearly as dangerous.

Once bombs left the planes, the bombers would leave the target as fast as possible. After dropping their load of bombs, air speed would improve and they would change altitude to escape anti-aircraft fire as they left the target. The success of the mission was sometimes observable by the tail gunner if visual contact was possible. The best confirmation of success or failure at bombing was verification by P-38 reconnaissance planes used to photograph the results.

The scheduling of missions was intense, as the Allies were intent on destroying Germany's capability of continuing the war. Because of the frequency of flying, an occasional day off permitted a trip to Naples or a nearby community. After completing one-half of their required missions, they received a two-week rest and recreation trip to the Isle of Capri. Organized into small groups, they toured the island and took in all the sights.

Occasional trips to nearby towns exposed Dankbar to young beggars along the roads who were desperate for food and/or money. What they could not receive through begging, they would try to steal. Begging was a condition of human frailty that was difficult for an Iowa boy, who had survived the Great Depression, to accept. It was hard to make a comparison, though, because there was food on the farm and Haverhill had not been under military siege for three years.

Dankbar wrote home to his mother two or three times a week. His mother and a sister wrote him about once a week. He rarely purchased items in town to send home because there were no craftsmen in the area, and selection was very poor. Dankbar did appreciate the packages he received from his mother, which arrived with great regularity. In reality, his mother was probably the only person at home who really understood the degree of Dankbar's exposure to danger. Mothers can be very good at reading between the lines.

Each officer's allowance of two bottles of whiskey per month was welcome, and they attempted to stretch the contents to last for a month. It did not always work. Gin and vodka were not rationed, but these liquors were new to American tastes. "Bourbon and seven" was the drink of choice of the airmen at that time (and may well be the same today). Whalen did not drink, a restraint greatly appreciated by his fellow compatriots.

Navigator Whalen loved the opera and constantly tried to get members of the crew to attend with him. Dankbar decided to give it a try and, on a leave to Naples, went to see Wagner's great work, *Lohengrin*. The central theme of *Lohengrin* is "man's search for a woman who trusts him implicitly, and is faithful to the end." The Haverhill, Iowa, boy found the opera boring. Whalen later convinced Dankbar to accompany him to see Bizet's *Carmen*. Dankbar found this presentation "pretty good" because he could understand the story. It was also sexier. However, it did not convert Dankbar, who has not returned to the opera in the last fifty-eight years.

Whalen, who was on his second tour of duty, attended seminary and was ordained as a priest. He asked for a release from his vows to serve in the Air Force. After 100 missions, he spent his later years teaching Anthropology at West Texas State College, while maintaining the commitment of his ordination.

The officers played a good deal of bridge in their off time. A poker game was steady fare at the Officer's Club. Stakes were high, and a paycheck (paid in Lira) would be gone in a day or two. Dankbar played some bridge, but sent his money home to pay for an education when the war was over.

The B-24s were modified on long sorties by placing two auxiliary gas tanks in the second bomb bay, enabling the planes to fly greater distances. The added weight reduced the quantity of bombs transported to the target. Bombs contained a nose propeller that would spin in descent, arming them to detonate on impact. Anti-personnel bombs usually detonated above ground. Incendiary bombs were either impact-type or delayed-fuse type. The type and size of bombs selected by operations were specifically for the type of targets they were attacking. The bombardier would oversee loading the bombs into the plane. He would check the safety wires on the bomb propellers, to assure they would extract as they left the plane.

The airfield at Lecce had a 6000 foot runway, which was barely long enough for a takeoff when the plane was fully loaded. Runways were constructed of asphalt, but the taxi strips were gravel. The taxi strips caused problems in wet weather when planes with full bomb loads veered too far from the centerline. On takeoff, the pilot retracted the wheels as soon as possible to miss fences and obstructions at the end of the runway.

Wintertime in Italy, particularly December through February, was the rainy season and it dictated when missions could fly. A check of dates of missions almost describes the nature of the weather and the intense pressure to get airplanes in the air during marginal weather. Successive days of flying meant the fatiguing routine of briefing, early to bed, early to rise, and exposure to flak and fighters. With the strong sense of duty, flying crews responded.

Several targets were bombed many times. If you bombed a particular target and never went back, you knew you had done a good job. Several repeat trips meant a partially damaged target or that it was reconstructed.

The Avisio Viaduct at the south end of Bremmer Pass in the Alps was one of the worst trips for Dankbar. It was well defended with fighters and anti-aircraft gun emplacements. Damage to their plane was considerable, and one of the crew members wounded in the hand received the Purple Heart. The intensity of the flak for an extended period of time damaged the plane, but it managed to make it back to the base. For Dankbar, it was a trip still vivid in his memory!

The nearer airmen were to completing the required number of missions, the more apprehensive they became about flying. There were too many recorded instances of crews being lost with only one or two missions remaining. Difficult targets were usually assigned to crews with the most experience, which probably contributed to their presentiment. Crews would be more hesitant in carrying out routine tasks, which made them more vulnerable in execution and response. The last four missions that members of the "Badger Beauty" crew flew were credited as double missions, reflecting their difficulty and level of danger. Dankbar particularly feared the intensity and exposure in those last sorties.

Finally, the missions were over.

After a few days, Dankbar was taken to Naples where he boarded a French ocean liner, the Mariposa. They steamed across the Mediterranean, through the Straits of Gibraltar, toward the U.S. They landed in Boston Harbor, Massachusetts. It was May 1945.

*The wedding of Roman Dankbar and Audrey Welp took place in Haverhill on June 23, 1947.*

# DANKBAR
# CHAPTER FIVE

Mother's cooking was even better than he had remembered. Roman had never really complained about the food in the camp at Lecce, but now he found the contrast with his mother's cooking remarkable. Leave was spent visiting family and friends, who found Roman a bit quieter and more mature. Sleeping in a real bed, on a real mattress, in a house without canvas walls, was a welcome change.

After his leave, he reported to Santa Ana Rehabilitation Center in California where he was presented the option to continue as a combat bombardier in the Pacific Theater, or go to a training center for becoming an instructor. He opted for the instruction school and was sent to Midland, Texas, to begin training. While at Midland, the atom bomb was dropped on Hiroshima, and V-J Day was celebrated. He was given the option to continue in the service or be discharged. He chose to be discharged in order to return to college. It was late August 1945.

He returned home to discover that Iowa State College (Now University) had began the fall quarter. Waiting until winter quarter, he reentered the college taking refresher courses offered to returning servicemen so they could get back into the college mindset.

Roman's sister was working in Marshalltown, Iowa, for an insurance company as a bookkeeper. It was a period of big bands traveling across Iowa and playing in dance halls and emporiums in small towns. Roman's sister and her husband arranged for Roman to date a young lady working in the insurance office and to attend a big dance at the Marshalltown Coliseum. The band was the famous "Blue Baron and His Orchestra." The young lady was Audrey Welp of Haverhill. She had been only one year behind Roman in the parochial school, but they only knew each other casually. Audrey was a city girl, whose father ran the grain elevator and lumberyard in Haverhill. After parochial school she attended Van Cleve High School, then the American Institute of Business in Des Moines before finding work in the insurance office in Marshalltown.

After the big band evening, they dated regularly, with Roman driving home from college on weekends. The option of getting married while Roman was in college and trying to live on the GI Bill was squeaky at best, but love won out.

They were married June 23, 1947, at the Immaculate Conception Church in Haverhill. The church is reminiscent of the big cathedral in Dyersville, Iowa, except it has only one spire, and is a scaled-down version of that impressive structure; the beautiful interior has a high arched ceiling covered with oil paintings. Audrey's brother, Cyril, was best man, and Roman's niece Helen Engster (Severson) was the maid of honor. After a brief honeymoon at Lake Okoboji, they returned to a small apartment on Duff Avenue in Ames. The rent was cheaper for Audrey and Roman because Roman stoked the coal furnace that heated the entire building. He also carried out the ashes and tidied up the furnace room. Every opportunity for Roman to add to the family income was welcome.

Roman continued studying Civil Engineering at Iowa State College. The study of Civil Engineering is a sobering experience, as it dwells extensively on mathematics and theoretical and applied mechanics. Waste-water treatment and soils compaction demand undue concentration, but are not subjects that make the spirit soar. Roman dutifully carried his slide rule from class to class, and solved problems in deflection and fluid mechanics, did moment diagrams, and closed survey station points. Roman studiously applied himself and graduated at the end of the spring quarter in 1948.

During college, he worked summers at the Highway Commission and made many friends who would be helpful later on.

Upon graduation, Roman accepted an engineering position with the Illinois Central Railroad, who was looking for an engineer with knowledge in soils engineering. It seems that a new dam site was under construction in Granada, Mississippi, which required the relocation of eleven miles of rail line. Roman worked for the Illinois Central for four and a half years. From Granada, he moved to Tennessee to work in the rail design office, then moved back to Jackson, Mississippi, as the Assistant Track Supervisor. From there Roman and Audrey moved to Freeport, Illinois, where Roman worked for three and a half years as Track Supervisor of the rail line from Chicago, Illinois, to Waterloo, Iowa, with a spur to Madison, Wisconsin.

Roman and Audrey added Elizabeth Anne to expand their family April 18, 1949, when they were living in Granada. William Edward arrived November 7, 1952, and Diane Teresa joined the family April 29, 1955.

Roman and Audrey tired of moving every few years, and wanted to get closer to Iowa State College where there were more employment options. Roman went to work in Des Moines for the Pittsburgh-Des Moines Steel Company, one of the largest steel fabricators in the country. Roman worked in the Structural Engineering Department, working on steel bridges and water tanks. He took the opportunity to study for, and take, the Professional Engineering Licensing Examination to get his professional engineering license. He worked for Pittsburgh-Des Moines for four years.

Designing structural steel was really not Roman's main interest, so he applied at the Highway Commission in Ames, Iowa, (which later became the Department of Transportation) and was hired in the road design section. After one and a half years, he joined the Bureau of Public Roads, where he started work in 1967, and retired in December 1985. Roman and Audrey lived in Springfield, Illinois, for six years, Washington, D.C., for three years, and Homewood, Illinois, (location of the regional office) for three years.

The Department of Transportation learned that Roman had retired and lured him back to Ames for four and a half years to take advantage of his expertise. He retired for good in 1991. He now spends his time looking after the family farmland and an acreage in the Ames area.

Roman looks back on his service experience and commitment with quiet introspection. There was no fanfare, no major hoopla. It was like doing chores on the farm. It was a fact of life! It was a job that had to be done! There was no particular special feeling of patriotism. No altruism. He wanted to do something about the conflict, do what had to be done, and get it over with!

Roman's favorite song during the war was not sentimental or reflective. It was the Army Air Corps Song! "Off we go, into the wild blue yonder…" This probably says more about Roman's commitment to "getting the job done" than one might realize.

# BOOK FIVE

# KETELSEN

*Second Lt. Arthur Ketelsen*

*B-17 Pilot*

*Eighth Air Force*

*351st Bomb Group*

*510th Squadron*

*"You're from Regensburg?
We bombed Regensburg during the war!"*

—*Ketelsen*

# KETELSEN
# CHAPTER ONE

It was a gray somber day in Chicago, Illinois. The winds blowing off Lake Michigan coursed through the downtown area and into the suburbs, spreading the penetrating cold dampness of December air. The streets were slushy from the recent snow, and the plowed snow lined the streets in uneven piles. Dee and Art Ketelsen attended the church service at Our Saviour's Lutheran Church in Riverdale, Illinois, and afterward walked the three blocks toward their small one room apartment in Dolton, Illinois. They looked forward to an afternoon of browsing through the large Chicago Sunday paper, a pleasant task that would take most of the chilly afternoon.

Dolores Kipley and Art Ketelsen were married on October 25, 1941, in that same church and were still enjoying the newness of "wedded bliss." The small apartment in the Chicago suburbs suited their needs, and every workday Art and Dee commuted to their jobs in downtown Chicago.

The couple was married in Riverdale, Illinois, Dolores's hometown. The Kipleys lived in Riverdale for several generations, and were prominent in many community activities. Edward Kipley was the fire chief who married Dorothea Warning, whose family was also longtime residents of that community.

The man Art selected for his best man was in military service and unable to return for the wedding. The young soldier was working in a military supply depot in New Zealand, a long way from Riverdale. It was an unusual coincidence that military equipment was being processed in that area in October of 1941. It was also an unusual coincidence that the commanding officer of the supply depot was a gentleman named Alden Harrison who, after the war, would become a vice-president of the Union Story Bank in Ames, Iowa.

Art managed to find another best man, and the ceremony successfully united the couple in a marriage lasting over sixty years.

Art was born February 12, 1920, in Chicago, the son of Arthur F. Ketelsen, originally from Chicago, and Frieda Kuehl Ketelsen, originally from Oshkosh, Wisconsin. Mr. Ketelsen worked for Railway Express Agency (the early train version of UPS) and

*Doris Kipley and Art Ketelsen's wedding picture October 25, 1941, In Riverdale, Illinois.*

*Laird Hansen, the man Art wanted for his best man, returned on leave and met Art's son, who was seven months old. Art was on leave returning from overseas.*

traveled on trains sorting packages for delivery. Art Jr. attended school in the Logan Square area of Chicago, which was in a dense neighborhood district. For nine years, Art did not know that a baseball field had a right field and a left field; there was only centerfield—between the cars in the street they used as a ball diamond. Then one day his Uncle Bill took him to a Cubs game, and he actually saw baseball played on a grass field that was very big—and there were no cars parked on the field!

When Art was nine years old, the family moved to a new home, only six blocks from the Cubs' ball park. Art attended high school at Lane Tech High School, graduating in February 1938. He was unemployed until September, when he was fortunate to find employment at Hibbard Spenser Bartlett. Jobs were very hard to find, even though the economic depression had lessened somewhat. Hibbard Spenser Bartlett (HSB) was a wholesale hardware company servicing the central United States. Housed in a large building thirteen stories tall and almost a city block square, it was located in downtown Chicago—east of the Wrigley Building on the Chicago River. Art worked as a jobber, responding to orders from small hardware stores in several states. It was at HSB that Art first met Dee, who was working as a bookkeeper handling accounts for the state of Iowa. Ironically, Carr Hardware of Ames, Iowa, was one of her accounts, and forty years later she would be a part-owner of the store.

On this December day Dee and Art were looking ahead, making plans for the Christmas season, when early afternoon special reports interrupted the Sunday radio programming. Aircraft from Japanese aircraft carriers were bombing the navy base at Pearl Harbor on Oahu in the Hawaiian Islands. The degree of damage caused by the surprise attack would soon be available. They spent the rest of Sunday afternoon listening to reports in disbelief, apprehension, surprise, and anger.

When he turned eighteen, Art registered for the selective service draft as was required of all young Americans, but his draft number was not imminent. After he was married, his new number meant he would be one of the last persons called into service. He continued to work as a hardware jobber until he received notice of his draft in November of 1942. Art took his physical and passed it, but wanted to select his branch of service. The next morning he visited the Air Corps' Recruiting Office and enlisted. Getting out of his selective service commitment by taking his name off the Draft Board's list took considerable paperwork, but the Board finally acquiesced.

Art received his notice for active duty in January 1943, and reported to Miami Beach, Florida, for induction and Basic Training. Dee left her job at HSB to take a job at the Air Corps G.F.E. Depot Number Four on Michigan Avenue, in downtown Chicago. She remained there until she joined her husband at his service assignment.

Basic Training in Miami Beach was not the usual military situation. Instead of living in drab army barracks, soldiers lived in hotels on the beach. Instead of practicing marching and physical fitness on a dusty parade ground, they marched up and down Collins Avenue, the main street in the beach area. Local citizens complained constantly about the troops getting up at the first light of dawn, doing calisthenics, then shouting HUP-TWP-THRIP-FAR as they learned the fine art of close-order drill. The local citizens complained about the early morning interruptions to the point that a local newspaper issued a headline story stating, "BETTER U.S. TROOPS DRILLING THAN HITLER'S TROOPS!"

Completing Basic Training, Art went to North Carolina State College Training Detachment, where he took college courses in preparation for Cadet Training. There he took the math, physics, and core courses necessary for entry into pilot training. The physical education instructor for the detachment was Herman Hickman, a successful football coach at the University of Tennessee. Hickman noticed that during the training the soldiers gained strength, but not much weight, and was concerned about their health. Investigating their diet, Hickman learned the men were served pork at every meal, and when he insisted on a well-rounded diet including red meat, he saw the men finally begin to put on some weight.

After completing the course work at North Carolina State, Art went to Nashville, Tennessee, to take a series of tests to determine whether the candidates would become pilots, navigators, or bombardiers. Art was selected for pilot's training and went to Pre-Flight at Montgomery, Alabama, where candidates again took additional class work and were subjected to intense physical training.

After Pre-Flight, Art went to Ocala, Florida, for Primary Flight Training where they flew the PT-17 Stearman aircraft, a bi-plane with a 250 horsepower engine. It was a delight to fly the open cockpit airplane, which Art thoroughly enjoyed. It was his first opportunity to "fly by the seat of your pants."

It was also his *last* opportunity to "fly by the seat of your pants."

In Bainbridge, Georgia, they learned to fly the BT-13 two-seat enclosed-cockpit training plane. Dee left her job in downtown

Chicago and joined him at Bainbridge for his two-month training period; this made Art's life during training a good deal more bearable. The next training site was a short trip to Turner Field in Albany, Georgia, where Art flew the twin-engine AT-11, preparing for multi-engine aircraft. During flight training, the instructors' famous phrase when admonishing the cadets was, "If you screw up, you are going to wind up flying in a gunnery school!"

The cadet class successfully completed its training, and in February 1944, class 44-B graduated. At the graduation ceremony, Dee Ketelsen pinned on Art's wings and gold bars as a Second Lt. in the Air Force. They immediately boarded an Illinois Central Railroad train crowded with new Second Lts. and headed for Dolton for a two-week leave.

It was 798 days since the leisurely stroll from Our Saviour's Lutheran Church in Riverdale on December 7, 1941.

*Ketelsen's crew. Front row: Angelo LoPresto from Mystic, Connecticut; Dominic Nuccio from New York City; Jack Wright from New Albany, Missouri; Eugene Percy from Oxford, Iowa; Frank Julian from Nottenfort, West Virginia. Back Row: Ketelsen; Stan Enforth from Ollani, California; Jim Simon from Merced, California; Dick Famris from Livermore, California.*

# KETELSEN
## CHAPTER TWO

Ketelsen's next assignment was at Columbus, Ohio, where he had his first opportunity to fly the B-17 Flying Fortress. For two months, the new pilots practiced getting the big B-17 off the ground, and then back on the ground. The four-engine aircraft was a brand new flying experience, due to its size and power. Each instructor worked with five pilots and demanded their best efforts. They flew every day, with non-flying time filled with classroom activity.

After several months of instruction, a night cross-country solo flight was scheduled. The pilots took turns on each leg of the solo flight, and served as crew when another pilot flew. As it turned out, the destination was Chicago. By coincidence, the three pilots in Ketelsen's group were also all from Chicago. The trip from Columbus to Chicago went smoothly and, once over the city, each pilot took his turn flying over his neighborhood and house at 7000 feet. It was every pilot's dream.

At the end of their B-17 instruction, Ketelsen's instructor called the five married pilots in the training group into his office. The airmen did not quite know what to expect, since he had been one of their toughest instructors. The instructor cleared his throat, and started, "Gentlemen, at ease. Gentlemen, I am going to do you a favor. I am going to recommend you for Gunnery School."

The five pilots went to Gunnery School without "screwing up."

The other pilots in the training class became replacement pilots in the European Theater of Operations, and were pretty well shot up—or down, as the case may be. At that critical juncture of the war, there was a relatively high mortality rate among bomber pilots and crews. Most of the replacement pilots in Ketelsen's class did not return from their overseas assignments. The instructor had, indeed, done the five young pilots a favor.

The five pilots went to Tyndall Field, Panama City, Florida, in April 1944, where they flew B-17s that trained machine gunners in their various locations in the plane. The gunners would practice shooting air-to-air, air-to-ground, and high-altitude firing, while wearing oxygen equipment and coping with cold temperatures. They flew locally around Tyndall Field, along the coast of Florida at Apalachicola, and over the Gulf. Although they flew every day, it was good duty, since they flew mornings and had the afternoons off, or alternated mornings and afternoons—still working only half-days. It was good duty until a new Executive Officer decided they should have duties during the other four hours each day.

The Executive Officer assigned Ketelsen duty as the "Beautification Officer," who was ordered to paint each tree white from the base to four feet above the ground. In addition, each large rock defining a driveway, post, parking post, etc., was to be painted white. Ketelsen dutifully assembled his assigned soldiers and executed the order. The base looked like a city park when they were finished. Then one day, an Inspecting General visited the base and was aghast at the sight. "This is wartime. At night, this damned base sticks out like a neon light!" Ketelsen once again assembled his paint crew, scrubbed down the trees, and painted everything else camouflage. The Executive Officer was given a new opportunity at another base.

Dee did not join him at Tyndall Field, but lived with her sister in Riverdale, Illinois, instead. Housing was difficult to locate, and Ketelsen's schedule was too undependable to make moving there worth pursuing. She continued to work for the government, and wrote Art regularly. She knew that Ketelsen's flying everyday was not without some exposure to danger, but it was far safer than being 3000 miles away, exposed to enemy guns.

Returning from one of the target training runs, a young gunner wanted the experience of sitting in the pilot's seat to get the feel of flying a big four-engine bomber. After much pleading, Ketelsen finally acquiesced and let the young man climb into the pilot's location. As the plane entered a cloud formation, it began to bounce uncontrollably—with the tail section fishtailing violently. This caused the mounted machine guns to swing wildly, hitting two side-gunner cadets, banging them up pretty good. The co-pilot managed to get the plane back under control. When they landed, the gunner cadets reported to the base medical facility, and Ketelsen reported to the Executive Officer about the incident. The Officer was not pleased, and in proper military fashion, let Lt. Ketelsen know it.

Decisions were made that Tyndall Field should convert from B-17 airplanes to B-24 airplanes, since there were more B-24s being manufactured and made available for service overseas. The B-17s were relocated to Texas and New Mexico, and Ketelsen was assigned the task of ferrying a B-17 to Roswell, New Mexico. It took seven hours to fly the B-17 from Tyndall Field to Roswell to deliver

*Dee and Art just before he left for England.*

the plane. The return trip, by crowded train, took seven long, uncomfortable days.

Ketelsen then trained to fly as a co-pilot on the B-24, and continued flying in training machine gunners. However, there was a marked difference in the handling characteristics between the Fortress and the Liberator, which made Ketelsen very uncomfortable. He also did not like switching chairs from pilot to co-pilot, which lessened his perceived responsibility—and perceived prestige.

This difference in the flying characteristics of the two planes and being a co-pilot was disconcerting enough that he decided to make a dramatic change. Ketelsen visited the Executive Officer and volunteered for overseas duty, so long as he would be flying a B-17 Flying Fortress. The Executive Officer accepted his offer without hesitation.

In November 1944, Ketelsen left Tyndall Field and went to Ardmore, Oklahoma, where he met his new crew, and they immediately began training for overseas service. They practiced formation flying, bombing runs, formation flying, cross-country exercises, and formation flying. Their last training flight was February 15, 1945.

The crew received orders they were going to England. They caught a train to New Jersey where they boarded the Queen Mary along with 10,000 other soldiers. The officers shared a crowded stateroom, where they spent eight hours in the stateroom, eight hours moving about the ship, and eight hours on deck. The enlisted men lived below decks where they slept on canvas bunks stacked five high. There was barely room to turn over. Meals were wonderful and served twice daily. After a few days they landed at the Ferth of Clyde, Glasgow, Scotland, where they disembarked and boarded a train for their new base.

Ketelsen and his crew were about to enter the shooting war.

# KETELSEN
## CHAPTER THREE

The train carrying Ketelsen and his crew left Glasgow and took them to Polebrook at Northamtonshire, north of London, and one of 150 airfields constructed in the area to house the American air armada. They were assigned to the Eighth Air Force, 351st Bomb Group, 510th Squadron, as a replacement crew. They arrived on April 12, found their assigned airplane, and flew practice flights for several days to become familiar with the landing strip, the field, and the area.

**Mission 1:** 16 Apr 44. Target: Rengensberg RR Marshalling Yards, Germany. Ketelsen flew as a co-pilot with his crew for experience over the target. The target was well defended and the crew discovered the meaning of the term, "walking on flak." The flight took 8:20 hours.

**Mission 2:** 18 Apr 44. Target: Traunstein, Germany, close to the Swiss border. Ketelsen again flew as co-pilot with his crew. They flew with the 351st Bomb Group over sunlit mountains, found their target, and dropped their bombs. On the return flight they inadvertently flew over Berchesgaden, Hitler's mountain retreat, which was heavily defended. The Bomb Group flew through a field of flak that was only momentary, but extremely intense. The flight time was over 10:00 hours, a long flight by any standard.

**Mission 3:** Apr 44. Target: Brandenburg on the outskirts of Berlin. Art was the pilot with his regular crew. It was heavily fortified, with lots of flak. Flying time 8:20 hours.

*Note: This was Ketelsen's last mission during hostilities because the conflict was winding down, and the Armistice negotiations were underway. Ketelsen's crew continued to fly and train everyday, to remain combat-ready.*

**News Release - Stars and Stripes - Undated**
   **8th, 15th AFs Have Finished Strategic Raps**
   In an Order of the Day commending all units under his USSTAF command, Gen. Carl Spaatz yesterday announced that the strategic air war of the 8th and 15th Air Forces is at an end and that from now on

they must "operate with our tactical air forces in close co-operation with our armies.

"The strategic air war has been won with a decisiveness becoming increasingly evident as our armies overrun Germany," Spaatz declared.

The Order of the Day was released shortly after 1,200 8th Air Force Fortresses and Liberators returned from attacks on German marshalling yards in the Regensburg area of southern Germany and blows against defense positions in the Gironde area north of Bordeaux.

Approximately 750 heavies, with 850 Thunderbolt and Mustang escorts, crossed the western battle line for the first time since Friday to batter rail targets and communications at Regensburg and at the junctions of Landshut, Plattling, and Straubing, to the south and east.

Fighter escorts peeled off to destroy 223 enemy planes at enemy airfields in the Munich area and as far east as Prague in Czechoslovakia.

Meanwhile, 450 unescorted Fortresses dumped high explosives near Point de Grave on the west side of the Gironde estuary in co-operation with elements of the French Army moving against the cornered Germans at Bordeaux.

RAF Mosquitoes raided Berlin three times Sunday night, reporting very little flak and no fighter opposition, although the Germans turned on the capital's searchlights for the first time in many weeks.

Ketelsen's crew flew a number of sorties over Germany that were not recorded as missions. The ground crews and base staff worked diligently to service the aircraft, working around the clock to have the planes ready for combat. Staff kept the personnel records, briefing, debriefing, and the myriad of other transactions—never getting to see the results of the crews they were supporting. Several B-17s were reconfigured to hold ten passengers, and the maintenance crews and staff were treated to a "Cook's Tour of the Rhine."

Squadron planes took off and assembled over the field, moved into formation, and the ground airmen were treated to the actual process of preparation for bombing. They then flew to Cherbourg,

*Bombing pattern over Regensburg Germany on Ketelsen's first official mission.*

Berlin, Dusseldorf, Hamburg, and other cities to view the devastation inflicted by their compatriots. They rarely flew over 1000 feet, so visibility was good, and there was no need for oxygen masks or cold-weather gear.

The "Cook's Tours" continued for seven days, and were very rewarding for the men who kept the crews in the air. It was a wonderful treat for the men, who had watched crews fulfill their missions and return to the States while they continued to labor away at their mundane tasks, day after day, for several years.

On the night of May 7, the air crews attended a briefing for the next day's "mission." The Armistice was going to be signed outside Paris on May 8, and pilots were told emphatically that there were to be absolutely no flights over the city at 3:00 P.M. The route over Germany was established, and the flight over bombed cities would continue as planned. Flights over Paris were "verboten," off limits—absolutely and unconditionally forbidden!

Leaving the briefing that evening, the pilot of the lead plane of the "V" of which Ketelsen's crew was a part, left this message: "For the other two pilots of my 'Vee': After we cross the channel, when the group turns left, we are going to turn right!"

The next morning, the bomb group took off as scheduled, assembled over the field, and headed in formation towards the continent. Ketelsen was flying wing on a three plane "Tail-End Charlie" location at the rear of the bomb group. As the bomb group crossed the English Channel into France and turned left, the last

"Vee" turned right. The three planes flew south over France to Barcelona, Spain, then turned up the north Mediterranean coast over Marseille. They proceeded to fly over Toulon and Nice, and when they approached Monaco, turned north. It was about 2:30 in the afternoon and Ketelsen had no idea where they were headed. Turning on the intercom, he called to the navigator, Jim Simon, and asked, "Where are we?" The navigator responded, "Looks like we are headed for Paris!"

The three planes flew to the outskirts of Paris and got their bearings. The formation dropped to 500 feet and flew up the Champs Elysees, over the Arch D' Triomphe, and then circled Alexandre-Gustave Eiffel's wonderful tower. They then set a course for a rendezvous with the bomb group that was returning from Germany. The three planes repositioned in their "Tail-End Charlie" slot and, supposedly, were never missed.

At the base, the airmen were required to turn in their side arms and Very pistols (flare guns) to ordinance. The supply officers would check them off, and since so many weapons were turned in, a pile of guns was started outside the window of the building. Many of the service men took the opportunity to retrieve their guns. The night of the Armistice signing, the soldiers consumed a fair amount of alcohol and started shooting their .45s in the air, as well as shooting off flares. It became quite dangerous, since soldiers were shooting up and down, with no one knowing who was shooting at what.

After the Armistice, the bomb group played a new role. Ketelsen's plane was stripped of all extraneous weight so they would have more load capacity. A partial crew of pilot, co-pilot, navigator, and radioman, went to Linz, Austria, to ferry French laborers back to France. The landing fields were very short for the bombers, only about 4000 feet long, which made taking off with a full load even more difficult.

Landing in Linz, they loaded their passengers and taxied to the end of the runway. Locking the brakes, Ketelsen gave the four big engines full throttle. The big plane kicked and bucked until the engines reached their maximum revolutions per minute (RPM), then the brakes were released, and the B-17 rolled down the runway—barely clearing the obstructions at the end of the field.

As the plane climbed for altitude, Ketelsen suddenly had difficulty getting the tail up, and the airplane dangerously approached the angle for stalling out. The radioman checked the rear compartment, only to find that all of the Frenchmen had scooted to the tail of the aircraft so they could look out the window at the scenery—suddenly placing over 2000 pounds in the tail of the airplane. The radioman had to threaten physical harm to get the French passengers back to the middle of the airplane over the bomb bay, in order to balance the plane for the return flight to Paris.

Once the plane landed in Paris, the Frenchmen endangered their lives by leaping out of the airplane before Ketelsen could get the engines shut down. Fortunately, the men—who were running wildly in all directions—in the euphoria of being on French soil again, managed to avoid running into the propellers.

Ketelsen and his skeleton crew continued to fly every day in order to continue training as required. They practiced formation flying and worked on instrument flying under overcast conditions. Preparing to return to the U.S., Operations discovered that Ketelsen did not have enough instrument time, so they required a skeleton crew to fly at 5000 feet in overcast. When Ketelsen and his crew took off, they discovered there were 250 planes in the air in pea-soup fog at that height. Ketelsen found it safest to fly south to the Mediterranean, circle the coastline, and return. He logged enough time to meet instrument requirements. The paperwork was completed. A trip home was a definite possibility.

The orders to return to the United States were finally issued, and May 24 was the day of departure for Ketelsen's crew of ten, plus ten passengers. Instructions included flying at 5000 feet so oxygen masks would not be necessary on the way home. They left Polebrook on May 24, and flew for one and a half hours to a base in Wales, where they put down to top off their gas tanks. It was unusual to fly such a short distance for topping off. They flew from Wales to Iceland in seven hours, arriving on the twenty-fifth. The next day, they flew to Goosebay, Labrador, to a large airbase. On the twenty-seventh they flew to the U.S. over Bangor, Maine, to Bradley Field, Connecticut. However, Bradley Field was socked in with bad weather, and they were forced to return to Bangor.

There were fifty planes arriving from Goosebay, and fifty planes returning from Bradley, all circling for a landing in Bangor. The control tower was frantic, as it was pure bedlam. However, all planes landed safely with no mid-air collisions, but there were plenty of frayed nerves. The next day the weather in Connecticut was clear, and the planes returned to Bradley Field where the crew found food and a clean bed for a long sleep.

Ketelsen's overseas tour of duty was short and sweet. And safe.

*Ketelsen in front of his airplane for the return trip home. His crew painted "Ket's Kids" on the plane to indicate Art was the only crew member who was a father.*

# KETELSEN
## CHAPTER FOUR

The processing of returned airmen was expedited because of the large numbers en route, and Art was accelerated through the paperwork. He received a two-week leave and immediately boarded a train to Chicago. He had called Dee from Bangor during the layover, and indicated he did not know how long or where processing would take place. Although the train was crowded, it was an express train hitting only the major cities along the way. As the train neared Chicago and slowed to a snail's pace as it approached Union Station, Art recognized it would pass within two blocks of their residence. The train barely crawled along, so Art had a friend throw off his B-4 bag, and he jumped down to the adjoining tracks. He walked to his home and completely surprised his family who was still awaiting notification of his arrival. He got to see his son for the first time, and learned the two most feared words in the raising of young children—diaper pail!

While on leave, orders arrived assigning him to the air base at Sioux Falls, South Dakota. He reported there when he completed his leave, and immediately began training, flying B-29s bound for the Pacific Theater.

On August 1, after six weeks of flight training, he went to Roswell, New Mexico, for deployment to the Far East. Five thousand pilots were awaiting orders when the first atom bomb destroyed Hiroshima. Suddenly, there were 5000 pilots doing absolutely nothing. Processing for separation from service was immediate and swift. Art was again on a train headed for Chicago.

Arriving home, he wasted no time contacting Hibbard Spenser Bartlett to see if he could have his old job back, and if so, when he could start work. The answer was, "Yes, and right now!" Instead of putting him to work in-house, HSB sent him out on the road. He was the first veteran to return to the Iowa division. Most of his accounts were on Highway 6 from eastern to central Iowa.

He traveled by train and bus for the first few weeks. After scouting communities for several months, he finally located a Chevy four-door sedan in Iowa City that was within his meager budget. He then began looking for a house he could rent, searching for an affordable one in towns along his route. Housing was still in short supply, made worse by the influx of returning veterans. Dee and Art finally located a home in Newton, Iowa, and moved there in October, 1945.

Traveling every day did not permit Art to spend much time with the family, and this began to bother him. His first son, Randall, was born in Blue Island, Illinois, on November 11, 1944, while Art was stationed in Columbus, Ohio. Art was denied leave to be present at the birth of his son, since he was training with an active combat crew preparing to ship overseas to the European Theater of Operations. Art did not get to see Randy until May 1945, when he returned from England. Their second son, James, was born May 28, 1947, in Newton.

As Art traveled his hardware route, he observed the operations of several of his larger accounts for nine years. One of the largest hardware stores was Carr Hardware in Ames, Iowa, owned by Frank Rodgers. In July 1954, Frank made an offer for Art to join Carr Hardware, and Art saw an opportunity to enter the retail business. As Art later stated, "I left traveling to spend more time with my family. I got into retailing and spent less time with them than I did when I was traveling!"

Art entered retailing and worked hard to maintain a quality facility in downtown Ames. He ultimately purchased the store from Mr. Rodgers and, in later years, sold it to his son, Randall.

Dee and Art attended a party at a friend's house in Ames, where he met another WWII pilot. In the course of getting acquainted, they discovered they had graduated in the same cadets' class, 44-B, on the same day, in Albany, Georgia. Tom Jellinger was a professor of Building Construction and Architectural Engineering at Iowa State University. He later initiated the Construction Engineering Department in the College of Engineering. From Albany, Jellinger went to Barksdale, Louisiana, for additional training as a B-26 pilot. One day for a lark, he hitched a ride on a B-26 Martin Marauder as a passenger. The plane crashed on landing, and Jellinger was severely injured. Tom barely survived with his life, and after much time in the hospital, lives with the permanent deformation of his leg and the loss of several fingers on one hand. Professor Jellinger was a very popular teacher, "Professor of the Year" at Iowa State University, and the recipient of many accolades from the construction industry. Tom and Art shared many memories about their days in flight training.

Son, Randy, graduated from college as a pharmacist. After several years in that field, he returned to work with Art and Jim in the hardware store. The boys were avid outdoorsmen and active hunters and fishermen. In November 1986, Jim was duck hunting along the Des Moines River by himself, when he apparently accidentally fell overboard. His empty boat was found floating downstream; attempts to find Jim's body were unsuccessful. Finally, his remains were recovered on February 20, 1987, when his body was found on the river bank. The period while Jim was missing was the most difficult period in Dee and Art's life.

Randy and his wife Mary (Hagie) purchased the store from Art and Dee in 1994 and opened a satellite store at 24th Street and Grand Avenue. He later closed the downtown store and now operates the store on 24th Street in Ames.

In 1995, Art was playing golf at Ames Golf and Country Club and, as he approached the second tee, was introduced to the guest of a member. The guest was Ludwig Zoellner, who was visiting from Germany. When Art asked Ludwig where he was from, Ludwig indicated he was from Rengensberg.

Art said, "Oh! We bombed Rengensburg during the war!"

Zoellner replied, "I want to talk to you."

Further conversation produced a picture of Zoellner's home in Rengensberg, a lovely house with a large swimming pool. Zoellner explained, "The pool is so big because we used a bomb crater for the excavation. Couldn't you have dropped a bomb that made a *square* hole?"

Ludwig served in the German Army, but never mentioned where or in what capacity. His wife, who was thirteen years old during the war, served as a translator for General George Patton immediately after the war. The Ketelsens and the Zoellners have become good friends, and still exchange Christmas cards to this day.

Art Ketelsen has many memories from his service experience, not all of them pleasant. Like the day he was going to take out a BT-13 that had been repaired and needed a flight check. It had been some time since he had flown one, but it was a fun plane to fly, and he wanted to take advantage of this opportunity. He crawled into the cockpit and gave the "wobble pump" several vigorous pumps to get gas into the cylinders to start the plane. He had forgotten that two pumps were adequate. When he started the engine, the excess gas caught fire and the engine blew up.

Most persons remembering their military experience forget the many hours spent standing in line, the nature of the food at various bases, the training films, and the faces of many in various squads and barracks. A few of the names return, a few outrageous moments are recalled, but with the passage of time most specifics become a blur. The anticipation of a letter from home, the packages of cookies that became packages of crumbs, the unique smell of woolen blankets, and the shock of loss of privacy in the toilet, are all experiences that fade in the memory.

Boarding the train to leave home was probably more disconcerting to those staying behind, than to the youngster entering a new and dangerous world. Leaving a pregnant wife to fly over hostile country is not without apprehension. Those fears are placed on a back shelf when you are responsible for the lives of nine other men, for keeping your place in formation, for herding a monster plane through unfavorable weather, and for remembering all the instructions that get you to the target and back safely.

Although Art did not fly fifty combat missions, his sense of duty and responsibility reflected the attitude of a young Chicago lad turned professional soldier, fulfilling his role.

In the whole scheme of things, you could ask nothing more.

*Bombers over English countryside.*

# BOOK SIX

# UNDERHILL

*Capt. Robert Underhill*

*B-17 Bombardier*

*Fifteenth Air Force*

*5th Wing*

*2d Bomb Group*

*96th Squadron*

*"We had an enviable lifestyle and looking
back at our conduct,
we were really a bunch of smart-asses!"*

—*Underhill*

# UNDERHILL
## CHAPTER ONE

Who would have thought that Fiorello La Guardia was born in Prescott, Arizona?

Certainly, the consummate Italian mayor of New York City during the depression and the war years should have been born in "Little Italy," in New York City. The popular mayor who read the comic papers on the radio to entertain children during the newspaper strike in New York City in 1940—from Arizona? No chance. Mama Mia! What will happen next?

La Guardia, a republican, was elected the Mayor of New York City in 1933, when the country was in the throes of the depression. When Franklin D. Roosevelt, former Governor of New York, instituted his "New Deal" programs to get the country moving again, Mayor La Guardia adopted the role of an "urban democrat" and initiated little "New Deals" within his city. They were very successful, because "little, hen-shaped" Mayor La Guardia was adamant that there was no graft, and the programs were "clean." La Guardia was outspoken, direct, and honest.

When the U.S. was mobilizing for the war, Roosevelt appointed La Guardia as head of the Office of Civilian Defense. When an aluminum pot and pan drive was initiated, they piled up around county courthouses all over the country. It seems the going rate for scrap utensil aluminum was twelve cents per pound, but junk dealers were selling it for forty cents per pound. La Guardia brought pressure to bear, agreements were made, and the pots and pans ultimately became shiny new airplanes.

When he initiated a blood drive in his town, the first person in line was Mayor La Guardia.

He was Mayor of New York City for twelve tumultuous years. "Through it all, flashing the personality that had endeared him to New Yorkers even when they were weary of his clowning—fussy, dumpy, outgoing Mayor Fiorello La Guardia never once lost the spotlight he loved." says a 1945 *Time Magazine*. It goes on to say, "As usual, he had enraged thousands of New Yorkers, but tickled thousands, and fascinated thousands. Perhaps that was his secret, even more than his withering frankness, and his relentless fight for honest government. Whatever it was, the people knew one thing for certain: After twelve years New York City was losing the best mayor it ever had."

In 1942, Fiorello La Guardia was an impressive American; he was impressive enough that, later, an airport was named after him.

To a young shoe salesman spending the week in Prescott, Arizona, the fact that Fiorello was a native of Prescott was not lost.

Robert Underhill had left college to become a traveling shoe salesman. He had been attending Manchester College, in North Manchester, Indiana—a conservative, strict, Church of the Brethren college. His small scholarship entitled him to no dancing, no cards, no games, no alcohol, and chapel four mornings a week. The attendees were mostly pre-law, pre-medicine, or pre-ministry. The curriculum offered numerous science classes that did not appeal to, or tempt, the young scholar. For two full calendar years, Bob made his own curriculum: humanities, literature, biology—but no tough stuff like math or physics. He was not particularly interested, or excited, about excelling in academics.

And then there was the young lady. George Bernard Shaw, once said, "It is the desire of every young lady to get married as soon as possible, and for every young man to delay it as long as possible." The young lady was interested in "sooner."

So, in 1940, Bob Underhill had an opportunity to take a traveling sales position with Mishawaka Woolen and Footware. He acquired a 1939 Chevy Coupe with a huge trunk that held samples of men's work shoes, waterproof footwear, women's footwear, woolen sox, and Red Ball sport shoes. For three months he traveled northern Florida, Alabama, Mississippi, Texas, and eastern New Mexico.

And he was free! There were no church restrictions, and there was dancing, and cards, and alcohol. He enjoyed the freedom of a traveling salesman, being on the road, seeing new country, and having a good time. And he enjoyed making good money now that the depression was nearly over, money that was his own to spend as he pleased.

Bob was born June 10, 1920, in Van Buren, Indiana, the second son of Tony Dale and Celeste Marie Anderson Underhill. Tony worked on the railroad moving as his job dictated, to Michigan City, Peru, and Kokomo.

Bob graduated from high school in Silver Lake, Indiana, in 1938 with no particularly outstanding accomplishments. He much preferred trapping muskrats, and hunting rabbits and squirrels.

As a young lad, he discovered he had a minor speech impediment, a medial lisp that made the letter 'c' come out with a soft 'sh.'. While hawking newspapers in Michigan City, Indiana, he would stand on a street corner selling them for three cents, and folks would give him a nickel and say, "Keep the change."

One day, a "well-heeled" gentleman came by and said, "I will give you a quarter if I can bring some friends by and you shout your sales pitch." The gentleman showed up with friends a few minutes later and Bob gave a lusty, "Get your copy of the Michigan City News," with a pronounced lisp. The gentleman and his friends all got a good laugh, and Bob got his quarter. A doctor later told Bob he had a lazy tongue. A few weeks of therapy made "city" sound quite acceptable.

After a few months selling shoes in Alabama and Florida, Bob was transferred to a new sales territory that included New Mexico, Arizona, and the desert area of California. Promoting new accounts, Bob made a call at the sales department of Davis-Monthan Air Base. Watching the planes take off, circle overhead, and land gave him the inspiration to learn to fly. He wrote a letter to the recruiter at the air base inquiring about becoming a flying cadet.

Bob was once again making sales calls in Prescott, Arizona. Once again he tried to understand how Fiorello La Guardia could migrate from then tiny Prescott to become the mayor of the biggest city in the U.S.—Bob was intrigued. Would Robert Underhill have the opportunity and ambition to do what La Guardia had accomplished?

On December 7, 1941, Bob was in Prescott, Arizona, selling footwear. On December 8, he contacted the head office of Mishawaka, gave his territory report, and informed them he had enlisted as a flying cadet. Driving back to Indiana, Bob found a response to his recruiting letter waiting, directing him to report to Baer Air Field, Fort Wayne, Indiana, to take a physical examination and several written examinations.

Two days after the examinations, he received orders to report to Santa Ana, California, on January 2, 1942.

Bob spent Christmas at home with his three brothers, all of whom would see service in the military. The next day, he boarded a Pennsylvania Rail Road train, along with new acquaintances, Dick Phelps and Jim Snyder—on track for new adventures. The paths of the young men would intersect several times during the next three years.

# UNDERHILL
## CHAPTER TWO

Traveling to Santa Ana, California, took Bob from the Pennsylvania Rail Road to the Santa Fe Rail Road line through New Mexico, Arizona, and southern California; he passed through towns he knew very well from his shoe-selling days—just two weeks previous. Bob arrived in Santa Ana wearing a heavy tweed suit, and he sweltered in the desert climate.

The camp was still under construction when the thousands of young recruits arrived, and there was confusion at all levels of organization. Cadet housing consisted of newly-erected tents located in a large bean field, which caused many problems. The winter/spring of 1942 was one of the wettest periods on record, causing the dry soil to turn to soup. There was more rain than the desert area had received in years. One of the camp newspapers reported that "since it never rains in southern California, the heavy dew washed out three bridges yesterday."

Cadets went through the usual processing: shots, clothes, movies, long lines, and learning to be a soldier. With hardly any training, the recruits were put on guard duty patrolling the Pacific's beaches, fearful that the Japanese might invade, or try slipping spies into the country.

Bob, as well as the other young recruits, was given a bolt-action Springfield .30 caliber rifle and placed on overnight patrol. Bob was stationed on guard duty along Jones Beach. Early one morning as it was starting to get light, he heard a ratcheting sound. Peering over the sand dunes, through the grass, he could see the silhouette of a small shack with a figure moving about and making hand signals. The rattling sounded suspiciously like a machine gun, and the activity at the shack became more pronounced. He was convinced that it was a Japanese person directing something coming in from the ocean. Bob had been given three bullets, to be used to alert the Corporal of the Guard in that sector. He assumed a prone position, peering through the ragged beach grass atop a sand dune. Slipping a bullet into the chamber, he quietly slid the bolt forward and peered down the gun sight. He was about to pull the trigger, when he realized the shadowy figure was not a man but a woman, and her frantic hand signals were the act of attaching clothes to a clothesline. The rattling sound was her washing machine. His military career had had a dubious beginning—almost ending in tragedy.

Bob was quite taken with southern California. Santa Ana was close to Hollywood, and it was a short hop for the movie stars to visit the base and entertain the troops. Bob Hope, Bing Crosby, Jack Benny, and Rita Hayworth were frequent visitors. Bob was definitely impressed by the beauty and allure of Rita Hayworth. The young lad from Indiana had never seen carrot-colored hair before, and it made a smashing impression.

During his early military training Bob learned that if he became a bombardier he would get his commission six months earlier than if he opted for pilot training. He could then apply for pilot training and be paid as a Second Lieutenant while attending flight school. That seemed like a propitious opportunity, so he volunteered for bombardier school and was sent to Victorville, California, for training.

Bombardier school was very challenging for Bob. It was hard, even exhausting, but he liked the discipline. He was weak in mathematics, which made it even harder. One day in class he was asked what "sine" was, and was totally dumfounded, thinking it was "sign." When his discrepancy in math was exposed, he immediately took remedial classes in math and trigonometry. He had a good memory and memorized trig tables in order to better respond to formula for bombing angles.

Practice missions were flown in a Beechcraft AT-11, with two 450 horsepower Wright-Curtis engines. The planes were stable airplanes that held a pilot and two bombardier cadets and contained two bomb racks with five bombs each. They dropped practice bombs (MS38A2) that held ninety-seven pounds of sand and three pounds of black powder. On the practice range, they were graded on Circular Error Probable (CEP) for accuracy on a target. The target consisted of a 12 foot square "shack," surround by concentric circles of 100 feet, 300 feet, 500 feet, and 1000 feet. Passing the course meant recording a certain number of hits that fell within acceptable limits.

The Air Corps had been using the Sperry Bombsight, and was in the process of converting to the Norden Bombsight, which was considered a vast improvement. A bombsight needed a level platform from which to drop bombs with any degree of accuracy. A major problem was that planes might be tilted front to rear, or have a wing tilt, which would require mathematical adjustment to identify a perpendicular for releasing bombs. This was hard to maintain and to calculate. The Norden Bombsight's virtue was that it told the bombardier not only how to solve the alignment

*The bombardier's view out of the plastic nose cone, showing the Norden Bombsight.*

problem, but when to drop the bombs. It had two gyroscopes that stabilized the craft fore and aft and laterally, establishing a consistent bombing platform. The system called "synchronizing" was a vast improvement. The right side of the bombsight had a special device for coordinating the information, and this was highly secret. There was considerable effort to maintain the secrecy of this portion of the bombsight.

Bombardier school was a special time for Bob. As his knowledge and confidence grew, he thoroughly enjoyed the learning process, and it would remain with him the rest of his life. He had a grand time as a cadet, and thoroughly enjoyed the mental discipline and the satisfaction of applying his knowledge for predictable results.

On September 4, 1942, Bob Underhill received his bombardier wings, and a commission as Second Lieutenant in the U.S. Army Air Corps (O-729520). Eight of the graduates were selected to become instructors. The remainder of the group would join crews being assembled in the U.S., or be sent overseas as replacements in existing crews. The young man with not enough mathematics and questionable trigonometric skills was retained to become an instructor of other young men learning a new trade, dropping bombs.

Underhill's pay went from 75 dollars per month to 300 dollars per month. Suddenly, he was a rich bachelor with the whole west coast for his playground. Cadets were required to take test flights at the end of their training, so Underhill would volunteer to go along. It was an opportunity to visit numerous big cities. He visited Dallas, Boise, and San Francisco. He learned he could enter most of the private and exclusive clubs in big cities due to his officer's uniform, be genuinely welcomed, and treated to only the best. It was early in the war and officers were relatively few at that time, so they attracted special attention. He took every advantage of the situation, and loved the attention it brought.

After Victorville his next assignment was Hobbs, New Mexico, as an instructor in a relatively new installation. Rigid military discipline had not yet arrived, and the officers were casual in their dress, wearing sheepskin flying jackets and flying boots around town. A favorite hangout was the Line Café. Hobbs was on the New Mexico/Texas state line, and the structure sat directly over the state line. When it was closing time in Texas at midnight, you picked up your drink and walked four steps to New Mexico where the closing time was 1:00 AM.

The next assignment was Roswell, New Mexico, where he taught two sessions of bombardier training. Again, it was a new installation, and they were free of rigid military discipline. From Roswell they were assigned to Deming, New Mexico, close to El Paso, Texas, instructing classes on how to drop bombs. He had been an instructor for a year and a half, but was sent to Instructors' School at Carlsbad, New Mexico, for two weeks, and then returned to Deming.

Gas rationing limited their mobility until they learned they could drive to Mexico, thirteen miles away, and get all the gas they needed. They even brought back fruit jars full of gasoline to share with other officers.

The cadre of young instructors lived a very idyllic existence. They possessed an abundance of arrogance, and were an unlikable, raunchy lot. They were isolated in the military, and comported themselves as dilettantes, above the surrounding military "rabble." They had an enviable lifestyle, and looking back at their conduct Underhill commented, "We were really a bunch of young smart-asses!"

Christmas 1943 was spent in La Junta, Colorado, where Chinese pilots were flying B-25s. Flying low-level sorties and bombing runs, they were preparing for a different type of engagement with the enemy. Since Underhill was the only English-speaking instructor on the airplane, except for one interpreter, he learned the Chinese words for up, down, drop, turn right, and turn left. He seemed to get by. He did not like dropping bombs from altitudes so low that debris would hit the airplane. Skip-bombing was particularly worrisome.

While in Deming, New Mexico, in late 1943, two or three of his earlier students returned from their tour of duty with thirty-five missions and chests full of ribbons. Underhill started to feel uneasy about it, since former students were overseas getting shot at and Underhill was in the States having a wonderful time—with absolute freedom, lots of money (saving none of it), and living the good life. Underhill realized he had obligations to fulfill his role in the military, and he volunteered for overseas service.

First, he had to attend radar school. He was sent to Boca Raton, Florida, and was housed in the exclusive Boca Raton Country Club. He lived in the clubhouse, which was very elegant. His room was one of seven or eight located off a large lounge that contained a billiard room and bar. The dining room had a large window below water level, looking directly into the Atlantic Ocean so you were able to watch exotic fish "au natural." Boca Raton Country Club remained very exclusive, and a few years later when he visited the facility, they would not permit him access.

Underhill had been promoted to First Lieutenant in early 1944. Completing radar training, he was assigned to Langley Field, Virginia, an established base with brick buildings and a permanent airfield. Underhill was assigned to train in B-17 airplanes, doing exercises in radar navigation with 150-mile trips over the ocean.

In May, 1944, he went on leave for ten days back home to Indiana. He had been in service two years and five months, spending most of his time instructing bombardiers. Now he would have an opportunity to apply what he had taught.

Knowing he was going overseas, Underhill acquired a .38 caliber "police special" that he wore in a shoulder holster. He had only six bullets for it. A police chief in Indianapolis, who had a son in the Eighth Air Force, had each of his officers donate three shells apiece, so when Underhill left the U.S. he was the proud owner of twenty-four bullets for his gun.

Embarkation point was at Camp Patrick Henry in Newport News, Virginia. Underhill boarded the Admiral Mann, a light cruiser-class navy ship, and five unescorted days later landed in North Africa. Aboard ship, six officers shared a wardroom. Four air officers and two paratroop officers shared Underhill's cabin. During the trip, the two paratroopers got into an argument and exchanged blows. One trooper started to beat the other's head against a steel post, and almost killed the soldier. It took two

*Captain Robert Underhill prior to going overseas. After a year and a half of instructing bombardiers and having a very good time, he volunteered for overseas duty.*

airmen to pull the trooper off to avoid a homicide. Underhill was only a First Lieutenant, and was not certain he should interrupt the two officers from another branch of service during their confrontation.

The Admiral Mann docked in Oran, and the officers headed to their respective assignments. Since Lt. Underhill did not yet have specific orders, he was assigned six privates, six metal detectors, and sent to an area on the base to clear it of mines. Underhill was not certain there were mines on the site, but it kept an officer and six men busy for several days.

After two weeks in Oran, North Africa, they boarded a British cargo ship bound for Naples, Italy. It was a dirty, unkempt ship that wallowed along in the Mediterranean and Tyrrhenian Sea, making everyone on board seasick.

Disembarking in Naples, all radar navigators boarded a "forty and eight" train and headed west. He was assigned to the 2d Bomb

Group near Manfredonia, a cape on the Adriatic Sea. The train was so slow the airmen would get out and walk along side it. It took two days to get to an air base near Foggia, Italy. Local women sold fruit along the way, and the airmen welcomed the opportunity to feast on fresh fruit. Unfortunately, after eating the fruit they all came down with dysentery. Lesson learned: always wash fruit before consumption.

As the airmen reached their destinations, Underhill was pleased to learn that his good friends from cadet class, Dick Phelps and Jim Snyder, would be stationed together at the 99th Bomb Group, only two miles from Underhill's base.

Underhill would be serving in the Fifteenth Air Force, 5th Wing, 2d Bomb Group. He was happy to learn that a former student was the group bombardier. The Fifteenth Air Force had been formed in North Africa, and bombed Italy, Ploesti in Romania, and Yugoslavia, prior to the Allied invasion of Italy.

Now that the Fifteenth was located in Italy, Ploesti would be a regular target. The oil refineries continued oil production until late in the war, and missions to Ploesti remained as dangerous as ever.

*The remains of a B-24 that Underhill's plane escorted back from a mission. Damage to the plane was so severe, you could see through the fuselage while the plane was in the air. The plane landed safely before collapsing.*

# UNDERHILL
# CHAPTER THREE

## LT. UNDERHILL'S MISSIONS

Underhill was assigned to the Fifteenth Air Force, 5th Wing, 2d Bomb Group, 96th Bomb Squadron—one of the six B-17 groups in the Fifteenth. There were also four bomb groups of B-24s, and a fighter command with P-38s and P-51s. There were a number of airfields in the Foggia, Italy, area, and this field would accommodate two squadrons: B-17s on one side of the field, and British aircraft on the other side.

The number of missions for a tour of duty in Italy was different than the requirements in England. In England, the tour was originally thirty missions, later changed to thirty-five. In Italy the duty tour was fifty missions, with thirty over the target. Airmen got credit for two missions if it was a long distance to the target, or if they were exposed to flak both going to and returning from the target.

The first five missions Underhill flew were trips to Vienna, Munich, and Ploesti, Romania—all heavily defended and considered hot spots.

As the radar operator, Underhill sat in an enclosed space inside the plane watching the screen and trying to define landfalls and identify landmarks. The rest of the crew were observing the countryside, watching for bogeys and making comments about the flight and/or the fight.

Notes from Underhill's records describe some of the activities and actions; the notes are abbreviated, yet descriptive:

**Mission 1&2:** 16 July 44. Target: Vienna, Austria. Flew wing, 6:40 hours in the air.

**Mission 3 & 4:** 18 July 44. Target: Munich, Germany. Flew wing. 8:25 hours in the air.

**Mission 5 & 6:** 19 July 44. Target: Munich, Germany. Flew wing. 8:10 hours in the air.

**Missions 7 & 8:** 20 July 44. Target: Memmingen, Germany. Flew Wing. 7:00 hours in the air.

*Note: Underhill did not like being the radar navigator. He was essentially out of the action. If there was cloud cover and the bombardier could not see the target visually, he would communicate with the bombardier and feed data to him to adjust for bombing. He would hear flak hitting the ship, and the crew identifying "fighters at three o'clock," but was totally in the dark. In addition, visual bombing proved to be more accurate. They used PPI (Planned Periscope Interpretation) to identify objects. Early radar made mountains look like buildings, and needed a constant, uniform, electrical supply. Unfortunately, the electrical supply on planes varied, or went out at critical moments. Because accuracy was in question, Underhill went to the Operations Officer and requested changing to bombardier. Since one of squadron lead bombardiers had returned to the States, Underhill was moved into his position. His first mission as bombardier was the very next morning.*

**Missions 9 & 10:** 21 July 44. Target: Brux, Czechoslovakia. As far north as the 15th has flown. Lots of flak, but not on the B-17s. Most of it hit the B-24s below. Two bombers shot down. Flew wing, 8:40 hours.

**Mission NS:** 22 July 44. Target: Ploesti, Rom. Had just rendezvoused over the Adriatic Sea, and cleared machine guns. Suddenly an object penetrated the plastic nose cone, hitting Underhill in the head, causing extreme blood flow. It seems a .50 cal. shell casing from the tail gun of an airplane ahead was the missile. Because of Underhill's injury the mission for the crew was aborted. They managed to get the bleeding to stop while in the air. Once on the ground Bob sported a large oversized bandage that somewhat embarrassed him.

*Note: A training trip to Bari, Italy, prepared Underhill to become a lead bombardier. He managed to find a restaurant for a meal, only to be served a watery soup and fried Spam. The harbor was closed, since the Germans had scuttled two ocean ships at the harbor entrance to block the Allies.*

*Underhill returned to Foggia for duty. The mission to Ploesti scheduled for July, 31 was scrubbed.*

**Mission 11:** 22 Aug 44. Target: Railroad Marshalling Yards, Portes Les Valences, France. Was squadron leader for first time. Site was next to Rhone River. No flak at target, but hit crossing the coast both ways. Had a good bomb run, and was complimented by Commanding Officer. 8:25 Hours.

**Mission 12:** 13 Aug 44. Target: Gun emplacements at Savona, Italy. Squadron Leader. Target hard to see. Heavy concentration of bombs. Plane was hit several times, with three big holes in rudder. As they crossed the Isle of Corsica, they saw a large collection of ships in convoy. Something big was about to happen.

**Mission 13:** 14 Aug 44. Target: Gun Emplacements, Tulon France. Dropped two 2,000 lb bombs. As they turned to the IP (Initial Point for bombing run) the ships below started a white smoke screen, which obscured the target. Saw the red bomb blast through the smoke. A piece of 2 inch long flak hit the navigator's machine gun. Their speculation was confirmed. The invasion of Southern France was August 15th.

**Mission 14:** 15 Aug 44. Target: Gun Emplacements, Tropez Gulf, 28 miles east of Tulon, France. Up at midnight. Breakfast at 01:25, take off at 02:15, assembled at 03:20 at 6,500 feet. Each ship had thirty-eight 100 lb bombs. IP was over water. Bomb spacing to land fifty feet apart, dropped at 180 MPH with 3 1/2 degree drift. Pilot was Major Jordan, co-pilot was Col. Jack Ryan who Bob knew at Deming NM, commander of the 5th wing. Six bombs got hung up, and were late in dropping, so the whole squadron was late in releasing bombs. Only two planes over the target hit it. Light and inaccurate flak. Every kind of airplane in the air; 17s, 24s, 25s, 26s, A20s, P-38s, P-51s and navy dive bombers. On route back, saw fifty landing craft going in. Really bushed, three missions the last three days.

**Missions 15 & 16:** 18 Aug 44. Target: Romano American Refinery, Ploesti, Romania. Lots of flak at 27,000 feet. Anti-aircraft (can) shoot higher then we fly. Dense smoke screen. Could see the target six miles west of Ploesti. Coming back over Yugoslavia, lots of flak.

**Missions 17 & 18:** 22 Aug 1944. Target Oil Refinery, Odertal, Germany. Roughest mission yet. Fighters attacked at Balaton on way in. The home crew that I went overseas with went down. Chuck Duncan, Hal Bogie, Wilbur Clark, navigator, all tent mates. Waist gunners saw two or three chutes. The lead pilot got excited at flak and salvoed bombs while getting set up on IP. Should not have done that since all other ships in squadron dropped their bombs. The other three squadrons turned and got better results. The 96th was badly split up by fighters and were sitting ducks. Me 109s hit at Balanton on way back and that is when Duncan went down. Lots of flak. Ed Harris, our navigator, got hit in chest by shrapnel that bent his wings, though did not break skin. Mission not successful and three friends gone.

**Missions 19 & 20:** 24 Aug 44. Target: Pardubice, Czech. Carried thirty-eight 100 lb RDX bombs. Jordan was pilot and navigator Capt. Tibbets was on fiftieth mission. 8:00 hours. Was deputy Group Leader.

**Mission 21:** 26 Aug 44. Target: Viaduct at Venzone, northern Italy. Was Group Leader on 6:25 hour mission. Navigator was desperate, used Astro Compass Box for commode.

**Missions 22 & 23:** 29 Aug 44. Target: Privoser, Czech. Fifty miles west of Moravska-Ostrava. Left at 06:25 carrying twenty 300 lb bombs. IP was Neutitscein. Col. Cunningham, Deputy Commander, was in charge. Had an escort of P-51s. Twenty minutes before IP, were hit by Me 109s and FW 190s. Three ships down in their first pass. Fired more rounds on this trip than others to date. In five minutes the entire 20th Sqdn was shot down. Saw more enemy planes than any single raid. The waist gunner shot one fighter down. While searching for the IP the waist gunner said, "There's a whole shit-pot of fighters coming in." Col Cunningham asked for a damage report. When he asked for the 20th Squadron, there was silence. Then a southern drawl reported, "Colonel, you ain't got no 20th no more!"

*Note: When they landed, a bombardier from another group said, "I will never fly in a bomber again. You can court-martial me first." He was assigned a desk job. The planes were so badly shot up the group could not fly for a week. Because of the number of missions flown, Underhill and several others were given a break for Rest and Recreation (R&R). They proceeded to Rome and caught a plane to San Marcigliano Airport. As they got out of the airplane, they learned that a crippled B-24 had landed just ahead of their airplane. The three men went to the aircraft and helped load two badly wounded airmen into an ambulance. They caught a ride into town and stayed in the Regina Victoria Hotel. Underhill wanted to see the sights he had read about in "Ben Hur" and "Quo Vadis" when in college. Underhill started scouting for the Coliseum and discovered he was standing next to it.*

*Harris, Mike Weinman, and Underhill met three Italian girls along the way, and invited them to dinner at a small restaurant. After the meal, the young ladies wanted to negotiate an arrangement, but Underhill had seen so many GI films on venereal disease that he was too scared to try anything. The girls showed the airmen their papers that said they had physicals and were clean, but the papers were one day old and the men didn't trust them. The soldiers finally managed to convince them they were not interested.*

*Underhill went on a tour of the Vatican, and was awed by the ornate richness and pageantry. Having attended a poor, spartan, strict, religious school, the opulence of the Vatican was overwhelming for a simple Indiana boy. Children surrounded the buildings, begging, and the contrast was most disconcerting. Finally, inside the Basilica, Pope Pius arrived with an entourage of Cardinals and gave a prayer in Italian. A chorus sang, after which the Pope addressed the assembly, first in Latin, then Italian, French, and finally English. His voice was soft and he had an unusual accent.*

*The next day, the three airmen caught a bus to Naples and toured the city. There were a lot of Allied soldiers on leave, and a lot of Italian children begging. The highlight for Underhill was the trip to Pompeii. In 79 A.D., the people of Pompeii were instantly killed by toxic gas, then covered with ashes from the volcanic eruption of Mt. Vesuvius. Underhill visited the homes of wealthy people that had been uncovered and were on display. The citizens of Pompeii seemed to be preoccupied with sex and male symbols of sex. Signs and ceramic tile-work had phallic symbols everywhere. At a house at Vedii, a wall-tile display showed a man with his penis on weighing scales, with weights on the other side. The Latin inscription said, "Worth its weight in gold." The guides asked nurses in the tour group to step aside, for fear they could read Latin.*

**Mission 24:** 6 Sept 44. Target: Aradea, Romania. Bombed at 25,000 ft, and carried twelve 500lb bombs. Before reaching the IP, the tail gunner said, "There's a whole s—pot of fighters at nine o'clock." It turned out they were P-51s, right where they were supposed to be.

**Missions 25 & 26:** 10 Sept 44. Target: Vienna, Austria. Lobau Oil Refinery. Flak batteries were as bad as those in Berlin. The Danube is not blue, but a muddy brown with yellow streaks. Flak was heavy when they started their bombing run. When I saw the aiming point, a B-24 flew under our plane and blew up. I could see it in my bombsight. Flew wing in the 7:40 hour flight. Flying was very cold so we may get some electrically heated suits.

**Mission 27:** 12 Sept 44. Target: Lechfeld Air Field, Germany. Flew sqdn lead in 7:20 hour mission. Thought they saw some jet fighters on the ground.

**Mission 28:** 14 Sept 44. Target: Railroad Bridge in North Italy. A milk run. Dropped six 1000 lb bombs, destroyed it.

**Mission 29:** 17 Sept 44. Target: Budapest, Hungary. RR marshalling yards. Chadwick was the pilot. Five 1000 Lb bombs. Over Hungary, you could see the onion topped buildings. Buda on one side of river, Pest on other side. 7:30 Hour flight.

*Note: Enoch Broyles, whom Underhill knew as a cadet, had been the group's designated lead bombardier. He finished his missions and left for home, and Underhill was designated the group bombardier. It meant he conducted the pre-flight briefing, review of the flight, targets, and passed on other pertinent information.*

**Mission 30:** 18 Sept 44. Target: Subotica, Yugo. RR Marshalling yards. Fifty miles south. Major Jordan was the pilot. Dropped twelve 500 lb bombs in 6:30 hour flight. Flew as Group lead bombardier for this and remainder of missions.

**Missions 31 & 32:** 22 Sept 44. Target: Brux, Czech Major Jordan was pilot. Flew as group leader. Mission was 9:30 hours.

Note: The next day, after the scheduled mission was canceled, Major Jordan traded gold leaves for silver Lieutenant Colonel leaves. Underhill found a B-17 that needed a flight check, so he and Jordan took a jeep to the flight line. Jordon flew and Underhill served as the co-pilot. The air was smooth over the Mediterranean and they had a full tank, so they flew west over to Anzio and Fifth Army troops—who waved back when they buzzed them. They flew over Pisa, saw the leaning tower of Pisa, and went in for a buzz job. They could see the Germans soldiers on the top balcony—who waved to them. When Jordan and Underhill returned to the airfield, Commanding Officer Cullen was waiting and proceeded to give them a good bawling out for their lack of judgment. A few days later, Cullen flew with Underhill's crew as commander of the group, and he was a perfect pilot—extremely courteous, and never mentioned the incident. Lt. Col. Jordan left soon after, because he had completed his tour of duty.

**Mission 33:** 12 Oct 44. Target: Bologna, Italy. Bivouac of German troops. Dropped fragmentation bombs, suspended vertically, which give unpredictable trajectories. Anti-personnel bombs. Tactical support.

**Missions 34 & 35:** 13 Oct 44. Target: Florisdorf, Austria. Oil refineries. Carried twelve 500 lb bombs. Flak thick and accurate. Ten miles from target, commander ordered a full 360 degree turn for another pass over the flak. Turns out that Commander Cullen saw a group of B-24s directly underneath the flight. After dropping, another group went in, and they saw a 17 explode in mid air. Flight was 8:40 hours.

**Missions 36 & 37:** 23 Oct 44. Target: Pilsen, Czech. Armament works. Beautiful weather, smooth run with fighter escort. Beautiful day for flying, beautiful day to bomb. Friend Dick Phelps and Jim Snyder were leading the 99th.

Note: The 5th Wing was considering performing a night mission. They proposed to load two B-17s with 100-pound bombs set to detonate in a thirty-minute sequence after first explosion. It would last all through the night to disrupt production. As one officer said, "It was probably dirty pool, but gallantry be dammed."

**Missions 38 & 39:** 28 Oct 44. Target: Munich, Germany. RR Marshalling yards in west Munich. Bill Salmon pilot, Toten was navigator. Took off at twilight, in the air the sunset was thrilling. Took off alone, another ship five minutes behind. Outside temp was minus 40 degrees. Had electric flying suit. Base altitude 27,000 feet. Daytime bursts were bright red, but through smoke they showed bright yellow. Bombs away at 04:30, turned left. Two bombs still aboard plane. Underhill hooked up to his portable oxygen bottle, crawled back to the bomb bay, and standing over the bomb bay opening, kicked them out. When they returned to the base, Underhill got a royal chewing out for using "poor judgment." He was told, "You will never make commander."

*Note: Every airplane was different: some were gas-guzzlers, had low voltage, auto-pilot controls didn't work, or the bomb sight was not working. The Group Lead Plane was named "Frankie," and was Underhill's favorite. A mechanic named the plane for his girlfriend in Foggia who was actually named Francesca. The mechanic claimed it took a bottle of Four Roses whiskey to convince the young lady she needed a plane named after her.*

**Missions 40 & 41:** 5 Nov 44. Target: Vienna, Austria. Very heavy flak. The Germans had two anti-aircraft guns. The 105mm shell exploded with a gray-acrid smoke. The 88mm shell gave off black smoke. The 105s could reach bombers at 30,000 feet. The mission suffered heavy losses. When on target line, they overran the IP, and followed another group in. B24s slid under them, and they had to do a 360 degree turn for a final run. 7:45 Hour mission. When they returned, Bob went to the Red Cross for some cookies, and met Dick Phelps and Jim Snyder, who were hoping to leave any day for home.

**Missions 42 & 43:** 16 Nov 44. Target: Marshalling yards west of Munich, Germany. George Redden CO of 96th was commander. Navigator Harris was on final mission. Hit RR stock. Came home via Insbruck, lots of flak.

**Mission 44:** 18 Nov 44. Target: Visograd, Yugoslavia. Orders came in at noon for a tactical raid to bomb town the partisans were about to capture. Carried twelve 500 lb bombs. Were at IP at 16,000 feet and circled 360 degrees to get to 20,000 feet for bombing run. The automatic pilot (C1) went out and had to contend with excessive drift. I decided to make another run on PDI (Pilots Direction Indicator). Made a pretty good run. Returned to base and had flak over Sarajevo. Some holes in plane but nothing critical.

**Mission NC:** 19 Nov 44. Target: RR Bridge at Ferrara, Italy. Target to be bombed visually. When reached IP, such a heavy undercast could not bomb, so returned to base with the bombs. No credit for mission.

*Note: The Eighth Air Force never returned with their bombs, but dropped them over the channel or the North Sea instead. One of the theories of Bandleader Glenn Miller's disappearance was his plane was hit by bombs being jettisoned by another bomber overhead.*

**Missions 45 & 46:** 20 Nov 44. Target: Brno, Czech. Primary target was Blechhammer South, and oil refinery in Silesia. We were last group in the wing. Maj. Redden was pilot, Toten navigator, Weinman was mickey and I was bombardier. About 30 miles south of IP ran into high cirrus clouds and decided to take alternate target at Brno. Could bomb by radar, made run without flak and dropped sixteen 250 lb bombs. On return trip, had heavy flak at Bratislava, Gyor and Lake Balaton. Were glad that no fighters arose from there. One man on board wounded in the arm.

**Missions 47 & 48:** 12 Dec 44. Target: Oil Refinery at Regensburg, Germany. Took off in bad weather, with frontal system closing in fast. Redden was pilot, Toton navigator and Weinman was mickey. Col. Cullen, our Base Commander, was co-pilot and we felt comfortable about decision to hit alternate target because our judgment not questioned. Group got split up. 90th and our 96th sqdn were together. Bombed on radar synchronization and as a result our hits were not observed. While watching bombs going down, Chadwick's plane took a hit and went out of formation. Radar went out, and we turned south through thick soup all the way. Two of us separated, not a good practice in case we meet fighters. Got a glimpse of ground and got back on course. Finally in a break in the clouds, we saw Trieste Harbor below us, and set a course for Foggia. Clouds thick and made an instrument let down. Other planes came in later. Two ditched at sea and another was lost. Our reliable plane 715 brought us through eight and a half hours of difficult flying.

As group bombardier, Underhill had additional duties and did not fly for several days. One afternoon, he went to a nearby fighter field that was home base for a squadron of P-38s. The P-38s flew in a three-ship formation, and the lead ship had installed a plexiglass nose and a D-8 bombsight made by the National Cash Register Company. The standing joke was that if you missed your target, a little red flag would come up registering "no sale." The bombsight was for low-level bombing. The P-38s were called "droop snoots." They were looking for a bombardier, so Underhill volunteered to fly one mission, even though it would not count as a mission.

The three P-38s took off for a target in north Yugoslavia, and the planes were so fast they were at 15,000 feet before you could get your oxygen hooked up. They stayed at that altitude until they were over the mountains. When it came time to bomb, they dropped to 12,000 feet, so they were only 3,000 feet above the target—a Railroad marshalling yard. The pilots saw flak at a distance and got nervous. These crazy guys were afraid of flak, but looked for fighters so they could jettison the bombs and go after the fighters. That would have made Underhill an observer to a dogfight, which did not please him because he never saw a fighter he did not fear. They got to the target, circled it once, then dropped to the proper altitude, and flew in at three times the ground speed Underhill was used to. At that altitude, you could not miss the target. The pilots complimented him on his accuracy and results, which Underhill modestly accepted. It was Underhill's only ride in a P-38.

It was Christmas, and thoughts returned to home and events in the States. The weather was cold and rainy. There was a constant poker game at the Officer's Club. Underhill's tent mates, McCook,

Jones, and Radtke, had scrounged some cake from the mess hall and goodies from packages from home, and they decided to have a tent Christmas party. To make it official, Underhill and Radtke drove thirty miles to the mountains to cut a scrawny eighteen-inch-tall fir tree. They brought it back to the tent and decorated it with radar tinsel. When the guests arrived, the tent bulged like an accordion, but the guests soon became emotional and did not stay long. They returned to their tents to write sentimental letters home to their families, or to one or two girlfriends. One fellow in Underhill's tent wrote the same letter to three sweethearts, changing nothing but the addresses.

Christmas day was a stand-down because even the commanders felt the nostalgia of the day. Late in the day, the next day's mission was posted. Pilot Redden, Toten, Weinman, and Underhill were scheduled in old reliable 715. The target was Blechammer, Germany.

It would be Underhill's forty-ninth and fiftieth mission. He had not made it home for Christmas, but he would soon complete his tour of duty and be on his way home.

Just one more mission.

# UNDERHILL
## CHAPTER FOUR

**Mission 49, 50:** 26 Dec 44. Target: Blechhammer, Germany.

Captain Underhill was called to Group Headquarters, where Major Redden and Commanding Officer Lt. Colonel Cullen were waiting for him. They discussed the target for the next day—the synthetic oil plants at Blechhammer. Up to that time, Ploesti had furnished about one-third of the gasoline, benzene, oil, and other products for keeping the German military functioning. Ploesti had been the target for numerous raids—with its production substantially reduced—and now the focus was the next main refinery in the chain of German production, with several plants along the banks of the Oder River.

Underhill had hoped his last mission would be a milk run, off early, back early. He noticed on the huge map that the target was only twenty miles from Moravska-Ostrava, where they had lost the entire 20th Squadron. Surely it would be well defended because it was one of the last production locales for petroleum products.

Underhill stayed at the headquarters late that evening, studying routes to and from the target, Initial Point (IP), bomb loads, fighter escort, expected flak, and specific aiming points for the bombardiers. He would be the bombardier in the lead echelon taking the group of thirty-six bombers over the target. Their plane would be the main target of the German defenders trying to disrupt the bomb run.

The next morning, they went to the supply room to draw their electric flying suits, K rations, Mae Wests, and parachutes. The supply sergeant joked with one of the crew that he had given him a new Polish parachute, "It's guaranteed to open on impact."

Underhill would be flying with his friends, Redden as pilot, Weinman as mickey (radar operator), Liberto was flight engineer, and Toton was navigator. The co-pilot was Lt. James McHood, a pilot on his first mission, and Lt. Sol Azar was the tail gunner, who kept track of the formation and reported to the commander. They would be in Underhill's favorite airplane, *715 Frankie*, which was kept in the best condition possible for a lead plane. Liberto knew how to maintain the proper voltage in the electrical system, to guarantee that variations in voltage would not affect the delicate instruments in the bombsight and radar.

The take off was on schedule; they cleared their guns over the Adriatic, and at 5000 feet assembled in formation. Underhill checked to see that the arming wires on the bomb racks were properly looped on the twelve 500-pound bombs. One bomb had "Merry Christmas, Adolph" written on it in chalk.

They passed over Brno, Czech, on the way to the IP. Visibility was perfect, but as they turned to the target they could see the dirty brown smoke from oil pots ignited by the Germans to conceal the targets. "Target sighted. Bomb bay doors open. We're on the run," Underhill reported to Redden.

Looking up from the sight, Underhill saw a group of FW-190s lined up for a frontal assault with another group of Me-109s right behind. The FW-190s flew right through the formation, and the plane shuddered as all the guns opened up on them. The first fighter-flurry ripped holes in *Frankie's* fuselage. Underhill went back to the eyepiece of the Norden and focused on the storage tanks 30,000 feet below, adjusting for groundspeed.

They entered a heavy flak curtain, and the fighters dropped off. The plane was bouncing through the flak barrage as Underhill locked in the trigger so the bombs would automatically drop when the two indices crossed inside the bombsight. The flak was closer and murderous, when suddenly there was a loud explosion in the cockpit, and *Frankie* abruptly and violently shuddered. Then the plane lightened as the bombs dropped away. Underhill expected the engineer to call "All bombs clear," but there was no response. A call to the pilot, the engineer, and the navigator sitting next to him got no results. The interphone system was totally destroyed.

The plane's vibrations were now violent, and Underhill looked back into the tunnel where Liberto was waiving for him to come. He unhooked his oxygen hose, hooking it up to the green portable bottle, and crawled through the tunnel. Redden was frantically pulling back on the controls trying to keep the plane on an even keel. Liberto went back to adjusting the fuel mix, throttle, and pitch.

A large section of fuselage was missing from the right side of a jagged instrument panel, and cold air was rushing through the plane. Co-pilot McHood was not helping and was slumped in his seat. The big hole in the fuselage was next to McHood's right hip, and the hole extended down to a "bloody mixture of flesh and metal." McHood's head was on his chest and he was not moving.

Redden motioned for Underhill to get McHood out of his seat in the cockpit while he and Liberto fought the controls. Redden was also trying to deal with the number-one engine that was on fire. Underhill managed to unhook McHood's parachute, squeeze him past Liberto, and pull him to the deck behind the cockpit. McHood's leg was blown off below the knee, and his side had opened. He was not dead. His eyes flickered on his ashen face. He mumbled something and pointed to his breast pocket. Underhill reached inside and found a small leather-bound book, and pressed it in his hand. McHood passed out again. Underhill found sulfanilamide in an emergency packet and sprinkled it over the exposed wound. He also found a syringe that was marked "morphine." Liberto helped cut away three layers of clothing to expose McHood's thigh, and Underhill plunged the syringe into McHood's leg to relieve the pain, should he come-to again. They found a piece of nylon, and Bob made a tourniquet of sorts, to stem the flow of blood that increased as they lost altitude.

Underhill then crawled into the co-pilot's seat, where he could use the radio to call for help if fighters tried to finish them off because they were alone and separated from the formation. Redden had managed to put out the fire in number-one engine, but now number three was trailing smoke. Liberto shut off the fuel to those two engines, and they continued on the other two engines—fortunately, there was one on each side of the plane. They had lost 10,000 feet in altitude, and the altimeter showed 15,000 feet and falling. Lt. Azar worked his way from tail gunner's position, through the bouncing plane, over the open bomb bay doors, to the cockpit, and took over as co-pilot.

Underhill attended to McHood, and gave him another morphine injection—not realizing the first had not yet taken effect. He loosened the tourniquet, but blood was now pouring from other areas around the shattered knee. He readjusted the tourniquet as best he could to stop the rush of blood.

Pilot Redden decided to try to land the airplane, since he had wounded men on board, and asked the crew men to assume ditching positions. Weinman, the radio operator, two waist gunners, and Underhill huddled together in the rear against a stack of flak suits. It probably would have been easier for all to jump and take their chances on becoming prisoners of war, but the pilot's decision was to try to save the lives of nine men.

When they touched ground, the landing with wheels up was gentle, and they slid for some distance before *Frankie* plowed into the ground, standing on its nose. The men piled out the back door of the ship and saw a group of men running toward them, jabbering in a strange tongue. It was not German or Russian. Underhill recognized it as Polish. They motioned that a wounded man was aboard, and one of the group produced an axe and chopped through the Plexiglas nose. Underhill crawled inside, and they managed to get McHood out of the tunnel, loaded him aboard a nearby Ford pickup, and drove him to the hospital. Major Redden rode along, looking after his crewman.

Underhill and Liberto went back to the airplane, took an emergency axe and demolished the IFF secret system (identification friend or foe). Then Underhill took his .45 caliber automatic and put three shots into the bombsight in strategic points. The strangers did not like the action, but it followed standard procedures to avoid capture of valuable equipment by the enemy.

The men were led to a nearby farmhouse where they milled around, feeling relieved that that they had lived through the ordeal and wondering what would come next. Then one of the captors returned with a woman named Kathryn Bandelek who could speak English. The beautiful young lady had lived in Brooklyn for two years before the war, and returned to Poland to join her husband who was in the Polish army. She could also speak Russian. She mentioned that the plane had landed near a Polish army field hospital, and assured them that if they could not treat McHood's horrible wounds, they could take him to a nearby Russian hospital recently set up in Rzescow, the nearest town.

About dark, Major Redden returned to say they had taken McHood to the Russian hospital, and had given him many transfusions of real blood from volunteer donors.

The eight soldiers wondered where they would be spending the night. Liberto, Redden, and Underhill went with Kathryn to her house and the three men slept fully clothed in her extra bed. The others slept elsewhere. The next morning, the airmen were visited by a Russian Major. Through Kathryn's interpretations, he informed them McHood was getting the best of care, and when he was well enough he would be moved further back from the front. Redden and Underhill went to see McHood at the hospital, taking all the cigarettes and candy they could gather from the men. Underhill thought they might never see him again, even if he lived through the ordeal.

That evening, they were moved to a dugout with several dozen stalls filled with clean straw. The stalls in the dugout were separated by heavy planks and each stall contained two bunks. The officers continued to visit Kathryn's house in the evenings, where the extremely pretty Polish officer's wife would feed them headcheese and bread. Kathryn paid special attention to Underhill, and engaged him in conversation whenever possible.

The Russians were with them constantly, more as guards than companions. The Russian officers insisted on sharing their vodka with the airmen, who were familiar with beer, whisky, and bourbon, but not with this clear substitute for water. Every drink of vodka required a toast: "Roosiky-Amerikanski" or "Hitler Kaput," or "Stalin, Churchill, and Roooskevelt."

Two days later, they again visited McHood. His leg had been amputated above the knee, and he could utter a few words. The doctor indicated he was still being given blood, and that he was still critical. He still looked bad and was in poor condition.

The Russian Major invited Major Redden and Captain Underhill to his home. The Russians were very rank conscious, and tried to match their guests, rank for rank. The attitude of the American crew was different. Major Redden, as pilot, was the commander and members of the crew were treated as equals. In the air, flak did not discriminate. In the Air Corps, commissions were given on the basis of technical training, rather than command potential. Some of the best leaders were enlisted men who stepped forward when the situation demanded it.

The next day two American GI's walked into the dugout and indicated they had been sent to find Redden's crew. They were arranging for the airmen to fly out, and had apparently been in the area for some time, performing this service for other downed airmen. They would arrange for downed crews to be flown to Poltava in Russia, where they could get clean clothes and beds.

Redden and Underhill continued to visit at the Russian commander's house, almost daily. On one occasion, they were served small fish, the size of minnows, to be downed with vodka. Underhill tried them, but the scales bothered him, and he couldn't swallow the "poor little critters" that looked like crappie bait in America. The commander informed them that a "Dooglas" would be arriving as soon as the weather cleared to take them to Poltava. He then brought out some small thimble glasses and served slivovitz, a fiery and potent liquor. Kathryn had told them to watch out for it—the warning came too late.

They stopped by Kathryn's house on the way back to the dugout, and Liberto played with Kathryn's two children while Underhill tried to find the floor. Had Liberto not had the vodka or slivovitz? Underhill never thought he would find the dugout so inviting. Instead of the dugout, Kathryn took Underhill into her bedroom and held him close until his dizziness subsided and the sun came up.

More American airmen joined them at the dugout. Five crewmen from a B-24 shot down on December 28 were added. They had parachuted from their airplane, and the whereabouts of the rest of the crew was unknown. Without much to do, the crews exchanged stories and accounts of missions. Liberto found some C rations in *Frankie*, which were shared. The hard crackers from C rations made good checkers, and they fashioned a checkerboard to keep occupied.

Kathryn tried to teach Underhill more about the Polish language, and Underhill was a good student. They wandered the hills, away from the other men, where they could openly laugh and flirt with one another. Deep inside they were sad, knowing that their time together was short lived.

Another crew joined them and soon it was getting crowded. They kept waiting for the "Dooglas," and about a week later, a C-47 landed nearby. The plane could only take ten or twelve healthy people plus the wounded, so they flipped coins to see who would go. Underhill flipped the coin for his crew, lost the toss, and suffered their abuse until they could fly out.

For Underhill, it meant a few more days with Kathryn, before having to say goodbye. When that moment came to leave, they steeled themselves from any emotional display. Underhill could not bear to look back for fear of meeting her beautiful eyes. It was time to go.

Several days later, another C-47 landed and all of the Americans crawled aboard. They headed for Poltava but when they reached the area, the weather was so bad they could not land, so they turned around and headed east, at an extremely low level. At one time they must have hit some birds, because it sounded like flak. Liberto went to the cockpit and returned, saying the "The Russian pilot is flying with his flight gyro and instruments caged. This pilot is the original "mad Russian." After a half-hour of foolhardy flying, they landed at Mirograd, and spent the night in an unheated house with no electricity or water.

The next morning they were tired, stiff, and eager to get going somewhere—anywhere. Breakfast was sauerkraut, pickles, fried barley (groats), tea, and some leftover C ration crackers. The C ration crackers were really starting to taste good.

Late afternoon, they reached Poltava, where there were still a few Americans stationed. They were able to shower, get de-loused, and given clean clothes. Feeling one-hundred percent better, Underhill suddenly realized how fortunate they had been. They had survived a potentially disastrous crippling of the plane. Their durable ship had lasted until their emergency landing. They had fallen into friendly hands with adequate food and, perhaps, too much vodka. The Russians were most considerate in caring for McHood. The airmen were hosted by an extremely attractive lady whose linguistic skills saved countless confrontations. She had singled out Underhill, and shared her affection without demands or reservation. She was a remarkable lady.

The best of all, perhaps, was having two quality men like Redden and Liberto, who performed substantially beyond the call of duty. They deserved accolades far beyond promotion, medals, ribbons, or a pat on the back.

They stayed in Poltava for nearly a week before an American crew in a C-47 took them to Tehran, Iran, for transport back to Italy.

With luck, Underhill would get credit for the mission, and, just perhaps, leave for the United States.

They stayed in Tehran for several days, eating in a mess hall, at tables with linen napkins, served by pretty Polish and Iranian girls—a far cry from their weeks in Foggia or Poland. From Tehran, they were flown in C-47s to Cairo, Egypt.

While waiting for transport back to Italy and their base in Foggia, Underhill ran into an acquaintance from Manchester, Indiana, named Harry Grossnickle, who served as a Finance Officer and was returning to the U.S. Since he lived only ten miles from Underhill's home, Underhill asked him to call his mother and report that Bob was safe and returning to his base. Harry did so when he returned, and it was the first word that Mrs. Underhill had received about her son—other than the standard War Department telegram that her son was missing in action. A few days later, Mrs. Underhill received word from the Red Cross that the Polish Red Cross had contacted them reporting her son was alive and well. It was another week before the War Department sent a telegram informing her that Underhill was safe.

Several days later, they caught a C-47, which stopped at Bengazi, Italy, then went on to Bari Italy, the Group Headquarters, as well as the Fifteenth Air Force Headquarters. There, they boarded two jeeps for Foggia. Underhill returned to his tent and was welcomed by Bob McCook, who shouted, "Bob, you're alive!" It was the most honest, happiest expression of appreciation Underhill had ever experienced.

Underhill was offered the opportunity to continue flying, with a strong recommendation for promotion to Major. Underhill declined the opportunity for advancement, and decided to go home. He caught a flight to Naples, where he waited for two weeks for a flight back to the U.S. It gave him an opportunity to visit Pompeii and he did—twice. Waiting provided him with two educational trips he thoroughly enjoyed. Underhill called it a "fabulous place!"

The return trip was made on a sister ship of the one he took to North Africa, the Admiral Meigs. They docked in New York Harbor and were given a wonderful welcome. However, Underhill was anxious to return home, and caught a service plane close to home. He was home a few days, happy to see his family, but his friends were all away, in service and other activities. He became bored with his hometown. Except for seeing his parents, Manchester was dull.

# UNDERHILL
# CHAPTER FIVE

Captain Robert Underhill was given a thirty-day leave, plus travel time, for rest and recreation in Santa Monica, California. He was a bachelor, had lots of money, no responsibility, and the prospect of fighting the battle of Japan. He had been scared in combat and might be exposed again, so it was time to live it up. And live it up he did. He could not handle liquor very well, but he tried. He ate at the best restaurants. "For a few weeks, I became a wastrel."

En route to Santa Monica, Bob decided to stop in Chicago and visit the parents of Dick Phelps, his friend from service. Bob was staying at the Sherman Hotel, and went to visit the Phelps. They called their daughter, Margaret, and asked her to come home to meet Bob. Margaret had an excellent job, serving as personal secretary to the vice president of the Mayflower Corporation. She returned home to meet her brother's friend from service. Bob immediately canceled his date for that evening and took Margaret out instead. Marge was an interesting, unusual young lady who made quite an impression on Bob.

After living it up in Santa Monica, Bob was assigned to Midland Field in Midland, Texas. He flew to Midland via Chicago, where he had two more dates with Margaret. Bob returned to Midland and they started writing each other at least twice a week. After three weeks, he was transferred to Big Springs, Texas. Bob considered it, "a virtual hell hole; they had the biggest, noisiest cockroaches I have ever seen or heard."

From there, Bob was transferred to Yuma, Arizona. The letters to Marge took on a more serious nature. For the first time, Underhill started thinking about what might happen in the war, and what might happen after the war. He invited Margaret to Yuma for a visit.

Bob later reflected it was Margaret who turned his life around. She gave him purpose and a future on which to focus. He would probably have become a derelict without the change of heart she generated in him.

Bob was training flying in B-25s in Yuma, Arizona, on August 5 when they received word about the big bomb that had been dropped in Japan. Bob knew they were working on bombs with higher explosive capacity such as the RDX (Rapid Detonating Explosive), but he knew nothing about the atomic bomb.

Three days after the war ended, a directive was issued stating three classes of military could get out of service early. The categories were prisoners of war, escapees, and/or evadees. Bob was considered an evadee because of his experience in Poland, and was eligible for discharge, so he decided to pursue getting out of service. Marge was considering the visit to Yuma when he called her and indicated he would be returning to Chicago, if Red Ball would rehire him.

He wrote to the Mishawaka Corporation to see if he could have his old job back, and they welcomed his return. Bob took his discharge on August 20, and with accumulated leave and travel time, final separation was scheduled for September 29, 1945.

September 29, 1945, became a very special day. Bob, on that day, separated from service; he officially entered the payroll of the Mishawaka Corporation, and Margaret Phelps and Robert Underhill were married in Manchester, Indiana.

When Bob was attending Manchester College, although he was not a member of that church's faith and resented the compulsory chapel, he had a good deal of respect for a bible instructor, Reverend Robert Miller. He contacted Rev. Miller and asked him to perform the wedding ceremony. All of Bob's friends were gone from Silver Lake, so Margaret and Bob drove from South Bend to Manchester, where they were married. They then returned to South Bend where Bob was to resume being a traveling salesman.

Bob started a six-week training program to learn the various lines of Red Ball shoes, the manufacturing processes, and their marketing strategies. During the training, he suddenly realized that he had a lovely young wife, and the prospect of being a traveling salesman would take him away from home for extended periods of time. Perhaps now was the time to evaluate his future and develop a different philosophy about life.

He discovered that with his past college training and the credits earned from his Army training, he was only three months away from being a certified high school teacher. He resigned from Mishawaka Corporation, and went back to Manchester College. Since housing was very tight, he had the opportunity to live with the Rev. Miller's family, and he and Margaret rented a bedroom from them for the three-month period. Living with a very strict Church of the Brethren minister had certain limitations. But, when they would occasionally sneak a drink of liquor in their bedroom, Rev. Miller never acknowledged he was aware of their imbibing.

Wedding picture of Margaret Phelps and Robert Underhill. They were married the memorable day of September 29, 1945: the same day Bob separated from service and began to work for Mishawaka Corporation.

In June of 1946, Bob completed his student teaching and received his certificate to teach high school, but he never used it. In June 1946, Bob got a scholarship to Northwestern University, in Evanston, Illinois, where he intended to pursue a course in radio production. Instead, he got much more interested in rhetoric and public speaking. He coached the debate team and, in 1947, received his master's degree; he learned he could teach at the college level, as well as the high school level. One of the colleges interested in Bob was Iowa State College (now University) in Ames, Iowa. He met with Dr. Fred Lorch, who was in Chicago on a recruiting trip, and Dr. Lorch asked Bob out for a visit of the campus in February 1947. Bob accepted a position that would allow him to start teaching during the summer session, 1947.

He was an instructor in English and Speech and, as most young faculty did, lived in Pammel Court housing for a year and a half. Their first child, Susan, was born there. Bob decided that if he were to climb the academic ladder, he would need a Ph.D, and proceeded to attend summer school at Northwestern University.

When Bob separated from service, he signed a good number of papers that took him out of the Air Force Reserve and transferred him to the Army of the United States. He thought nothing about it, assuming his service responsibilities were completed.

One day in February 1951, Marge called him at the office, and said, "Bob, you have a very important official-looking document in the mail." She opened it and read it to him. It stated that Captain Robert Underhill will immediately report to Rantoul, Illinois, for examination and entrance into active duty. Bob took the letter to Dr. Lorch, who called the proper military commander and indicated that Bob was needed as an instructor at Iowa State College. Dr. Lorch received a letter a week later from the Army saying Bob was needed in service, and they did not care about Iowa State's instructorship. On March 15, at the end of the winter quarter, Underhill went back on active duty.

He was first ordered to Mather Field in Sacramento, California, where he thought he would be taught on new radar equipment. Instead, he found that they were using the APQ13 equipment left over from WWII which he last used on his first three flights, before he became a full time bombardier. It took a while to adjust to reading the radar, but the west coast was full of contrast, and the Pacific was easy to read on the screen.

After six weeks, he was transferred to Randolph Field near San Antonio, Texas. Their second daughter, Sandra, was born by then, and Marge and the two children came down to live in a little rented house. Bob was assigned to a B-29 crew, who trained on missions twelve and thirteen hours long. They loved Randolph because it was a permanent base with permanent buildings and facilities.

The crew was preparing for a move to Korea, but was first sent to Mountain Home, Idaho. Bob was apprehensive about flying more combat and, with a young family, did not want to leave them behind. At Mountain Home, Bob applied for an area called Psychological Warfare, because of his interest and background in rhetoric, and transferred from the Strategic Air Command (SAC) to Air Re-supply and Communication. He was then sent to Washington, D.C., for six months' training in Linguistics and Language, at a branch of Georgetown University. Bob considered it some of the best instruction he had ever had in all the schools he had attended. He studied Geo-politics and European History, responding to the excellent instruction, and graduating with honors.

He was picked to attend schooling in the Polish language at Indiana University in Bloomington, Indiana. He packed the family and went to Indiana U for eight months, where he did nothing but study the Polish language. There were three students and five instructors for around-the-clock study of the language. Naturally, they became reasonably proficient in reading and conversing in the language.

He then received notice that his commission had expired, and if he wished to continue in active duty he would have to re-enlist for seven years. He liked the service, and was interested in continuing in the service, but he recognized that you moved up in rank only if you were a pilot or regular army. As a bombardier, he would have limited potential for moving vertically in rank. Bob was notified he had been appointed an associate professor at Iowa State College, meaning he was tenured. After a good deal of sweat and confusion, he decided to turn down his commission and return to civilian life as a professor at Iowa State.

Bob and his family returned to Ames in the fall of 1955 and, not long after that, he was named a full professor and head of the Department of English and Speech. As the years progressed, he became more involved in administration and less in teaching. In 1969, Speech was separated from English, became a department on its own, and Bob was elected chairman. For five years, Underhill administered several areas under the broad umbrella of his department, including rhetoric, public address, drama, tele-communicative arts, and speech pathology.

While this was going on he tried to sandwich time for writing articles, but also wanted to write a book. He became interested in the life of Harry Truman. During 1979/1980, he applied for a faculty improvement leave, and spent a year at the Truman Library in Independence, Missouri, doing research and writing. This produced his first full length book, *The Truman Persuasions*, published in 1981.

Back at Iowa State he returned to the classroom, rather than administration. From 1955 until his retirement in 1986, the Iowa State student body increased from 6,000 students to over 24,000 students—severely taxing all facets of academia.

Margaret had experienced a series of illnesses that were difficult to diagnose, and in 1983 had a major colostomy, which was most debilitating. She recovered physically, but never fully recovered mentally. She was soon diagnosed as having Alzheimer's disease. Bob retired from teaching in 1986, and gave Margaret home care until 1992 when she was moved to Greenhill's Care Center in Ames. No two cases of Alzheimer's are alike. Margaret's condition continued to deteriorate as she lost her faculties in the reverse order she had attained them. Memory and communication skills were the first faculties to go. She chose to move to Bethany Manor in Story City in 2000.

This was extremely difficult for Bob, since Margaret was so important in giving his life direction and purpose, and two wonderful children. "Without Marge my life would not have amounted to a tinker's damn."

Bob continued to pursue his interest in Harry Truman and in 1988 wrote *The Bully Pulpit*.

In 1994 he completed, *FDR and Harry: Unparalleled Lives*.

Then, in 1998, he produced a biography, *Alone with Friends: the Biography of W. Robert Parks*.

He wrote a novel based on his personal experience being shot down over Poland, published in 2000, entitled, *Blechhammer on the Oder*. The book was reissued in 2002 under the title, *I'll See You Again*.

In 2001, Bob completed a biography of an Ames physician entitled, *A Doctor and His Wife*.

A new biography, written by Bob, about a long-time WHO Radio news broadcaster was introduced in the summer of 2002. *Jack Shelley and the News* includes a compact disk containing the complete broadcasts from four major news events Jack Shelley observed first-hand. Included are: The Battle of the Bulge, the interview with pilot Col. Paul Tibbets after dropping the atomic bomb on Hiroshima, the signing of the Unconditional Surrender aboard the USS Missouri, and some observations during an Atomic bomb test in Nevada. The book carries the inimitable style of a thorough, accomplished, scholarly writer.

A number of years ago, Bob's bomb group publication asked him to recount his experiences in Poland in an article for their magazine. In that article, he commented on the demise of Lt. McHood, who was so severely wounded and who was cared for in Russian hospitals. It was reported that McHood was sent to an American hospital in North Africa, where after additional amputations, he passed away. After publication of the article, Bob received a letter July 27, 1994, from McHood who stated, "Like hell I'm dead. I'm an electrical engineer practicing in Decatur, Illinois." It seems McHood not only survived, but attended the University of

Illinois, worked for the Illinois Power Company, and was married, with two children.

Bob appreciated the time he spent in service: the travel, the comradeship, the friendships, the opportunity to learn, and the exposure to the world as it exists. He did not enjoy being shot at, and he never moralized his responsibility to disable the enemy's ability to conduct the war. He may have been carried away with his newfound freedoms, and experienced a few extraneous excesses in his comportment. Too many young men would stare death in the face and perform their duties as everyday tasks. Under the circumstances, the indiscretions can be overlooked.

The motto of the U.S. Military Academy is "Duty, Honor, Country." Most of the young men and women focused on "Duty." The rest took care of itself.

Captain Robert Underhill received a number of medals and awards. They included:
- The WWII Victory Medal
- The American Campaign Ribbon
- The Arno River Campaign Medal with five stars
- The Air Medal with four Oak Leaf Clusters
- The Distinguished Flying Cross with one Oak Leaf Cluster.

He also received a wonderful education, which he shared with thousands of students over the years. And he continues to share his story-telling abilities through recent and future volumes.

# BOOK SEVEN

# BAILEY

*Sergeant Merritt Bailey*

*S-2 Intelligence*

*Fifteenth Air Force*

*49th Wing*

*484th Bomb Group*

*"With censorship, soldiers often claimed that the only items in their letters that survived were 'Dear Mom' and 'Your Loving Son.'"*

—*Bailey*

# BAILEY
# CHAPTER ONE

If you were to hear the song, "The Old Lamplighter (of long, long ago)" you would probably picture a European nineteenth-century tradition for illuminating major streets. In the late 1920s, Merritt Bailey lived, as a child, in a neighborhood of St. Louis that was late in installing electric lights and he observed first-hand the activities of the town lamplighter. The lamplighter cleaned the glass surround and put a flame to the natural gas that would burn through the fading daylight and into the night. Early the next morning, he would repeat his route, turning off the gas supply. It was a task that happened 365 days per year, every evening and every morning.

The Bailey household had electric lights, and the local power company encouraged an increased use of electricity. When a lightbulb would burn out in the Bailey household, it was young Merritt Jr.'s job to carry the bulb to the power company, where they replaced it with a new bulb, free of charge. The late twenties were a period of great technological transition. That period saw rapid improvement in the motorcar, electrical distribution and electric motors, movie theaters, highways, aeroplanes, and public and private conveniences. You could still turn in a used light bulb for a free replacement well into the late 1930s.

Merritt Jr. was born in Denver, Colorado, on February 24, 1921. He was the only child of Merritt and Edwina Bailey. His father, Merritt Sr., who was Missouri born, originally worked for an Alton, Illinois, bank and later worked in Denver, Colorado, as a bond salesman. That ended when the stock market crash caused thousands of investors to lose their hard earned money. After the crash of 1929, Merritt Sr. became a typewriter salesman, moving from job to job frequently during the depression. The family lived mostly in large cities—Minneapolis, Pittsburgh, Denver, and St. Louis (three different times)—primarily because people in big cities bought typewriters. Merritt Sr. operated an appliance store in Alton, Illinois, for two years, but found selling typewriters to be more profitable. Each move for Merritt Sr. usually meant a raise in responsibility. It was in Alton that Merritt met Edwina Fox, who was born in Tennessee, but at the age of eighteen had moved to Alton to find work.

While growing up, Merritt Jr. attended eight different grade schools. The moves were mostly during the school year, so Merritt joined the class at whatever stage the curriculum was in at that particular time. As a result, Merritt felt that his schooling was better in "readin' and writin'" than in 'rithmetic."

On December 7, 1941, Bailey was visiting at his grandmother's house in Denver, Colorado. After high school, he attended the American Institute of Business (AIB) in Des Moines. He worked at several jobs in Des Moines: for a credit bureau, *Look* magazine, Westinghouse Electric, and then for a company in Kansas City, Missouri, that made storage tanks. When the war started and American business converted to making military components, the storage tank company got a contract to make landing carriages for B-25s.

While working in Des Moines, he found that life does follow popular songs, particularly if the song goes like this:

> *"While strolling through the park one day,*
> *In the mer-ry month of May,*
> *I was taken by surprise, by a pair of roguish eyes.*
> *In a mo-ment my poor heart was stole away."*

It seems the eyes belonged to Grace Crabtree, a young student nurse from Sheldahl, Iowa, who was training at Iowa Lutheran Hospital in Des Moines. After nine months of courting, they decided to marry. There was one major problem: student nurses were not allowed to be married. Merritt and Grace decided to elope, and drove to Greenfield, Iowa, where the Presbyterian minister, Reverend Hanks, performed the ceremony. The witnesses were Reverend Hanks' wife and their two babies. After a whirlwind twenty-three-hour honeymoon in Omaha, they returned so Grace could be at work Sunday afternoon. The marriage remained a secret until Grace graduated in her white starched nurse's cap.

In Kansas City, Merritt worked as a stenographer, and his prime ambition was to make as much money as an engineer, a whole 3,000 dollars per year. By that time, he and Grace had a child on the way, and knowing he would soon be called in the Selective Service draft, he enlisted in the Officer Candidate School program, hoping to get into chemical warfare.

Grace stayed with her parents in Sheldahl, Iowa, and found employment at Mary Greeley Hospital in Ames, Iowa, while Merritt went to basic training.

*Grace and Merritt Bailey in a picture taken several months after their marriage. They eloped, so no formal pictures were taken.*

Merritt reported to Camp Sibert, near Gadson, Alabama, for basic training and chemical warfare training. However, the Officer Candidate School (OCS) program for chemical warfare training was phased out, and he was reassigned to a heavy weapons company: training on mortars, machine guns, and projectiles. During the training, he contracted Poliomyelitis and spent one month in the hospital. Since the OCS program was no longer available, Merritt was discharged as provided for in the OCS conditions of enlistment.

While at Camp Sibert, Merritt was housed in a barracks with thirty-nine other men, all from rural Arkansas. It seems none of them had ever worn a tie. Merritt was ordered to put his "talent for tying" to use, with the threat that "failure to teach them immediately" would result in permanent Kitchen Police (KP) duty. Merritt discovered early in his military career the basis of military motivation.

Merritt later learned that the heavy weapons company saw extensive combat in Europe, resulting in over sixty-percent casualties.

*Attempts to make a tent more livable involved putting up the side flaps and building make-shift walls out of scrounged materials.*

# BAILEY
## CHAPTER TWO

Bailey stayed in Kelly, Iowa, for five or six months, until he was drafted and sent to Fort Leavenworth, Kansas, for basic training. The military rotated branch of service assignment on a daily basis: infantry, artillery, mechanized, etc. He was lucky. The day he was processed was Air Corps' day, so he was selected for training in staff activities. He went to Buckley Field, Colorado, to experience basic training for the second time. After the second time, he felt he could march and salute with the best of them. From Buckley Field he went to Jefferson Barracks, Missouri, which served as a replacement depot and experienced more basic training. Now he could really march and salute.

Bailey was reporting to Norfolk, Virginia, (he was scheduled to go to England with replacement troops for the Eighth Air Force) when he received word that Grace was quite ill. He returned home for a short leave, and while in Iowa, his assigned group left for England.

Returning to Norfolk, Bailey was reassigned to a group going to Italy. The replacement group boarded a Liberty Ship and set sail for Italy as part of a large convoy. A few lucky crews were selected to fly the squadron's B-24s from America to Italy, while the remainder of the squadron enjoyed the thirty-day convoy across the Atlantic, through the Mediterranean to the east coast of Italy. The major excitement of the trip came one night as the convoy entered the Adriatic Sea. As the convoy rounded the "boot" of Italy, it was attacked by German Ju-88 bombers. One of the convoy ships was sunk, and a number of the bombers were shot down in flames. One person on Bailey's Liberty Ship was hit by gunfire, but it was not known if it came from a bomber or was a stray shell from an adjoining ship.

They made port in Bari, on the east coast of Italy. As they disembarked, they were issued either carbines or side arms to wear as they marched from the docks to the railroad yards. The air corps did not give them any ammunition for the guns, which certainly reduced the aura of being triumphant invaders.

They were loaded aboard boxcars, reminiscent of the old "forty and eight" boxcars of World War I fame. The ancient steam engine labored as it moved along the coast and climbed through the

Italian hills—past farms, woodlands, and grain fields—finally reaching Cerignola on the Foggia plain. From the rail yard they boarded trucks to their new base, still under construction. It was located on a farm that contained a few farm buildings surrounded by a large wheat field where a "tent city" was in the process of being erected. A few hundred yards away the airstrip was nearing completion and soon would house a squadron of heavy bombers.

The Foggia area contained eight or ten air bases that included both heavy bombers and fighters. Bailey was assigned to Torretta Field, which accommodated the 49th Wing, 484th Bomb Group of B-24 Liberator Bombers. Bailey arrived at Torretta Field in March 1943; he served there until spring 1945.

Bailey was a member of S-2 Intelligence at the squadron level, which was very grass roots in Italy during WWII. Not being part of a flying crew meant he was out of the loop for the glamour of being a prime target of the Germans.

Bailey lived in a tent with five other men, who worked at various locations on and around the base, so the only opportunity to build rapport was after hours—mostly late hours. The flying crews trained together, flew together, and lived together—and as a result, they developed a team concept that bound them as friends. Bailey had no such luck. He managed to make a few friends at the Non-Commissioned Officer's (NCO) Club, but the spirit of crew never developed. He suffered the ennui of base living, doing routine tasks—watching while other men risk their lives.

When they first arrived, they lived in tents in the middle of a wheat field. The tents were on the ground, unheated, without bunks. The description of the basic tent as a "six-man tent" was a violation of reality. Six men sleeping on the floor literally filled the tent. One of the first tent improvements was a stove fabricated from a fifty-five-gallon oil drum and shell casings, which burned aviation gasoline. Keeping it lit and serviced kept the men warmer than the actual BTU's generated by the functioning stove.

Since the tent mates worked at different locations during the day, there was little opportunity to work together to fix their tent up. They did manage to find some packing crates to build walls, and by extending the side flaps they doubled the size of the tent. After a few months' occupancy, they installed their first single-light socket, and had the luxury of a sixty-watt bulb. It was an occasion for electric celebration.

A rut down the edge of the tent, left by a truck, served Bailey as a bed for several weeks. Bailey endured sleeping in the depression as it helped to contain body heat. The later addition of canvas cots was not nearly as cozy. The winters in Torretta were very uncomfortable, as the winds off the Adriatic Sea were damp, cold, and penetrating.

Initially, rats were a major problem. They would get into tents every night, and the chaos of pursuit would result in a frantic rearrangement of the occupants' possessions as well as the occupants themselves. The rats chewed on everything, including toes. The rat problem was eventually resolved by devising a special trap. Each tent had a fifty-five-gallon barrel full of water outside the entrance. The water was for fire protection, and reflecting usual military planning, there were no pails to draw water from the barrels. The men contrived a device, wherein the rat would fall into the water and drown.

Mission instructions were handed down from the Air Force, through the Wing, then to the Group, and finally to the Squadrons. A chain of command this long provided ample opportunity for Axis sympathizers to leak information to the Germans. The staff soon learned that if you wanted to know the next day's mission, you listened to "Axis Sally," the German lady reporter on the radio, who would give the mission, the target, and what groups were flying it. If you missed the radio report, mission information would be common knowledge in Cerignola, the nearest Italian town. It was even more disconcerting to hear a certain bomb group would soon have a new commanding officer, Col. Xxxxx, and that the bomb group would be welcomed with heavy flak and fighters on the next day's mission.

Outgoing mail had to be censored, and the individual censor used whatever criteria he thought was appropriate. Censors read between the lines to determine what was sensitive or secretive, or what breached security. The slashing black deletions were often ludicrous and frustrating to the recipient. Soldiers often claimed that the only items in their letters that survived censorship were "Dear Mom" and "Your loving son."

Since Bailey learned shorthand at AIB, he would take testimony at court trials on the base. Bailey served as an interrogation reporter on a case where an airman had stolen a quantity of gold-seal currency. This currency was American paper money that promised redemption in gold bullion, making it legitimate currency. Most flight crews carried a small packet of currency to use in the event they were shot down over enemy territory. The airmen could use the currency to bribe their captors. This thieving airman was cornered in a latrine, and as the Military Police closed in for the arrest, he disposed of the stolen currency by dumping it in the latrine. Part of the resolution of his case resulted in his descending into the latrine pit to recover all of the stolen currency.

*The tents afforded minimal housing for the soldiers. Maintenance and permanent staff spent two to three years in this environment.*

Sergeant Bailey's tasks involved a myriad of activities. He worked primarily with the Squadron Adjutant, typing reports. He maintained the personnel reports for the Adjutant, attending pre-mission briefings and post-mission debriefings.

At first his assignment was interesting, then routine, and finally totally boring. At the NCO club there was little excitement to share with the airmen returning from their dangerous missions. Getting to know non-commissioned crew members was tenuous, since their future was perilous. It was difficult to build friendly relationships, as the camp non-coms (non-commissioned officers) involved in maintenance, armament, and transportation were scattered about the base and had little in common.

Ultimately promoted to the rank of sergeant, Bailey noticed a promotional bias in his squadron. It seems that the Commanding Officer (CO) was from Texas, and promotions appeared to go to Texas boys. The Executive Officer, the first sergeant, the master sergeant, and numerous staff sergeants also happened to be from Texas. The situation caused a good deal of grumbling by the other soldiers who never seemed to get promoted.

Bailey would occasionally be in charge of several truckloads of Italian workers brought in each day to perform a variety of menial tasks. They were presumably officially screened as potential spies. They were, however, primarily scavengers. At the end of the day, when leaving the base, they were thoroughly searched for contraband, or parcels of food they had salvaged from the mess hall trash barrels. Recovery of personnel items was understandable, but the troops did not understand why the Air Force was so adamant about their not taking food that was being thrown away. Certainly, the prospect of food contamination and sickness might become a problem, but much good could have been done by sharing it with starving families in the community.

In every war since the dawn of man, there has been one consistency: Wherever men congregate, there have been camp followers and prostitutes who plague armies. They were constantly being rooted out and sent packing. The two main reasons for their dismissal were, first, hygienic, and second, to cut down the transmission of "secrets" an aroused airman might confess during moments of passion.

As noted, the squadron was located in the middle of a former wheat field, and without fencing, security was virtually nonexistent. Local farmers farmed the fields during the day and, during harvest, gleaned every last stalk of wheat the machines had missed. At night the base was visited by the ladies of pleasure, who always found a way into camp (probably with some assistance). Access by saboteurs was equally easy. Bailey remembers only one event attributed to saboteurs. It seems that eleven of the planes in one squadron slated for a mission crashed at takeoff on that day's mission. Information regarding the event was suppressed by the Commanding Officer, but flight crews who heard the rumor were very nervous about flying for several weeks.

The Air Corps, as a reward for their flying crews, developed a tradition of providing alcohol for the crews after each mission. Upon return, the crews would line up outside the Headquarters building and each airman would receive one one-ounce shot of rye whiskey. The Executive Officer decreed that the whiskey had to be consumed on the spot. The airmen used all sorts of stratagem to try to smuggle their liquor back to their tent, to be saved for a major event. Since each man received one ounce of rye, the pourer was required to certify that twenty-five drinks had been served from each bottle. A careful pourer could pour twenty-five ounces, leaving a remainder in the bottle for the pourer. After serving several hundred men, the residual rye would permit the pourer and his closest friends a cheerful evening—and maybe even a slight buzz.

The airmen often wondered why inexpensive rye whiskey was the liquor of choice; it seems the higher echelons got Johnny Walker, befitting their status. The only other liquor available was the four bottles of beer dispensed by the squadron Post Exchange (PX) each week. Each soldier could also get two cigars and a carton of cigarettes. One night a week the bar was open, and a soldier could buy shots of Italian "brandy" guaranteed to be at least twenty-four hours old. Consumed in any quantity, the "brandy" would almost guarantee blindness.

For a period of time, a British anti-aircraft unit was stationed near the squadron to provide protection in case of a German air raid. The British food—at its best—was even less palatable than the American food, which U.S. soldiers considered only marginally palatable. The Brits, however, had a variety of liquors available to them, with more options than the Americans. One American mess sergeant did a brisk business exchanging American food with his British counterpart for some fine liquor; that is, until the Commanding Officer found out about it.

The squadron surgeon was a disappointed and disillusioned man. The good doctor anticipated performing a variety of surgical procedures that would be extremely useful upon his return to civilian life. Although he would occasionally work on wounded airmen following a mission and had the occasional chore of dealing with the dead, most of his work dealt with sick call, venereal disease (VD), stomach disorders, and the usual servicemen's maladies. There was not the unusual and intense surgery that he had anticipated. His extreme disappointment was a reflection of most airmen's good fortune.

As in any unit, there were the special characters who sort of "just wandered about." One young airman was an alcoholic, and for two years did nothing but perambulate about the base in his inebriated condition. No one knew his assignment, specialty, or who he reported to—he was just *there*. Rumor was that he was once a staff sergeant, and had done some stockade time, but no one knew his actual history.

One night, Bailey and his tent mates were called out to assist in searching the camp for a "body." The Officer of the Day reported he had run over someone while making the drive around camp in his jeep. As the searchers discovered, he had run over a soldier. It seems the body belonged to the camp drunk who had passed out in the middle of the road and was difficult to see because of the dirty jeep lights. The soft mud, and the soldier's relaxed condition, saved the soldier from serious injury.

# BAILEY
# CHAPTER THREE

One of Bailey's tent mates spoke fluent Italian and made friends with several families in the town of Cerignola. They were occasionally invited to family dinners, not for their charm, grace, and good manners, but because they would bring gifts of cigarettes or clothing. The local citizens were also short of food, but the cigarettes were a valuable trading commodity, enabling them to expand their bartering power. Thanks to the Italian-speaking tent mate, there were weekly deliveries of eggs and fresh vegetables in exchange for cigarettes.

Local customs prevailed as the war swirled around the local citizens. German occupation caused a jejune existence, depriving them of most of the necessities, but they struggled on as best they could. Bailey remembers walking along the waterfront, watching women beating squid on the rocks to tenderize them before cooking them.

Several Italian "tradesmen" were given permission to set up shops in the squadron area. One tradesman, a barber, charged ten cents for a shave and fifteen cents more if you also wanted a haircut. Bailey remembers the barber had only cold water, and would spend fifteen minutes lathering a face for a shave. The resulting shave was the best in Bailey's experience.

Cerignola was a "Jekyll and Hyde" sort of town. Bailey and his tent mates' visits to families were a pleasant experience, but not without some fear. Recent publications indicate Cerignola was considered a "Rest and Recreation Community" developed by the Red Cross. During fourteen months of service nearby, Bailey was never aware of Rest and Recreation (R&R) facilities. During his tour of duty, soldiers were discouraged from visiting the community because of the number of attacks on airmen by Italians who were still Axis sympathizers. This was not uncommon in small Italian communities, resulting from reaction to Allied bombings that attempted to dislodge the German occupiers. Some towns were totally destroyed by the attacks, with many innocent civilians killed or wounded.

As their lists of missions grew longer, flight crews became increasingly occupied with the chances of completing their tour of duty. On mission days, attendance at sick bay increased rather significantly. One gunner "accidentally" shot himself in the foot while "cleaning his gun." Sore throats or ear infections were another way to avoid missions. One young gunner, for reasons unexplained, sprayed the encampment with bullets from his airplane's nose gun one morning, ventilating a few tents and the latrine in the process. The only injuries were to the pride of the officer who had to explain this occurrence to higher echelons.

It is fairly safe to say that wherever there is a concentration of soldiers and it is payday, games of chance will suddenly appear. This truism is not scientifically factual, but has been observed for several millenniums. The base at Torretta was no exception. Several enterprising airmen set up a roulette game in their tent, and after every payday the action was hot and heavy. As usual, some soldiers exercised discipline in their gambling while others lost everything—spending the rest of the month borrowing money to get by. Sergeant Bailey decided to outsmart the operators, and diligently worked out a formula for beating the game. He immediately put his sophisticated system to work and proceeded to lose all of his money, as well as that of his tent mates, before discovering one major flaw in the formula.

Rumors were that the enterprising gamblers had amassed several thousand dollars, which they intended to use as a nest egg when they returned home. However, when it came time to leave, all soldiers were required to turn in military script money for American money. The higher echelon issued a directive establishing an exchange limit at fifty dollars per person. Bailey remembers the astonished look on the faces of the gamblers—who were holding thousands of dollars of script that became essentially worthless.

Bailey learned enough Italian phrases to work with the laborers who came into the camp daily, but was not very fluent in the language. While in high school, he was required to take three years of Latin, and he enjoyed the class. On one trip into Foggia he met a Catholic priest, and tried to engage him in conversation. Rather than use his broken Italian he decided to impress the Priest with his mastery of Latin. The conversation fell flat, since the Priest had only memorized the Latin prayers, and was totally unfamiliar with Latin as a means of communication.

Staff members who drudged away on their ground assignments would attempt to go on missions with flight crews for a change of scenery. Bailey made friends with one crew and managed to sneak aboard a B-24 on a "milk run" to Yugoslavia. He was not prepared for the cold air of the open waist gunner's position. The bouncing of the airplane flying through clouds or "prop wash," caused him to fill his steel helmet with his breakfast. When typing up the flight report he learned the pilot had listed additional cargo as an "additional gunner."

Many attempts were made to take the soldiers' minds off of the war, and a variety of sports activities were available. There were numerous football, baseball, and basketball games, with some inter-squadron play. There were also contests where the winner would win R&R trips for a week. Bailey entered a bridge tournament with a partner who was loaded with confidence, but had absolutely no experience in the game. They were soundly defeated in the first round. So, Bailey entered the chess tournament and ended up taking first place.

The reward for his victory was a week's pass to Nice, France, which had been liberated by the Allies by that time. He caught a plane to Nice, and for thirty-six hours reveled in all that Nice had to offer. However, he was recalled to Italy because his squadron was being demobilized with the air crews destined for the United States with the balance of the support staff assigned to other bases at Casablanca and Dakar, North Africa. Bailey was re-assigned to the Air Transport Command in Dakar. The reward for winning a prize at chess for R&R lasted barely two days. Bailey, after two days, went from a knight to a pawn.

Victory in Europe Day (V-E Day) was cause for a big celebration in camp. The ground war in Italy had been a long and difficult one. The terrain favored the defensive position of the retreating Germans who gave ground grudgingly. There was much relief at the airbase and surrounding communities that the shooting war had finally ceased. As soldiers started rotating back to the U.S., an accumulated point system indicating length of service and other considerations was used to select returnees. Since air crews were rotated after fifty missions, several generations of crews arrived and left while the base staff continued their boring routine. Bailey continued from May to September, reporting incoming and outgoing flights, determining reasons for flight delays, and performing the usual military documentation of activities.

When the squadron finally transferred, part of the troops were stationed in Casablanca, while Bailey and others were sent to Dakar. The pilot of the DC-3 transporting the troops boasted that he was capable of taking off and landing the DC-3 on one engine. Leaving Casablanca the plane was substantially overloaded, and they were two hours out when the port engine coughed, sputtered and quit. The pilot's boast was put to the test. They managed to find an obscure landing strip in the desert, and landed for several hours of repairs before continuing on their way to Dakar.

Dakar was home for a plethora of mosquitoes, and fear of coming down with malaria was a major concern. All soldiers took a pill called Atabrine to combat the disease, in case of exposure. Soldiers were required to take it as they left the mess hall after meals. It was a wonderful drug, but had a side effect of turning the recipient's skin a deep yellow hue. Most soldiers took the pill, faked swallowing it, and upon leaving the mess tent, spit it on the ground. After a few weeks, the soil outside the mess tent took on a yellow pallor—approximately equal to that of some of the soldiers.

Another malaria fighter was a directive to always wear calf-high boots after 6:00 P.M. A soldier might be wearing khaki shorts, but the directive assumed this breed of mosquitoes only bit below the knees. New arrivals in Dakar would contract with pilots ferrying planes back and forth from Brazil, to bring back boots from Brazil. Bailey paid five dollars for a fine pair of boots that he wore long after he had separated from service. In the U.S. the boots would have cost over 100 dollars.

The Commanding General at Dakar was determined to preserve the base's record for having the lowest venereal disease (VD) rate of the bases in the area. Punishment for contracting VD was extremely severe. The French government cooperated by registering all of the "pavement princesses" in Dakar and requiring them to have weekly health exams. Bailey was in charge of preparing the weekly reports of base VD, and found the General's approach to be most effective in curbing disease. The results were the best of any of the bases where Bailey was stationed.

The "black market" did a brisk business in most of the bases in Italy. Even though money was in short supply, the bartering and selling of items with resale value was fairly common. In Dakar it reached new heights. A Colt .45, or carbine, or even a Jeep would find a flock of buyers. The main black market item for most GI's was a carton of cigarettes. A two-dollar carton of cigarettes would bring twenty dollars on the streets of Dakar. A soldier never went into Dakar alone after dark, or after having too much liquor. Too many soldiers found themselves in a remote alley stripped to their shorts—and sometimes without shorts.

Bailey's squadron received seven Battle Stars, and two Distinguished Unit Citations. And Bailey never fired a shot in anger.

When Bailey finally received orders to return to the United States, he boarded a huge new C-54 transport and flew a direct route from Dakar to the Canary Islands, and on to Miami Beach. In Miami, Bailey lived on the seventh floor of a hotel in which the elevator did not function. They learned it was being saved for postwar activity. The soldiers trudged the seven floors several times daily, which certainly kept them in the physical shape necessary to discharge their Air Transport Command duties.

From Miami he went to Missouri. After a few days processing, he separated from service and returned to Ames.

He would get to see his wife and daughter, who he had not seen in over two years.

# BAILEY
# CHAPTER FOUR

Grace Bailey worked as a nurse in Mary Greeley Hospital in Ames, Iowa, while her husband was overseas. Her parents had moved from Sheldahl to Kelley, Iowa, which made it convenient for Grace to continue working. Their daughter was born three months after Merritt entered the service. He got to meet his daughter, Shirley, when he was home on leave when she was very small, but did not to get to see her again until she was three years old. Grace had moved to Kelley to live with her mother, who baby-sat while she worked at the hospital. Later, Grace found an apartment in Ames.

Merritt considers the three years he spent in service the best investment he ever made. In his high school graduating class of 500 students, only two students were planning a college education. The depression had created an attitude that education was affordable only by the wealthy—a misconception accepted by most students with indifference.

Merritt was grateful for the opportunity offered by the GI bill, and enrolled at Iowa State College in the chemistry curriculum. Merritt and Grace moved into Pammel Court, several acres of corrugated aluminum, minimum housing, erected during the war as temporary living quarters. The units did prove to be temporary—as they lasted only sixty years. The two-bedroom units were very small, with a kerosene stove and practically no kitchen, a bathroom in which you could not turn around, and a smoky, inefficient oil heater.

This was compensated for by being cold and drafty.

Merritt noticed that every night when he staggered home with a load of books, studying past midnight, his duplex neighbor was relatively relaxed about college, studied only occasionally, and went to bed early. The neighbor's major was journalism. Merritt, after much consideration, decided that perhaps he was cut out to become a journalist, and changed majors with the intent of teaching in that area. Since Iowa State College (now University) did not have an advanced degree in Journalism at that time, Merritt took a double major in Economics and Journalism, ultimately getting a master's degree in Economics and Journalism. When he received his undergraduate degree, he graduated with top honors in his curriculum.

Living in Pammel Court was an interesting experience. Returning veterans had preference for living there, and the readjustment to civilian life while exposed to academic pressure resulted in interesting situations and many wonderful stories. Pammel Court housing was separated from the campus by the longest two-track railroad system in the U.S., running from Omaha, Nebraska, to Chicago, Illinois. There were numerous trains daily, and it was universally accepted that the whistle of the "City of San Francisco" as the train flew through Ames at 3:00 A.M. (at seventy miles per hour) was responsible for causing more progeny than any other train!

The returning veterans and their exposure to the outside world introduced an interesting amalgam of societal change in the conservative Iowa community. The drinking habits and social interaction were new to the community, but it was mollified by the income level of the veterans. The married students also fell outside the watchful eye of Dean Helser, who frowned on consumption of alcohol in any form. Pammel Court was too much of a challenge for police, with residents too worldly in their ways. There were social adjustments, however. Several couples allegedly met monthly at one couple's residence, and exchanged house keys and spouses for an evening's entertainment. Merritt's observation is that, "It was just like Peyton Place."

A young married couple in an adjoining unit had a weekly confrontation, loud enough that surrounding units could hear every word. The verbal and minor physical abuse usually ended with the husband being physically thrown out of the house, finding refuge by being invited into another unit until things cooled down. The husband would return late at night, ready for another week's academic application—until the next Saturday night fracas. The final resolution of their relationship is not known.

One lovely young wife would sunbathe in her back yard wearing only a very small washcloth towel, much to other wives' consternation and their husbands' delight. In the afternoon the young lady would dress in her most revealing outfit, leave in a taxi, and spend the afternoon out and about. It was an interesting way to supplement her husband's GI bill.

In spite of Pammel Court's marginal housing and crowded living conditions, it fostered many successful marriages, careers, friendships, and memories.

Parenthetically, the GI bill, that permitted veterans to further their education, was probably the greatest social engineering in history—helping to build the most creative, technologically-advanced nation ever.

The return of veterans to college was most perplexing to teachers and instructors in academic institutions. Most of the instructors had no service experience and were apprehensive over how the students might respond in the classroom. Young men and women students had been exposed to horrors difficult to comprehend, and had attained a certain degree of independence, as well as self-dependence. However, the veterans were eager to take advantage of the educational opportunity and, for the most part, worked hard to acquire an education. The veterans were mature in many ways, and immature in many other ways.

While attending graduate school, Merritt was offered an editorial job with the Iowa State College Press; though a publishing arm of the college, it was separate and distinct. The press published textbooks and scholarly books written by college professors. The Press was self-sustaining, funded by the profits from book sales. The *Iowa State Daily* student newspaper and other student publications used half of the Press building. Both the books and the student paper were printed by presses owned by the Iowa State College Press.

Merritt was promoted to Director of the Iowa State College (now University) Press after fourteen years as an editor. The Director also had a half-time appointment in the Department of Technical Journalism. During his tenure, the Iowa State College Press underwent several changes due to economics, the organization of the university, and the nature of the publishing business. Bailey retired from the University Press in 1985, after thirty-seven years of service.

Grace and Merritt's only child, daughter Shirley, has presented them with two grandchildren and one great-grandchild. Shirley received her bachelor's and master's degrees in Political Science at Iowa State University; she works for the Rand Corporation, a public "think tank." Shirley's husband, Jonathan Ruhe, recently retired from the office of Health Education and Welfare in Washington, D.C.

Merritt has never attended a reunion of the 484th Group since the ground staff was not particularly close, and because he could not "swap lies" with the flight crews. Recounting "rats in the tent biting my toes" is not nearly as exciting as "There I was at 20,000 feet..." He has followed the 484th, to some degree, on the Internet. His one regret is that he learned of the fiftieth reunion of his high school graduating class on the Internet, after it had occurred.

For each soldier who served in the air, there were one or two representatives on the ground performing the seemingly menial tasks of maintenance and operations that permitted the airmen to perform at their best. Those "menial tasks" were monumental in assuring the safety and security of the airmen and their equipment. In every instance, while talking to pilots, navigators, bombardiers, and gunners, the topic of the ground crews and operations not receiving adequate credit for their unfailing support was mentioned. While the men in the air received the accolades and returned home after completing their required missions, the ground personnel continued to wade through their daily routines, meeting the challenges of the day, until the war was over.

They, too, are heroes in their own right.

# BOOK EIGHT

# PENKHUS

*Lt. Floyd Penkhus*

*B-25 Pilot*

*Twelfth Air Force*

*12th Bomb Group*

*81st Squadron*

*"On missions I carried a .45 caliber automatic pistol and made the decision that if I were to be isolated in the jungle, I would use it on myself."*

*—Penkhus*

# PENKHUS
# CHAPTER ONE

Floyd Penkhus was born in Carroll County, Iowa.

That is not an astounding fact, but it certainly prepared Floyd for an interesting and adaptable life.

Carroll County is probably a perfect example of a medieval satellite community. Carroll County was settled by German Catholic agrarians who were attracted to the rich, black soil on the western edge of one of one of the most fertile edaphic areas in the world. The county seat is Carroll, which is surrounded by smaller communities—each of whom's main focus is a large Catholic church. The towns are evenly spaced six to eight miles apart. They include Willy, Dedham, Roselle, Templeton, Halbur, Breda, Manning, Mount Carmel, Lidderdale, Glidden, Lanesboro, Ralston, and Coon Rapids. The first eight communities listed have large, beautiful, ornate Catholic churches; all the churches were built around 1910–1920, and were designed by a priest who traveled through the area. The remaining communities allowed a few Protestants to live in the county.

In 1920, Congress passed a law for "Prohibition of Domestic Sale of Intoxicating Beverages." The year 1920 also saw the ratification of the nineteenth amendment providing for "Women's Suffrage." It was also the year of the first meeting of the "League of Nations," and three years before Adolph Hitler, an un-employed paperhanger, would write "My Struggle" (*Mein Kampf*).

The farmers around Templeton faced all of the issues of 1920, but were particularly incensed by prohibition. They were so incensed they decided to be innovative and produce some intoxicating beverages of their own. The result of their activity was so successful that soon "Templeton Rye" became one of the staples of a well-known distributor in Cicero, Illinois, named Al Capone. Most of the distribution was local, but an occasional truckload found its way to an adjoining state.

Federal officials worked closely with local officials to locate the stills in the county, but were always unsuccessful. Sheriff Frank Bucheit, the Carroll County Sheriff, cooperated fully in trying to identify those involved. When the Federal agents visited his office to discuss the situation, the Sheriff usually had a list of possible bootleggers. When they left the County Courthouse, if the Sheriff had his hat on there was not going to be a raid. If he had his hat in his hand, a telephone tree would alert the producers to take down their stills because the Federal Officers were visiting local farms.

There was one recorded instance when a farmer emptied his still into a local creek, and a group of cows downstream got quite drunk on a lovely summer afternoon.

Floyd Penkhus was born and raised in Templeton. His birthdate was June 19, 1919. His father and mother, Henry G. and Kathryn Lippold Penkhus, ran a general store in the small town of 350 people. Both of their parents had come over from Germany. Henry's father was a bricklayer until his later years when he bought a saloon.

Henry's general store survived during the depression because he gave the farmers credit, and waited for payment until the crops came in, or the chickens matured for selling—whichever came first. Floyd had an older brother by two and a half years, Jerry, and a younger brother, Bob, who was two and a half years his junior. When the young men reached ten years old, they were involved in helping service customers at the store. They would bag groceries, carry in thirty-dozen egg cases and candle them, peel the eyes from old potatoes, and sweep the store.

One job Floyd did not relish was buying chickens. It was his job to go into the dirty, dusty chicken house with a wire hook to get the chickens. It was a most unpleasant job, but picking up chickens meant that the farmer would have money to pay his grocery bill, and that made it *barely* tolerable.

The Penkhus family lived in a house in town that had running water. Floyd's father had installed a big metal horse tank in the attic, and water was pumped from a cistern to the tank. The cistern, a below-ground plastered brick container, caught rainwater from the roof; one of Floyd's jobs was to crawl in the cistern every spring to clean it out. The water system worked for flushing a real porcelain toilet, and furnished cold water to the kitchen sink. Somehow, Henry managed to locate his septic tank on a vacant lot across the street from their house. The well water on his property tasted pretty good.

Growing up in a small town, the boys had simple homemade activities. They would walk to a creek a mile south of town, dam it up and wade in the two-foot-deep water. In winter, they would tie their sleds to the back of a horse-drawn bobsled for a mile or so out of town, where they would hook a ride with another bobsled going into town. Floyd liked to build model airplanes, then slide them down a string from his second floor bedroom window to a stake in the ground some distance away. The sliding airplanes first got him interested in flying.

Floyd's father took the boys hunting every fall. They regularly hunted rabbits, squirrels, and chicken hawks. Pheasants were in abundance, and several farmers would let them hunt on their property. On one such excursion, as they neared the end of a field, Floyd was stomping the bushes along a fence row when his leg suddenly dropped about two feet, catching the barbed wire and severely cutting his leg. It seems that one of the ways the bootleggers sold whisky was to place it in a hole "next to the fourth wooden fence post from the corner" where a person could pick up his liquor without exposing the maker. It seems Floyd had discovered a "sales area." He still has large scars on his leg from the barbed wire—sixty years later. It was the first time Floyd had heard of the "local product." Carroll County boys were known to become familiar with the "local product" at an early age.

Floyd attended the parochial school in Templeton. However, when he was ready to enter the tenth grade, his father recommended that he attend Manning High School, a larger consolidated school that offered more classroom opportunities. He left a class of ten students and found a huge class of thirty-six students in Manning. He loved baseball and stayed after school till 6:30 for practice, then would hitchhike home. Floyd graduated from Manning High School in the spring of 1936 at the age of sixteen.

That fall, Floyd attended the American Institute of Business (AIB) in Des Moines. He was surprised to find recent graduates in Engineering and Agriculture from Iowa State College attending so they could try to get a job in an office. He took Accounting, Business Law, and a little shorthand; he wanted to have a broad background in order to have numerous qualifications for a job—any job.

The session at AIB lasted a full year, and as Floyd was about to leave he met a new student from Spencer, Iowa, named Margaret Siebel. Floyd found work handling insurance for a large real estate company, Chamberlain and Kirk. He managed to stay in contact with Margaret while he worked in Des Moines—well, fairly close contact. They were married October 5, 1941.

After the December 7, 1941 surprise attack, it was obvious Floyd would be called into service. He knew he wanted to fly in the Air Corps, so he decided to prepare for his future. Not having had the required two years of college, he entered night school at Drake University taking two-month crash courses in history, geometry, trigonometry, and geography. Floyd's tuition at Drake was paid for by a local Elk's Club in Des Moines in a generous gesture of fellowship. On April 1, Floyd took the flying cadet examination and was one of the few in the group to pass it.

*Margaret Siebel was attending the American Institute of Business when she caught Floyd's eye. Floyd was working for an insurance company in Des Moines when they decided to marry.*

Floyd was told to get his affairs in order, since he would be called into service soon. However, it was not until August that he was finally given orders to report to Pre-flight Training. Accepting a married recruit into cadet training was rare at that time.

In 1931, the Wickersham Report on Prohibition indicated that "local enforcement was impossible," but opposed the repeal. In 1932, Franklin Roosevelt was elected president and, within two months, the Twenty-First Amendment had been repealed. The "Roaring Twenties" had ended, and alcohol was once again available with state-directed controls. Liquor by the drink was not available in Iowa until the late 1950s. In Carroll County, it was readily available during the 1940s in several local establishments—unimpeded by state law.

What ever happened to "Templeton Rye?" Some say it never really disappeared. Some say it has been gone for years. Ask in certain quarters, and you will only get a "wry" smile!

*A twin-engine B-25. The B-25s were the first planes to bomb Japan when Col. Jimmy Doolittle took off from the aircraft carrier Hornet on their now famous mission.*

# PENKHUS
# CHAPTER TWO

In August 1942, Floyd boarded the train in Des Moines for Santa Ana, California, for Basic Training. Basic Training involved not only learning military conduct, but a spending a good deal of time in the classroom and getting into physical shape. The pay was all of twenty-one dollars per month. After two months of preparation, they moved to Thunderbird Field, Phoenix, Arizona, for Primary Training. Here, they learned to fly the Stearman Airplane, and after nine weeks of training and sixty hours' flying time, they were sent to Pecos, Texas.

Primary Training at Thunderbird Air Force Base was not without incident. On December 2, 1942, the *Arizona Republic* Newspaper carried the following item:

**FLIERS ESCAPE IS MIRACULOUS**
*Flying cadets at Thunderbird Field had a candidate yesterday for the title of the world's luckiest man.*

*He is Floyd F Penkhus, aviation cadet of Templeton, Iowa, whose complete escape from personal injury and damage to his training plane in a forced landing was little short of miraculous.*

*Cadet Penkhus was on one of his final training flights just before graduation, when engine trouble forced him to make an immediate landing near the intersection of Northern Avenue and Mission Drive (27th Avenue).*

*The young flier's troubles began immediately after he put his ship down in a lettuce field. The plane bounced directly into the middle of Northern Avenue, barely passing under telephone wires bordering that street. Then it bounced again, once more clearing the wires by the slimmest of margins and also hurdling a wide irrigation ditch. Finally it came to rest in a cotton field.*

*Military authorities towed the ship back to Thunderbird behind a light truck and placed it in a service field. A thoroughly frightened Cadet Penkhus also returned to the field—for dinner."*

In Pecos, they flew low-wing BT-13 planes and had their first training experiences in cross-country flying and night flying. If they passed the required flying skills, they moved on to their next location. The cadets flew seventy-two hours in and around Pecos, met the requirements, and were sent to La Junta, Colorado, for Advanced Training.

Flying the twin engine AT-9s and AT-17s was a big change for the cadets. The additional preparation for flying and added horsepower in the airplanes' engines was a challenge. They did a considerable amount of cross-country navigation and night flying. They were kept extremely busy. After four weeks, Floyd had flown 128 hours, about twice as much as Primary and Basic Trainings combined.

On April 12, 1943, graduation was held, and Floyd Penkhus received his wings and a commission as Second Lieutenant in the U.S. Army Air Force. Since Margaret was not in attendance, wings and bars were pinned on by his Commanding Officer. The officer who addressed the graduating class reminded them that "a Second Lieutenant was in a class with warm beer and wet toilet paper." The new officers thought they "had it made."

It so happened that in April of 1943 the Air Corps changed the base at La Junta from an Advanced Training site to a training site for B-25 bombers. Penkhus remained in La Junta, assigned to begin training on the two-engine bombers. They started training nine days after graduation, on April 21.

The B-25 had achieved notoriety just a year earlier, when General Jimmy Doolittle and fifteen other pilots took off from the carrier Hornet to bomb the Island of Honshu, Japan. After the surprise attack December 7, 1941, military planners immediately recognized the need to bolster U.S. morale by retaliating against their aggressor. In January they devised a plan, and immediately started training for a mission to surprise the Japanese populace and military. On April 18, 1942, the sixteen planes left the Hornet, 620 miles from the coast of Japan, and arrived over Tokyo—coincidentally, they arrived just as the Japanese were completing their first practice air alert. The Americans had missed their control point, an island off the coast of Japan, and, as a result, approached Tokyo from several different directions. This proved to be fortuitous, as most of the Japanese thought it was part of the exercise. They released bombs not on the targets assigned, but on whatever targets they could find, and, as a result, were effective in serving notice that Japan was vulnerable. Two of the U.S. planes were shot down over Japan, but the remaining fourteen planes flew on to China, some ditching in the China Sea. The attack gave the American public and military a great boost in their preparations to defeat their enemies on two fronts.

The "Billy Mitchell" B-25 was a medium bomber manufactured by North American Aircraft. It had a gross weight of 33,500 pounds, was 52 feet 11 inches long, and had a wingspan of 67 feet 7 inches. Powered by two Wright R-2600 1700 horsepower engines, it could carry a load of 3,000 pounds. It could reach a speed of 272 miles per hour at 13,000 feet, with a ceiling of 24,200 feet and had a range of 1,350 miles. The armament consisted of a variety of combinations of firepower, usually twelve .50 caliber machine guns. It later replaced two machine guns in the nose with a seventy-five millimeter canon.

It was a well designed and effective aircraft for its purpose. For Penkhus, flying it was a thrill because of its power and handling. "The change from flying an AT-17 to a B-25 was like flying a tractor." They flew it almost every day.

On June 28, they were transferred to Greenville Army Air Base in Greenville, South Carolina, for more advanced B-25 flying, including bombing missions and formation flying. The B-25 was fun to fly, since it was so heavy that "it just stayed in formation." It also had the power to adjust speed, if there was "catching up" to do. They alternated their training time, one day in the classroom and the next day flying. They were now flying about 100 hours per month, sometimes two and three trips per day.

Penkhus was flying cross-country with his instructor one day, and flew to La Guardia Airport in New York City. The instructor decided he wanted to spend the night, so he "burned out a fuse" on the instrument panel, making the airplane unflyable. They wired Greenville for permission to Remain Over Night (RON) and return the next day. Permission was received. The next day was overcast, so they proceeded to operations to get clearance for an instrument takeoff. The instructor did not have his instrument clearance card along, but Penkhus did. The Operations Officer cleared their flight, Floyd flew pilot, and the Instructor flew co-pilot—which made Penkhus very happy. They took off with an 800-foot ceiling (the Empire State Building was 1200 feet), flew out over the ocean until they broke out of the overcast, and returned home.

Late in October the Commanding Officer knew orders for an overseas assignment were due at any time, and granted the pilots a cross-country flight anywhere they wanted to go. Penkhus chose to return to Iowa to fly over his hometown. They flew to Vichy, Missouri, where they refueled, and Penkhus called his parents to alert them that he would be over Templeton between 6:30 and 7:00 that evening. It was a thrill for him to see Templeton from the air, and he spotted twenty-five people on the south side of town. He could recognize Mom and Dad, Grandma and Grandpa, and other townspeople. He was so excited he flew over four times, once from each direction; he then waved goodbye, and headed back to Greenville Army Air Base.

Two days later, the servicemen received sad news. One of the pilots in their group, on his cross-country return to his hometown, had crashed in his parents' farmyard killing all seven on board. His home was Thornburg, Iowa, and he and Penkhus had planned trips home together. Two days later, Penkhus was assigned to attend the funeral, representing the Air Force. Penkhus, Margaret, and five other airmen from Greenville rode the train to Des Moines. Penkhus immediately went to Camp Dodge to make arrangements for the funeral, which was held in Keswick, with burial in Sigourney. The funeral was an extremely sad event for the family and friends in attendance.

Penkhus wired Greenville for a five-day pass and ultimately received it. His parents and Margaret's parents drove them to Des Moines to catch a train back to Greenville. The drive gave Penkhus an opportunity to say goodbye, since he probably would not see them before going overseas.

Penkhus returned to Greenville Sunday afternoon in time to receive orders to fly on Monday to Vichy, Missouri, for detached service, flying low-level bombing runs over the infantry at Fort Leonard Wood. The training prepared the pilots for tree-top flying, and trained the infantry for enemy planes coming in too low to be picked up by radar. They had a lot of fun dropping flour sacks on the troops below. They also flew to Fort Riley, Kansas, for training, and returned the same day. A cracked exhaust stack on the airplane caused them to remain in Missouri for several days before returning to Greenville.

On November 30, they received orders to report to Savannah, Georgia, for final staging before going overseas. They went through equipment screening for personal and flying necessities. Every item was laid out on the ramp for review. Penkhus learned that Joe Murtha had been assigned to the crew. He personally liked Joe, and felt he was an outstanding bombardier and navigator. Owen Mabry would be his co-pilot, and the remainder of the crew, a radioman, engineer, and gunner were also assigned. Lt. Penkhus felt he had a real good crew.

On December 5, Penkhus said his goodbyes to Margaret, who had driven to Savannah from Greenville. She would be driving home to Templeton. They knew it would be several months before they would see each other again, and the parting was most difficult. They were fortunate to have spent time together while Penkhus was in training schools.

On December 9, they received their new, shiny B-25 D with only sixteen hours on it, complete with all twelve machine guns. They took a two and one-half hour flight, calibrating the compass by following nearby railroad tracks; they also calibrated air speed. The next day, they flew a three-hour pattern over the Everglades testing fuel consumption, making certain they could fly across the ocean. This aircraft would literally be their home for the next three weeks.

On December 13, they left Hunter Air Force Base for Morrison Field, West Palm Beach, Florida, where they were briefed for their flight to Puerto Rico. Penkhus called his parents and Margaret to say one last goodbye. He was twenty-four years old, older than most of the pilots, and felt he could have handled saying goodbye in a more adult fashion. The intense training and prospect of flying into the unknown world of combat would certainly excuse the emotional display.

The prospect of flying overseas was actually quite a thrill. Floyd had accomplished what he had set out to do. He had studied hard and passed his entrance examination. He had made it through Primary, Basic, and Advanced Training. He had learned to fly. Now he would enter a new world of totally different experiences.

The morning of December 15, they departed from Morrison Field, West Palm Beach, and headed out over "the big pond" to Puerto Rico. They were informed there was weather moving in, and were to leave early the next morning. At 3:30 A.M., they were roused out of bed, and were airborne forty minutes before daybreak. They flew over Martinique and Trinidad, and hit the South American coast at British Guiana. They flew over solid jungle until Atkinson Field appeared, cut right out of the jungle. They had flown 1,175 miles through quite a bit of bad weather, but landed safely.

They were up early again on the 17th, and took off at 6:35 A.M. They landed at Belem, Brazil, at 11:20, flying 901 miles. It was overcast most of the way, but a break in the clouds enabled them to see the impressive Amazon River delta. They flew across the equator, a real thrill for an Iowa farm boy. They slept in tents on elevated platforms above the ground, and had their first experience with mosquito netting. They discovered the food was good, but the water was really bad—something they would experience numerous times in the following ten months.

After four days, they loved their airplane. It was everything they had expected, and more.

Early the next morning, the 18th, they left Belem around 6:30 A.M. for Natal, on the east coast of Brazil. They flew over solid jungle for some distance, then open desert. They followed the coastline for much of the way—it would provide a better landing surface than the jungle. The plane touched down about 12:10 P.M. on what proved to be a good field. They would have an extra day to rest up before an over-the-water flight of 1,400 miles. They next day, Sunday, Penkhus went to Mass, sent a cablegram home, and bought some hose and Chanel #5 perfume for Margy.

Monday, December 20, was a big day. They were up at 5:00 A.M. to take off at 6:00 for the Ascension Islands, a speck in the Atlantic Ocean only 1445 miles away. They flew from 6:30 A.M. until 2:25 P.M. when they let down through the clouds and saw the tiny island. Murtha had done his work from the nose of the airplane, getting his wind direction from the Norden Bombsight and the white caps on the ocean to get the drift. He was only five miles off target. There was a radio direction finder in the cockpit, but Murtha would not refer to it since he wanted to test his navigational skills. The only facilities on the island were a runway, a control tower, and a few barracks.

They had a good night's rest, and were up at 5:30 A.M. for a 6:30 A.M. takeoff, flying over water to Roberts Field, Liberia, West Africa, 1019 miles away. It was thrilling to see Africa, but they were getting a long way from home. The air was filled with mosquitoes, and suddenly they had a new worry—malaria.

On December 23, they laidover due to mud on the field at Dakar, the next stop. Joe, Owen, Wagner, and Penkhus walked two miles up the road to visit a Firestone plant and the native village. It was sad to see the natives living in such filth and poverty. They walked through their open-air markets and found them equally dirty. It was very disconcerting to the Iowa boy.

The crew pulled a fifty-hour inspection the next day, going over the plane from 9:00 A.M. to 4:30 P.M. Everyone was proud of the ship, and enjoyed checking everything in detail.

On Christmas day, they took off at 7:00 A.M., flying along the African coast, landing at Dakar around noon. The trip was 786 miles. They had a good Christmas dinner and then attended a briefing about their trip over the Sahara Desert. They were warned about a forced landing in the desert, since drifting sand could cover a plane in twenty-four hours.

The next leg of the trip started immediately the next morning, December 26, heading for Marrakush. They were amazed that flying over the desert looked like flying over water because of the waves of sand. One thousand miles of nothing but sand. They landed at field at Tindouf on runways of sand, where they took on 200 gallons of gas. They continued on their way, arriving at 2:45 P.M. after flying 1285 miles.

Marrakush looked very good from the air with its white buildings. It was most uninviting when they ate in a large hanger with the cold desert wind blowing through it. They spent a miserable night sleeping in tents in an olive grove, absolutely freezing with four blankets. They were happy to leave early the next morning for Casablanca, only 150 miles away.

Casablanca is another town typically of white buildings. The field was interesting because it had every kind of airplane imaginable. When they visited the town, they were disappointed because the buildings that looked so neat from the air were not. Some of the local Arabs were filthy and nearly all were beggars. He bought Margy a red billfold at one of the bazaar shops. He found the city interesting, "but not for me."

They spent the next seven days waiting for orders, cleaning the plane, and breaking down the machine guns in preparation for gunnery practice. January 4, they test-fired them over water, and were impressed with the seven guns firing forward making quite a splash in the water. With two guns in the top turret, two side guns, and one in the tail, the B-25 was a formidable fighting machine.

January 5, they left Casablanca and flew 660 miles to Algiers. They were to go on to Tunis, but the weather was bad. They went into town to spend the night in a hotel, only to find out it was unheated, and did not have the comforts of a normal hotel. January 6, they took time to look over the town, expecting to find it bombed out. It turned out the town had been captured by three soldiers and a newspaper correspondent. The harbor was full of British ships, some floating, some destroyed. They heard the story of how American and British officers walked into the main hotel, the "Alette," capturing it full of German and Italian officers.

Saturday, January 8, they took off from Algiers for Catania, flying along the coast, and were thrilled to see a convoy of thirty ships. When approaching Tunis, they saw the first evidence of action. The ground was covered with crashed airplanes, both Allied and German, and destroyed tanks and trucks. There were bomb craters in great abundance. From Tunis they flew to Panteleria, and again saw more debris, sunken ships, and the results of battle. Over Sicily, they experienced the true realization they were in a war zone. When they landed at Catania, the field was covered with wrecked German planes. Many were bombed on the field, and others looked like they had been shot down on takeoff. The hangers were all destroyed, and the town was "a pitiful sight."

On Sunday Morning, January 9, members of the crew got up from their freezing hotel room and went to church in a huge cathedral in Cantania. It was quite cold, since one corner of the walls and roof had been blown away, leaving a gaping hole in the building. They returned to a dinner of "chicken-fried Spam" which tasted quite good to the men. They then walked to town where they stood in line for the only hot-water bath or shower in town. The cost was twenty-five cents!

Monday they received orders to continue on to Naples, and left at 11:00 A.M., arriving at 12:40 P.M. They were to stay in town, which was in very poor shape. Buildings had been bombed and the streets were covered with mud, ruined by the Nazis to make it uncomfortable for their pursuers. They were now only about 100 miles from the front.

On January 11, they were informed that the Twelfth Air Force was on the other side of Italy's "boot" at Foggia, so they flew to their new location. Once they arrived, there was some question about whether they were to be at Foggia or Naples, so time was spent waiting for the decision. Finally, a decision was made for them to report to 12th Group Headquarters at Foggia. They were assigned to the 81st Squadron, one of four squadrons in the group. They moved into six-person tents and commenced unpacking their gear. The plumbing was the "outdoor type," cold and drafty. They ate out of their mess kits and canteens, and cleaned them in large cans of boiling water. They slept on canvas cots, and lived out of duffel bags. Their living conditions were quite a shock when compared to other installations where they were stationed.

Finally, all of the training, lessons learned, and flying techniques would be put to the test. There were no father-figures to prepare them for their first mission, no cards to punch, no training films on how to be cool. Within a day or so, they would see their name on a duty roster, attend an early-morning briefing, put on their flying suits, climb into a plane loaded with devices meant to damage, mangle, and kill, take to the air, deliver their cargo, and hope to return safely—in order to make another trip to damage, mangle, and kill.

# PENKHUS
# CHAPTER THREE

On January 12, 1944, Penkhus and his crew were assigned to the Twelfth Air Force, 12th Bomb Group, 81st Squadron, and immediately started preparing for their missions. Penkhus was assigned as co-pilot of another crew for nine missions, for exposure to battle conditions. Another pilot took over his crew to train them.

The missions of the B-25s were different than those of heavy bombers; the planes participating on a mission were fewer in number because they went after specific, small targets. They were more maneuverable, and could drop bombs from 12,000 feet or 300 feet. Carrying twelve machine guns meant more defensive firepower, as well as offensive firepower for strafing. Planes were later modified for armament, installing a seventy-five millimeter cannon in the nose by removing the co-pilot's seat. The cannon was armed by the radioman and fired by the pilot.

Some mission notes were from official transcripts and some from pilots' log books. The following are notes from Floyd Penkhus's personal diary (entries were made daily):

**Mission 1:** 14 Jan 44. Target: Faligero rail road yards. The nine planes flew in formation over the target.

**Mission 2:** 16 Jan 44. Target: Terni rail yards. Experienced two bursts of flak close by. Good coverage of the target.

**Mission 3:** 17 Jan 44. Target: Terni. Flew over town and could see local people walking to church. Plenty of flak—no fighters. Test hopped a plane that had been worked on.

*Jan 18th.* Moved to Salerno at the base of Mt. Vesuvius, Guardo Field. (This later proved to have repercussions.) Flew two loads of tents, equipment and supplies to set up camp. Is much warmer here.

**Mission 4:** 20 Jan 44. Thursday. Target: Railroad Bridge near Carsio. Wing plane took six flak holes.

**Mission 5:** 21 Jan 44. Friday. Target: Junction at Fillitti to cut off German retreat. Working in concert with landing craft invasion. Hits were good, some flak, no fighters.

**Mission 6:** 23 Jan 44. Target: Road junction to keep Germans from retreating. No flak. Bad weather 24th, 25th, 26th.

**Mission 7:** 27 Jan 44. Target: Orte. No fighters or flak. Another group on a morning mission was hit hard. Penkhus's co-pilot Owen Mabry was hit by flak through neck, out the back. Severely hurt, several transfusions. Went to aid station—Mabry doped up.

**Mission 8:** 29 Jan 44. Target: Foligno covered with clouds. Dropped on alternate target San Benedetto. Flak accurate, one hit, all returned.

**Mission 9:** 30 Jan 44. Target: Grotta-Fenuda road junction. Overcast, returned with bombs. Went to aid station to see Mabry. Was better—could talk to him.

*Monday, Jan 31st.* Stand down. Got paid. Was asked to work in Operations. Great opportunity. Scheduled planes. Called maintenance to see how many planes avail. Called armament, told them what to load. Group HQ tells us what to do, operations tell maintenance and crew what's on the line. Was Operations Officer for six months.

Major Sutton told us to stand down, that we were going to move, but not where. Feb 2nd, 3rd, and 4th, went to see Lt. Olin Mabry for last time before leaving. Feb 6th told we were going to leave by truck and to pack accordingly.

*Feb 6th.* Up at 5:00 am, loaded at 7:00 am drove till 8:00 that night. Drove through snow, ate C rations. Got to Taronto, unpacked and hit the sack. Next day cold and rainy, stayed in sack. Up to eat, bed at 6:00 pm. Feb 8th, got rations of 3 candy bars and 6 oranges.

*Feb 9th.* Boarded Polish boat Batoria, biggest boat I've ever seen. 14 Ship convoy, kept heading with small compass. Going back to US? Feb 10th. Played bridge all day. Feb 11th, 12th. Worst day overseas, woke up sick. Must have local disease.

Landed in harbor at Alexandria, to Cairo by train. Was held back as baggage officer. Went to Alexandria Hotel, met interesting English and New Zealand officers. Ali Baba fixed up crew member with lady. This crew member vowed to get laid on every continent.

*Feb 14th.* Tea at 7:30 am, docks at 8:30. Train to leave at 2:10 pm. Lunch at American Red Cross, had real chocolate ice cream. Saw irrigated land along the Nile, fruit, cotton, rice etc. to Cairo, beautiful city, beautiful houses and slums. Will be here two weeks at Camp Russell. Can get candy and ice cream. Bought perfume and ivory letter opener. Met guide to go to pyramids, sphinx and blue mosque. Played bridge four days. Sunday

27th, went to Mass. Saw movie with Betty Hutton "Miracle at Morgan Creek." Beer rations, six cans each.

*Feb 24th.* Got first mail from home, letter from Margy's mother. I wrote home every day, a V-mail.

*Feb 29th.* 3:30 am Boarded trucks for Suez for boat ride. English ship Dilwara. Got six letters at mail call. Second day on boat got English rations. Third day, smooth water, more English mutton. Fourth day, rough water, more mutton. Now I know what it means to be torpedoed. At 1:00 am, a large wave hit open porthole with water all over beds and floor. Crossed the equator. Landed at Port Aden. Stayed aboard, too hot.

*Mar 7th.* Leaving port, escorted by two destroyers. Two ships sunk last week. 8th, Evasive action all day, smooth as glass. 9th—going to Bombay. No excitement. 11th Started moustache. 12th To top deck to see Bombay. Sent cable to Margey, Mom, Dad.

*Mar 13th.* Off boat, to train. Train has wood lathe seats and shelf. Issued two blankets, sleep on hard wood slats. Supper on RR platform while ragged Indians watched. Beggars are at every stop. RR yards have wealth of iron, cotton, lumber etc, and poverty all around. 15th—Third day on train. Two hours to set up mess line to serve 1,000 troops on train. People look better, brats run around naked. 16th—Natives sell oranges, coconuts, bananas—one rupee.

*Mar 17th.* Pulled into Calcutta, RR siding, went 20 miles in 4 hours. Arrived at Galundo, off train to get on river barge, wait till morning to leave.

*Mar 19th.* Sunday, Breakfast at 7:00, barge 9:30, down Burmaputra River to Daka. Climbed on trucks, to Tesgaoun, home for the next few months. 20th. Monday. Saw field, will live in bamboo huts. Native boy couriers. Got to hut at 1:30 am, full of spiders and mosquitoes. 21st, cleaned up hut. Eat picnic style on ground. Beds are of rope. Keep pants tucked in sox and shirts buttoned, spray with mosquito repellent. Still afraid of malaria. Had a belly ache, Doc thought it was appendix, found something else and kicked me out of the hospital.

*Mar 25th.* Saturday. Have been overseas 3 months and 10 days. At mail call today and received 110 letters. 52 were from Margaret. Kept busy reading and writing.

*Mar 26th.* Sunday. Went to Mass. Got word that Mt. Vesuvius had erupted in Italy and ruined 25 airplanes, including all in our squadron. Spent next four days reading and writing letters.

Penkhus and his crew had entered a new theater of operations that few people knew about. The war in Northern Europe received all the press back home, because the war correspondents could hang out in the city of London with its culture and conveniences. They would not have to slug it out in the mud to get their stories. Even members of the Seventeenth Air Force in Italy complained because news coverage was practically non-existent. The China-Burma-India Theater of operations was rarely mentioned other than the early exploits of General Claire Chennualt and his Flying Tigers.

During Japan's expansion in early 1942, they pushed forward on several fronts. From January 1942 to May 1942, they captured Manila in the Phillipines Islands, then Malaya and Singapore, the Dutch Indies, North Borneo, Java, and finally Bataan, Corregidor, and Burma. Their interest was reaching India and parts of China where they could add oil and munitions to supply their expanding army.

Burma was comprised of thick jungle and rugged mountains reaching 5000 feet. The only all-weather connecting road and railroad through Burma ran from the Chindwin River through Imphal and Kohima to Dimapur in India. The only level ground adequate for an airfield was the plains area at Imphal. The Japanese needed to control the road and/or the railroad in order to supply their army.

British General William Slim and the Fourteenth Army had to defend the area from the invading Japanese. General Renya Mutaguchi a "fearless, ruthlessly ambitious man who reveled in war," was in charge of the occupation of Burma. He recognized that the mountainous, roadless jungle between Burma and India, the diseases indigenous to the area, and Japan's extended supply lines would make further advance perilous at best. In the face of all that, he decided to press on, and attacked the British bases at Imphal and Kohima.

General Slim responded by building defensive "boxes" around strategic points to stave off numerous attempts to capture the road and the towns. The fight continued for two years, under the worst of conditions. The jungles were impenetrable. The monsoons kept the ground impassable. Even with the hottest weather, nothing dried out. Trails through the jungle were few in number, and rarely useable because of the monsoon rains. The ground war fought by British, Indian, and Gurkha troops and the Japanese was one of attack and withdrawal.

Controlling supplies to keep the war effort going was a major strategy. The Japanese were isolated and had little air cover. The

*Penkhus's favorite plane. The maintenance crew renamed it the "Penkhus Peak Express" because of Floyd's numerous missions to bomb the same mountaintop that was inhabited by the Japanese.*

Allies could fly in supplies from India and disrupt the lines of supplies to the Japanese. The Allies bombed supply routes, railroad bridges, and the few river bridges in the area, in order to isolate the Japanese.

The strategy was successful. In prolonged engagement, the Japanese had 53,000 casualties with 30,000 dead, while the Allies lost only 16,000 men. Ultimately, the Japanese lost 92,000 dead, wounded, or missing in action. They were ultimately reduced to small groups on the verge of starvation, with small clusters of troops continuing to fight beyond the end of the war. General Slim paid them tribute: "We all talk about fighting to the last man, to the last bullet. The Japanese soldier was the only one who did it." He was also generous in praise of his own troops. "Burma was a soldiers' war. It was they who turned defeat into victory."

Flying over the rough terrain and thick jungle was not without its perils. A forced landing in the jungle meant survival would be marginal. If one survived a crash landing, they would have to live off the land while hiking forty or fifty miles to find a barely discernable trail that might lead to safety fifty more miles away. Eating bugs, lizards, or snakes in the steamy jungle did not appeal to Penkhus. On missions he carried a .45 caliber automatic pistol, and made the decision that if he were to be isolated in the jungle, he would use it on himself.

The Tenth Air Force, comprised of transports, medium bombers and fighters, controlled the air and provided tactical support for the ground troops. They literally bombed the tops off of mountains, and because of their successes on transportation routes, they gained the title "the Bridge Busters."

The 81st Squadron was recognized several times for its ability to fly tight formations. The tight formations discouraged Japanese aircraft from attacking, since each B-25 carried twelve .50 caliber machine guns. A normal formation consisted of twelve aircraft, that combined for a total of 144 machine guns. The enemy fighters would always be just out of range, hoping to find a wounded B-25 hit by ground fire and dropping out of the formation.

En route to the target, the squadrons flew at an 11,000 or 12,000-feet altitude. The altitude, heading, and airspeed were maintained until five minutes distance from the target. Anti-aircraft defenses had an opportunity to adjust their trajectory and height of air bursts during this time. To compensate, the Allied aircraft would change direction and drop 2,000 feet—gaining airspeed as they headed for the target—hoping to throw off the computations of the anti-aircraft guns. Following the lead bombardier in the lead ship, the bombers would fly straight and level, and when the lead bombardier gave the orders "Bomb bay doors down," the other eleven ships would follow. The plane was then an easy target as the bombardier gave commands of "Easy right," or "Steady," or "Nose up." When the bombardier said, "Bombs away!" the pilot hit the release button, and the trailing planes followed suit.

Then the pilot immediately closed the bomb bay doors, dove another 1000 feet, and used evasive action to get out of the vicinity and head for home as fast as possible.

They had a good team that was well trained, but this was a different kind of war than the war in Italy. Penkhus and his crew were immediately thrown into this new situation. They responded in typical Iowan fashion. They rolled up their sleeves and went to work.

# PENKHUS
# CHAPTER FOUR

Continuing with Penkhus personal diary:

*Mar 30th.* Started working Operations again.

*Mar 31st.* Friday. Started getting in new B-25 Hs and Js. 'H' has a 75 mm cannon mounted in nose. No co-pilot seat. Radioman loads cannon—pilot fires it. Pilot kept busy without co-pilot. April 3rd, some men flew missions, much easier here. April 4, flew two hours in new 'H' with cannon. A new experience with only one pilot per plane, may not get to fly as often. Today a lizard crawled from under my bed.

*Easter Sunday.* Flew with Roberts as co-pilot for 1 1/2 hours, and 1hour instruments. Got rations, two boxes of beer and cigs.

*Apr 11th, 12th, 13th, 14th.* Hard rains. Monsoons here. Twelve letters from Margy. Mail takes 12 days to reach us.

*Apr 16th.* Sunday. Squadron flew first mission today. Lt Roberts lost in storm.

*Apr 18th.* Tuesday. Squadron flew 2nd Mission, was on standby. Got 1 hr 40 min combat time.

*Apr 20th.* 81st flew mission. I went to town. Now have tables in mess hall, but is hotter than blazes. Flew instruments. Went to movie "Swing Shift Maisy." (Ann Southern)

*Apr 26th.* Got some ice. Finally a cold beer.

**Mission 10:** 27 Apr 44. Flew first mission over Japanese held territory. No flak, no opposition. Left town in flames.

*Apr 28th, 29th.* Flew over area where we thought Lt Roberts went down. No sign of plane. May 1st, got paid 1129 rupees ($341) sent $300 to Margy. May 2, 3. Practiced formation flying.

**Mission 11:** 4 May 44. Flew co-pilot with Capt Long, lead ship. Milk run. Have new mess hall and ate off plates at tables. Bought hand fan, boots and had pix taken with moustache.

*May 6th.* 81st flew mission. Three pilots down with malaria. Makes me nervous. 7th, Flew to Calcutta. 8th, Some guys going home. Maybe I'll get in some missions.

**Mission 12**: 9 May 44. Co-pilot to Commanding Officer. Nine ships—target—Ningthouk. Bombed at 2:30 pm, ground forces attacked at 3:00.

**Mission 13**: 10 May 44. Flew co-pilot with Capt Leo D. Smith. Target—road junction in hills, missed target.

*May 14th.* New lights in mess. Mosquitoes getting worse. Flew transition. Saw movie "Jane Eyre." May 15th, Monday. Left US 5 months ago. Five 'old dogs' leaving, now can fly more missions.

**Mission 14**: 16 May 44. Tuesday. Target: Tiddem-Imphal. Japanese trucks caught on road between two bombed out sections of road.

*May 17th.* Wednesday. Riots in Dakar. 18th, lecture on chemical warfare. Saw movie, Charles Boyer in "The Constant Nymph."

*May 20th.* All pilots to pack to go to Comilla to fly C-47s to supply troops. Flew as co-pilot, landed. Lots of pilots. 21st. Monsoons start in two weeks, fly day and night (to drop supplies to troops.) 22nd. Up at 6:30 am, flew rice to Imphal, brought back wounded Gurkas. At night, shot cobra in tree, seven feet long. 25th. Three missions today. Gas barrels up, grain for cattle, brought back wounded Gurkas. Saw spitfires land. Only eight miles from Japanese installation. 26th. Returned to Tezgaon in B-25s to pick up 20 pilots. Just got unpacked when they decided to use our barracks for another squadron, had to move.

**Mission 15**: 28 May 44. Take off 6:30 am. Target—Imphal—Tidon road. Some hits. Tailgunner mistook Spitfire for zero, shot and hit it. Too bad.

*May 29th.* Monday. Flew mission with Pitt. Nose gun not working, radio bad. Turned back. Would have been Mission 16. Voided.

*May 21st.* Wednesday. Mission 16. Target—Bridge at Shebo. Bad weather, turned back.

**Mission 17**: 1 June 44. Thursday. Target: river bridge at Monywa. With Lt Pitts (his 49th mission). Solid rain for 30 min, turned back. Brushed up on navigation.

*June 2nd.* Lt Pitts told me to practice formation flying, to fly as first pilot. He put me in for First Lieut. Flew 50 min in solid rain. 3rd Practice formations. 4th. Went to church and Officer's Club. 5th. Early mission. Stood by at 7:00 am heavy ground fog. Mission aborted. Flew to Calcutta, dinner at Grand Hotel. I've had [enough of] India.

**Mission 18:** 6 June 44. Tuesday. Target: RR north of Shebo. Bad weather, so dropped on alternate road.

**Mission 19:** 9 June 44. First mission as first pilot (group), Zentner (from Dubuque) was bombardier. Target: RR bridge at Wentho. Dropped at 300 feet, three 1000 lb. demolition bombs. Missed but damaged.

**Mission 20:** 9 June 44. 8:00 to 11:00. Target: Titedly-Imphal road. Heavy overcast, brought bombs back. Had meeting about C-47 trips. Got credit for missions. Now have 25 missions. Two pilots left for states.

*June 10th.* Stand down. Got 9 letters. No rain for 5 days. Played bridge. 11th. Instrument flying. 12th. (Dad's birthday) Moving 185 miles west. 13th. Six planes used to haul ammo to Imphal. Lost one plane that landed in mud. 14th. No mission. Moving to new base at Madhiagohj.

**Mission 26:** 15 June 44. Joe Murtha, navigator, our first mission together. Flew ammo to Imphal for British soldiers.

*June 16th.* Flew equipment to new field, hot 120 degrees, but drier. 200 Miles made a change in weather. Heard that B-29s dropped bombs on Japan. 17th. Moving. Flew load down, B-24 equipment back, personal belongings. Better housing and base. 18th. Busy in operations. 19th. My birthday. Lots of cards and letters. Four ships out for ammo run, returned because of weather. 21st. Monsoon rain, really hard. 22nd. Hot today, steamy. 23rd Stand down.

**Mission 27 & 28:** 24 June 44. 6:50 am. Two ammo runs to Imphal. Six hours flying time.

*June 25th.* Stand down. 26th. June rations. On move again soon, 50 miles from last base.

**Mission 29:** 27 June 44. Flew with Fred Underwood, gas cap off, lost 50 gal gas. Landed at alternate base, put in gas and gas cap. Landed at Comilla and RON. Stayed with RAF.

**Mission 30:** 28 June 44. Col Grubbs, Operations Officer of 3rd Tactical Air Force, took good care of us. Ammo run.

*June 29th.* Flew to Bangalore to get new aircraft. Pilot thought he saw smoke in engine and we returned. Got new typewriter for operations office. 30th. Started for Bangalore, landed at Bazwada because of bad weather. RON. Small British base. July 1st. Flew 1 hr 30 min. Landed Bangalore. July 1st, Sunday. G I truck into town, went to Mass. Mixture of people in India is amazing. 3rd. Planes not ready, saw movie "Adventures of Tartu [Tarzan?]. 4th. Checked planes, 10:30 take off. Landed at 3:30 at Pandavaswar. So much rain, no missions since we left.

*July 5th.* Operations officer Pitts on flight. 9 ships landed at Camilla for gas. Attended meeting at operations at group HQ to make up flying schedule. I made the flying team.

*July 6th.* Mission 31. Up at 4:45 am, to be a long day. Took off at 7:00, 245 miles for fuel. 11:15 am to target 430 mi to Myikina. Had to turn back because of bad weather. Counted as a mission.

*July 7th.* Friday. Stand down. Went to Osasol. Could not eat, no appetite because the smell was so bad.

*July 8th.* Saturday. Mission 32. Up at 4:45 am. Landed at Kurmatola to refuel. Left at 11:00 am, at target at 13:30. Hit it good with twenty-four 100 pound bombs. Returned to Kurmatola for gas, back to base. 5 hours in cockpit without a copilot is one long haul. McCutcheon landing in the rain cracked up a plane.

*July 9th.* On schedule, Woke up with a headache, hope its not malaria. July 10th. Stand down. Its been raining for a week.

*July 11th.* Mission 33. Nine planes to bomb Myitkyna. Dropped a lot of bombs on that little town. Had a plane shot down by a Zero. Pilot and crew made it to friendly territory.

*July 12th.* Mission 34. Myitkyna again in number two position. 8 hour jobs. Number 3 returned because engine was acting up. When returned, found out I was promoted to First Lieutenant.

*July 13th.* Nine ships scheduled, called off because of rain and weather.

*July 15th.* Stand down till moved. To move to Fenny about 260 miles east and 60 miles from Tezgon where we were two months ago. July 16th. Went to new field, and will have to learn to rough it all over again. July 17th. Moved in style with four C-47s and ten B-25 loads.

*July18th.* Twelve B-25s on move. One half went behind with Kimonathaniel. July 20th. Lots of personnel and baggage. Returned for my stuff. Stayed at new field. What a swampy field it was. Full of rice paddies and pools of water. No lights, nothing convenient.

*July 21st.* Scheduled for a mission. Rain. 22nd. Another nine ship mission. Rain. Briefing—rain. Stand in rain. Mission canceled. Fooling around like that, with all the toads, frogs, bugs, mosquitoes, and ants—enough to drive a man crazy.

**Mission 35:** 23 July 44. Sunday. Target: Myitkina. Quit raining long enough to get into the air. Nine ships. I flew Pitt's wing. We did a good job. Got back to field at 13:45 and had three letters from Margy, Mother and Dad. It is good to be 260 miles closer to targets—not nearly as tiring.

*July 24th.* Monday. Squadron put up nine ships today to Myitkina. Didn't make the team. Started up to Imphal to get Sauer, who landed there yesterday with a bad engine, but called back due to bad weather. Flew local with Martz and Torres to let them shoot a couple landings.

**Mission 36:** 26 July 44. Wednesday. Target: Myitkina again today. Flew on Lt Pitt's wing. No resistance—no trouble.

*July 27th.* Had a lot of mail tonight, nine letters. Flew transition with Harmon and Wright. Flew my 1000th hour today.

*July 28th.* Friday. Made the team today, briefed for Myitkina, but after waiting under plane during hard rain till 13:00, mission called.

**Mission 37:** 29 July 44. Saturday. Target: Myitkina. All nine of our ships along with nine from 82nd Squadron and nine from 83rd. Dropped 1000 pounders. That's 72,000 pounds of bombs. Landed in hard rain.

*July 30th.* Sunday. Joe and I went to Mass in enlisted Men's Mess Hall. August 1st. Would have had mission 38, but called off—rain. August 2nd. Same as yesterday.

**Mission 38:** 3 Aug 44. Target: RR yards at Mohnyin, Burma. Weather cleared and had clear sailing. Flew Leo Smith's wing in No 9 position.

*Aug 4th.* Friday. Slow timed a new engine on #21. Sent three planes to Ondal to bring back 32 ground replacements.

**Mission 39:** 5 Aug 44. Saturday. Target: Town of Pinbaw. Japanese are retreating from Myitkina to South. We are bombing ahead of their retreat. Ran into bad weather returning to base. I broke off formation, to 15,000 feet and came home alone.

*Aug 6th.* Sunday. On schedule again, but mission called—rain. August 7th. Same mission, but called off—rain. Two fellows quit today, now five waiting to go home. Saw movie, "Going My Way." Up till 1:00. August Eighth. Three days in a row called off. Gets monotonous-need something to do. Just sit and stare at bamboo walls. Can't play softball.

**Mission 40:** 9 Aug 44. Target: Town of Sittaung. Flew Major Sutton's right wing. Short mission, only 3 hours 15 min.

*Aug 10th.* Our squadron put up nine ships today. Saw two large river boats and dropped on them since target socked in. Murtha, flying with Smith, got a slug in his left wrist and above his heart. Smith landed at Agartala and took him to hospital.

*Aug 11th.* Friday. Bad weather again today. Major Sutton and Doc went to hospital to see Murtha. Is doing OK, back in a week.

**Mission 41:** 12 Aug 44. Saturday. Target: Railroad north of Mandalay. Low level bombing with 1000 lb. Bombs. My third bomb was a direct hit under bridge, knocking out one / two supports. Green camouflage on bridge flew in all directions. Three planes had small holes in them.

**Mission 42:** 13 Aug 44. Sunday. Target: Railroad north of Mandalay. A tragic day for the 81st. Flew on Leo Smith's wing. Twelve planes, only eleven returned. Squadron C.O. Maj Sutton was hit on a strafing attack, crashed and burned. Major Sutton had 88 missions. Harmon and two of his crew hit. Herzog returned on one engine. I guess I'm lucky. It was our roughest mission since we have been in India. Hope it's not what to expect from now on.

**Mission 43:** 14 Aug 44. Monday. Target: Tawlaik, a town along the Chindwin River. Dropped 100 lb demolitions and incendiaries. Did a good job.

*Aug 15th.* Stand down today. Flew formation for practice for lead plane. Flew to Comilia to see Joe Murtha. He's getting along OK, should be back in a week.

**Mission 44:** 16 Aug 44. Target Town of Tawlaik. Donohue lead and I was on his left wing. We really "pronged" the target with 100 lb. demolitions and 100 lb. Incendiaries. It's a storage area and rest camp for the Japanese from Tiddem and Chindwin Valley.

*Aug 18th.* Engineering called, had two ships to test hop....My assignment to Operations Office gives me priority when it comes to test hopping after planes are worked on. It may be other pilots do not enjoy flying as much as I do.

**Mission 45:** 20 Aug 44. Sunday. Target: RR Bridge at Budalin, Burma. We dropped four 1000 lb. Bombs from about 3000 feet but missed.

*Aug 21st.* Was scheduled to lead the 4 element and was really excited about the promotion. Bad weather and mission canceled.

**Mission 46:** 23 Aug 44. Target: RR Yards at Pinbaw, Burma. Weather cleared last night, got 11 ships off. I was moved up to lead the 2nd flight, an immediate promotion. Schenk was my bombardier and we really plastered the target. Six direct hits on the tracks and good pattern in the town. Easy mission.

*Mission Aborted: Aug 24th.* Thursday. Target: Town about 35 miles east of Mandaly. Each of four squadrons put up twelve ships, and we had 19 P-38s for escort. Weather over the target forced to return home with bombs.

*Aug 25th, 26th.* Bad weather both missions scrubbed at 9:30.

**Mission 47:** 29 Aug 44. Target: Took off with 4000 ft overcast, weather rough. After an hour in heavy weather, turned back. CO gave us credit for mission.

**Mission 48:** 31 Aug 44. Thursday. Target: Concrete RR bridge at Yeyu. Another rough weather day, alternate target was ship through thin overcast. Missed target.

**Mission 49:** 2 Sept 44. Saturday. Target: Town of Mawlaik. Capt Thompson led mission and I led 2nd box. Plastered the entire town with one hundred-twenty 100 lb demolition bombs. Good mission before going on leave.

**Mission 50:** 3 Sept 44. Target: Yeyu Bridge. I thought I was going on leave. Wanted bridge blown, took off at 8:05. Bombed in individual flights, both missed. Hit the road though. Rest camp tomorrow.

*Sept 4th.* No planes today, so a wasted day. September 5th. Took off for Calcutta at 11:00. Murtha, Schwartz, Bailey, Bell, Harmon and I. Went to show in air conditioned theater. Waited in Grand Hotel lobby from 4:45 until 7:45 when we finally got a room. All in the same room.

*Sept 6th.* Bought a couple of vases. Movie, took life easy. September 7th. Spent the day with a couple of British officers, one a pilot, and a Captain who has spent two years front line duty in Akyab and Imphal. Had a good time with them. September 8th. Went to Calcutta Swimming Club this afternoon. British Officers Club, but American officers invited. September 9th. Had more ice cream sundaes, averaging about four per day. Took in a movie.

*Sept 10th.* Went to a pretty nice church on a side street. People well dressed. Some pretty cute babes, but had to pass 'em by to get to field to catch plane home. Got home around 6:00, found lots of mail.

*Sept 11th.* Training mission. I flew lead ship for squadron formation, felt honored.

*Sept 12th.* Flew with Carter to get him checked out as first pilot. Capt Thompson asked me if I wanted to take over Operations Officer. I was thrilled. I said I would but would not promise to stay longer than it would take me to complete my missions. Normally you stay long enough to make Captain, but he said I could take the job and finish my tour.

**Mission 51:** 13 Sept 44. Had mission today. My first duty as Operations Officer was to brief the crews for today's mission. There are some 60 pilots, co-pilots, navigators, bombardiers, gunners, radiomen, etc. They are told what kind of bombs they will be dropping, what their target is, from what altitude and what heading they should be on to drop. They are briefed by intelligence officers about what is going on in the area and what kind of terrain to expect if they have to bail out—all those good things. I also tell them the exact time to take off, how they are to form their formation, what altitude to fly on course. And of course the navigators are briefed as to the course, distance, etc. This particular mission turned out to be a long one, to the town of Wauling, China. Joe Murtha flew with me. We led the second row. Got some pretty fair hits on the target. Turned out to be Joe's last mission.

**Mission 52:** 15 Sept 44. Friday. Target: I led the second box. Col Dalton led the first box. We hit weather so bad, had to break up our 12 ship formation. Really rough. Ships were all over the sky in clouds. We are told what to do in a situation of this kind but when it happens and the men have been staring at the lead ship for an hour, it is hard to go back to the instrument panel, flying instruments. Deckrow and I came out of the clouds in a two-ship formation. Went down on the railroad yards north of Yeyu and dropped bombs. Good hits on alternate target. When I got back I went to the makeshift tower to see how many ships had returned. Col Dalton was there and very worried. He did not have enough experience to be leading the entire formation, but when a full Colonel joins your squadron from the states, I guess you don't argue the point. He should never have taken a formation into weather that bad.

*Sept 16th.* Had a nine ship mission today. Murtha found out from Doc that he is through and going home soon. Both Mabry and Murtha, my co-pilot and navigator from the states, are purple heart men.

**Mission 53:** 17 Sept 44. Sunday. Target: Wanling, China. A long haul. Everything went well until Capt. Thompson started the bomb run through weather that was not good. It should have been canceled before we got that far into the run, because it was located at the base of a horseshoe mountain and to get in and out of the area, there just wasn't enough room. The pilots sort of panicked and broke formation. Torres, the right wing man of the second element nearly cracked into Wright, my left wing man. We bombed our alternate target, Bhamo, Burma.

*Sept 18th.* Monday. Put up nine ships today, to a closer target. Joe and I went to Mass. September 19th. Finally got to Stand Down. Have been really busy. September 20th. Mission scheduled, called off because of weather. Went to Mass at 5:00. September 21st. Bad weather, mission canceled.

**Mission 54:** 22 Sept 44. Target: Ye U road bridges. Put up twelve ships today. Since I am now making out the schedule for missions, I don't seem to have too much of a problem getting in on the action. Had been over target several times before and missed. Today we plastered it and blew out about 100 feet of it.

*Sept 23rd.* No mission today. We got a new pilot in our squadron today, a former A-10 instructor who had never seen a B-25. I took him up for an hour to start checking him out. Imagine me, checking out an instructor.

*Sept 24th.* Sunday. Put up a 12 ship formation today. Target was another bridge South of Mandalay. They saw quite a bit of flak, but not too accurate, no one hit. Went to Mass and communion after take off.

**Mission 55:** 25 Sept 44. Target: Railroad Bridge at Tautbin. First box hit bridge, our second box hit the approach, completely demolishing it.

**Mission 56:** 26 Sept 44. Target: In China but due to bad weather, bombed alternate target in Bhamo, Burma. Not too good but we did get some hits. Flew with Col Dalton. I have the feeling he wants more experience before leading full formation.

*Sept 29th.* Joe, Carpenter and I flew over bay and dropped 12 practice bombs. Really a treat to go flying on other than a mission.

**Mission 57:** 2 Oct 44. Target: Maugshi, China. Capt Thompson led the first box and I lead the second. Some bombs on target, and dropped a few on the Burma Road. Long day, five hours flying time.

**Mission 58:** 5 Oct 44. Target: Close by. What a day to be in India with my little gal 14,000 miles away. Our third [wedding] anniversary.

*Oct 8th.* Had a talk with Capt. Thompson tonight about my going home. He asked me to stay on as Operations Officer—fly until I get in three hundred hours combat time and the DFC. Quick as a flash I let him know what I thought about the DFC. He said I could write my own ticket if I stayed. Asked me to do about two or three more missions and he would put through my orders for sending me home. Just thinking about home is like seeing the light at the end of the tunnel.

**Mission 59:** 10 Oct 44. Tuesday. Target: Chaung-U Bridge. Capt Thompson was to lead mission, but he had a group meeting, so I led the whole show. It was quite a thrill as well as a responsibility. Did not hit bridge, but knocked out some tracks.

Oct 14th. Had our big wheel meeting at Group Headquarters. All squadron COs, all squadron Operations Officers and the CO from the P-38 squadron at Chittagon. Found out our targets were going to be Japanese Air Bases. Each squadron was to put up twelve B-25s—a total of 48 bombers and our escorts, twenty-four P-38s. We were excited because we felt if they were furnishing fighter escorts for only the second or third time in India we must be penetrating well into Japanese territory.

**Mission 60:** 15 Oct 44. Sunday. Target: Myktella Air Field near Rangoon. A big day—lots of excitement at our briefing—this is the first any of our squadron crews heard anything about the big mission. Capt Thompson flew lead of the squadron, and I flew lead of the second box. The 82nd Squadron tacked onto our squadron. We had ten P-38s for our 24 ships. We saw quite a bit of flak as we crossed the Irraway River, then more over the target. Our 2nd box bombed the Thedaw Airfield—did a good job.

Oct 16th. Our target today was the Thedaw Airfield, the one we hit yesterday. Very bad weather in the target area. All our ships split up because of clouds ahead and came back individually. I stayed in the control tower until 6:00 waiting for the last one. All twelve came back about 10 to 15 minutes apart. One had to land at Chittagong and one at Sillet—worried about fuel.

**Mission 61:** 18 Oct 44. Wednesday. Target: Prome, ninety miles from Rangoon. We had a good long target today. We were told we would get plenty of flak. Prome was weathered over, so we dropped on alternate target, Taungup and really smacked it. The 82nd Squadron came in over Prone about thirty minutes after us, found a hole in the clouds and dropped their bombs. Did a good job on it. I led the Squadron again today.

Oct 19th. In our meeting at Group today, our Group CO, Col Dalton said the 81st Squadron looked excellent yesterday in it's formation join up, it's bombing results and it's formation back over the field, then landing procedure. That was the good part. He then made it clear that everyone could expect to put in at least 75 missions.

**Missions 62, 63:** 21 Oct 44. Saturday. Target: Morning-Vital Corner. Afternoon-Kennedy Peak. We were called on to fly two missions today. Just short ones into the Chin Hills in close support with the drive around Tiddem. What we were doing is literally bombing the tops of these hills where the Japanese are dug in and firing down on Indian and British troops trying to get through.

*Oct 22nd.* Sunday. Had a big mission today with P-38 escorts. The 82nd and 81st flying together. Capt Thompson told me my orders would be going in any day now, so I'm hoping they will get back here by Nov. 20th. Went to 9:00 Mass. As Father Minahan was reading the gospel, we heard a loud explosion. He looked up and hesitated a moment—then went on. We found out later it was an 82nd ship with 4000 pounds of bombs that crashed.

*Oct 23rd.* Monday. Yesterday afternoon, Capt Thompson asked me if I would go with him to the site of the plane that crashed. When we arrived they were defusing the bombs. None of the bodies had been removed, so as soon as the bombs were defused, we began looking for the bodies. One of the bombs exploded when the plane crashed, really tearing up the plane so there was not much left of it. Four of the bodies were found whole. We carried the bodies to the jeeps, then by jeeps to ambulances. It was horrible—I held two bodies while Capt Thompson drove.

*Oct 26th.* We received information from intelligence that the Japanese had moved in a squadron of Fighter Bombers and that they were trained for night bombing. We were told to expect some scanty attacks because the moon was full.

*Oct 27th.* We had our squadron barbeque tonight. Mighty good thing the Japs didn't pay us a visit tonight. About 80% of the squadron was plenty "beered up."

*Oct 28th.* Had a stand down so everyone could recover from the good time at the Bar-B-Q last night. Tonight our lights were turned off twice because the Japanese were supposed to be heading our way. But they bombed Cox's Bazaar instead. Didn't do but little damage. Our fighters shot one down. Saw an 82nd plane crash and burn during takeoff. Actually, the right tire blew out on the take-off roll and when the pilot tried to brake his roll, he overheated the brakes and started the rubber burning from the flopping tire. The plane veered off to the right and as soon as it did stop the crew bailed out from the exits and were clear of the plane when the bombs really took off. They were loaded with 100 pound incendiaries which did not help any. No one hurt.

*Oct 29th.* The mission took off at 7:50. Tonight at the movie we were interrupted by the siren indicating the Japanese were within 50 miles of the field. We all hit for cover. We heard the ack-ack guns fire twice, which meant the planes were within twenty miles. We expected trouble, but nothing happened.

*Oct 30th.* I have reasons to believe my orders are going in pretty soon. Lt St. John was shot through the thigh on a hunting trip. Three or four of the fellows decided to try wild boar hunting. One of the men saw something move and fired his rifle at it. It turned out to be Lt St. John. It happened about 8:30 at night. By the time the Doc went out to get him and dress his wound it was midnight. I was asked to fly him to Calcutta in the middle of the night to the hospital there. Had another red alert today.

**Mission 65:** 2 Nov 44. Thursday. Target: Kennedy Peak. Had another milk run to Kennedy Peak. I led the Squadron formation. A group of the fellows decided to rename the peak "Penkhus Peak" because I have scheduled myself for so many missions there. In fact they lettered my favorite ship no. 27 the "Penkhus Peak Express."

**Mission 66:** 4 Nov 44. Saturday. Target: Myingyou. We were awakened at 03:00 hours this morning and ordered into the slit trenches. One Japanese plane actually got over the field this time. Dropped his bombs about a mile off target on the north of the runway. We were in the air early for our mission. Did a bang up job. I led a squadron formation of 24 ships, our squadron and the 83rd.

**Mission 67:** 9 Nov 44. Target: It looks like Lt Markel will succeed me as Operations Officer. This was the first time he led the entire squadron. Did a good job. Free ride as far as flak or fighters were concerned.

*Nov 12th.* Sunday. Went to Mass and communion this morning. Father Minahan gave me an all silver rosary made here in India to give Margaret when I get home. Had a big-wig Group briefing this afternoon—all four squadrons will put up twelve ships for a total of 48 and we will have P-47 fighter escorts. The P-47s are on our field ready for tomorrow, all 16 of them.

*Nov 13th.* It was a big show. Exciting to see 48 ships rendezvousing over the field, then see the P-47s take off to join them. The target was about 8 miles north of Mandalay.

**Mission 68:** 14 Nov 44. Tuesday. Target: Sagaing, a few miles SW of Mandalay. I wore my flak suit and, as Lt Balsinger used to say back in Italy, I sat on the chin strap of my steel helmet. We saw lots of flak, just like the missions back in Italy, but it was inaccurate and behind us. I led our squadron and Lt Cooper led the second box. I think this just might be my last mission.

*Nov 15th.* Group ordered a "big horse stand down" for training to include low level bombing, medium altitude bombing and 75 MM cannon practice.

*Nov 19th.* Up early to brief crews, put up a twelve-ship formation.

*Nov 24th.* Lt Sauer and I took off for Calcutta on a 3 day pass. Landed at Barrackpore at 11:00 am. Had my blouse cleaned and pressed, bought some insignia, then took in a movie. November 25th. We were sitting around the hotel room when a one of the bearers came up with a note from our squadron that our orders came back from 10th Air Force and we were to return at once to our squadron. Took off from Calcutta at 05:15 and landed in Fenny at 06:30.

*Nov 27th.* Monday. Up at 06:45 to see boys off for the last time. I stood at the rear of the briefing room and shook hands with all of them. We got on a truck at 09:45 and took off from our base at 10:00. Had mixed emotions—I have to admit I enjoyed doing what I was doing—flying, working in operations, scheduling the missions and working with engineering and the fellows on the flight line to schedule planes. I will miss all this—but I will be thrilled to be back home and have all this behind me. Landed in Calcutta at 11:00. We ate and reported to operations to put in our name for a ride home. We were called from the waiting room at 15:00 but didn't take off until 10:00 that night. Big thrill—our plane was to be a DC-3 with bucket seats.

*Nov 28th.* Tuesday. We landed at Agra, just south of New Delhi in central India, at 03:15. We were on the ground one hour, then off again at 04:15 and landed Kharachi, Pakistan at 08:45. Four hours in a bucket seat would be a long time for anyone other than someone returning home. We were assigned billets. I had just hit the sack when they told us to report for immediate take-off. Left Kharachi at 13:45 and landed on a little island—Masira at 17:15. Off again at 18:15 and landed at Aden, Aden, on the south tip of Arabia at 24:00. The change in time zone I guess would be about 20:30.

*Nov 29th.* Wednesday. We were in Aden about thirty minutes. Took off at 21:00 their time and landed at Khartoum in the central part of the Egyptian Sudan at 01:45, after setting our watches back another hour. We did get about four hours sleep here. Off again at 08:00 and landed 3:15 minutes later at El Fascher, still in Egyptian Sudan. With only fifty minutes on the ground we were off again at 11:35 noon and landed at Maiduguri, Nigeria, at 17:05 (16:05 their time). Left at 16:45 and landed at Accra on the southern coast of the Gold Coast Territory at 22:45. This is a large well-built airbase—we expect a layover here.

*Nov 30th.* Thursday. We were alerted to leave Accra at 10:45 and we did leave at 11:45 for that little rock in the middle of the Atlantic, Ascension Island. Arrived at 18:25. I sure thought about our landing here one year ago—going the other direction with lots of worries about what lies ahead. Stayed here but 35 minutes. Our next overseas crossing would be in a large C-87. Left at 19:00 for South America. After 6:50 minutes we landed at Natal, Brazil. Our time in the air was about the same as when we flew our B-25 going over. However, we were flying at minimum cruise to conserve fuel. We requested a day layover to rest up. Rest granted. We really needed some sleep after two nights with little or no sleep.

*Dec 1st.* Rested a lot and ate a lot of their delicious pineapple. I think I had it for lunch and dinner with little of anything else. December 2nd. Another day of rest and waiting.

*Dec 3rd.* Left Natal in a bucket seated B-24 around noon and landed in Trinidad about 5:45. No planes available so we spent the night here. I really think the pilot and crew wanted to spend a night in Trinidad. December 4th. Off again headed closer to home—landed in San Juan, Puerto Rico and again another overnight. Sure anxious to set foot on U.S. soil.

*Dec 5th.* Talk about excitement. Our last hop—next stop good old U S A. Landed at Miami and the first time we had a few minutes we headed for the restaurant on base and had a hamburger and a malt. Called Margy to let her know we were "home". She was excited. We were to leave by train for Des Moines Thursday. We had routine checking in to do here in Miami.

*Dec 6th.* On train to Des Moines.

*Dec 7th.* Thursday 1944. Our train pulled into Des Moines about noon—Margy was there to meet us. **What a Day!**

# PENKHUS
# CHAPTER FIVE

Floyd had two weeks of leave in Templeton with his wife and family. The December weather was certainly a change from India, but with the anticipation of Christmas, it was a welcome change. Automobiles were not readily available for purchase because there was a war on, but occasionally a few cars were released for civilians. In order to treat everyone fairly, the local dealers would hold a closed auction where sealed bids were submitted from prospective buyers. Floyd bid on a new Chevrolet coupe, and he estimated the high bid to be 850 dollars. Floyd submitted a bid of 855 dollars, and was the lucky winner.

Floyd received orders to report to Santa Monica, California, and he and Margaret proceeded to drive to California. They stopped to visit some Spencer, Iowa, friends then living in Los Angeles. During their visit, the building suddenly began to "shudder." Thinking it might be an earthquake, they ran outside to discover a B-36 with eight huge engines flying overhead, making the entire town vibrate. They then discovered that their new car had been broken into, and all of Margaret's personal belongings had been stolen: her clothes, hose, jewelry, ration coupons, shoes, and underwear. Floyd's uniforms and military clothing were not touched. Margaret had to buy an entire new wardrobe, a prospect most women would relish under other circumstances.

Reporting for duty, Floyd asked for duty in La Junta, Colorado. The Operations Officer, a Col. Wilcox from Oskaloosa, Iowa, found him a job as Operations Officer in Bakersfield, California. He would be teaching Chinese pilots how to fly the B-25, and he could fly whenever he wanted. He and Margaret purchased a furnished bungalow, and Floyd was able to live off base.

He managed to arrange to fly an AT-6 to Selma, Mississippi, to see his younger brother graduate from cadet school. It was a thrill to fly cross-country again. He flew brother, Bob, to Des Moines, and visited in Templeton for a few days before returning to Bakersfield.

They had lived in Bakersfield for almost a year when Floyd received his discharge from service December 22, 1945, with accolades for a job well done. In addition, they added their first son, Steven Dean, born August 22, 1945, while they were living in Bakersfield. They sold their bungalow, loaded up their possessions and dreams in the Chevy coupe, and drove back to Templeton.

Their second son, Mark Lippold, was born in Ames on April 19, 1949.

Floyd immediately went to Des Moines to find work. He decided to invest in a dry cleaning business, and soon Floyd owned a one-quarter interest in Artistic Cleaners.

Floyd and Margaret moved to Des Moines, and Floyd worked diligently to create a viable business. Things were going quite well, until representatives from a labor union dropped by to "unionize" Artistic Cleaners. Floyd, however, did not give them much encouragement. That night, the front windows of Artistic Cleaners were broken out, and dye was thrown over all the clothes in the store.

The next evening Floyd sat in the shop armed with a shotgun to defend his property. Again, the Union representatives stopped by, and when confronted said, "That's okay, Penkhus. We'll visit your wife at home." Floyd replied that he did not spend two years in service to come home and be treated like this. The response was, "We wish you would have been shot down!" Floyd had just fought a war thousands of miles away, and now had a bigger war in Des Moines.

He locked the doors to Artistic Cleaners, walked away, and the partners lost their investment.

In 1948, Jack Hoeppner, who worked for the Ford Motor Company, had an opportunity to open a Lincoln-Mercury dealership in Ames. He offered Floyd a one-quarter interest, and suddenly Floyd was in the automobile business.

The automobile business flourished for two years until the Ford Motor Company began shipping all of the dealerships their "fair share" of obsolete parts, and immediately started billing the dealers. Since most of the parts had little demand and were overpriced, it was an option that Floyd was not particularly pleased with. He suspected this would become a standard operating procedure for Ford, and was a losing proposition—he wanted no part of it, so he withdrew from the partnership.

Jack Hoeppner and Floyd's brothers, Jerry and Bob, teamed with Floyd once more to buy a skating rink in Colorado Springs, Colorado, which proved to be quite profitable. They then built a skating rink and a bowling alley in Ames. Brother Bob moved to Colorado Springs, Colorado, bought a used car lot, and purchased a Volvo franchise. Bob Penkhus now has the longest established Volvo dealership in the U.S.

The bowling and skating business went well in Ames for Floyd and Margaret, that is until a tornado hit the skating rink in 1968 and demolished it. Floyd then contracted to have a movie theater, with three in-house theaters, built next to his bowling alley in Ames. It was torn down in 2001. Floyd continued to operate the bowling alley until 1993, when he sold the operation, the building, and the land.

Floyd was always active in the community. He served on the Ames Golf and Country Club Board from 1973 to 1975. He served on the Board of Directors of Ames Building and Loan for over fifteen years, and was Chairman for four years. For two years he headed the State Bowling Association.

While Floyd was in service Margaret wrote every day, and Floyd responded almost every day. Floyd would usually get his mail in large batches, and always read them in sequence. They were very close. Margaret passed away February 6, 2000, after a lengthy illness.

During his overseas service, Floyd's favorite songs were "Once In a While" and "Sentimental Journey." Somehow, they both seem very appropriate.

Floyd has returned for many of his unit reunions: Newport, Virginia, Minneapolis, Minnesota, Kansas City, Missouri, and last year in Nashville, Tennessee.

During his service experience, Floyd always held a great deal of respect for the ground crews who looked after the airplanes, prepared the food, and made certain the needs of the air crews were taken care of. Floyd Penkhus has had time to reflect on his service commitment, and on what happened in America early in the conflict. Among his personal notes was the following tribute:

*"I am truly proud of our country...*

*"For planning for participation in the war effort.*

*"The overnight changing of our auto factories and manufacturing plants to build airplanes, tank, trucks, boats, ships, and all the items needed to conduct a war.*

*"For deciding where we needed air bases, ports, storage facilities, and such.*

*"Finding the engineers to build airports, miscellaneous headquarters for supplies all over the world; the many South Pacific Islands, England, Europe, North Africa, China, Burma, India, Alaska, and other locations.*

"The distribution of gas, plane parts, ship repairs, and ammunition to all these bases and ports.

"At the same time all this is going on, planning on instructors to train personnel. Thousands of people were hired to train 18, 19, and 20 year old 'kids' to fight a 'man's war.' The very thought of training our young men or adult kids to fly planes, pilot ships, drive tanks, and such, must have been a big challenge.

"I was older than most pilots. I was twenty-three when I graduated from pilot training. I was twenty-four when I went to get my plane in Savannah, Georgia, and fly it to over to Italy by way of Puerto Rico, Natal Brazil, Ascension Island, Liberia, West Africa, Casablanca, Algiers, Sicily, and finally Foggia, Italy.

"I was lucky. I was only overseas one year. Our excellent crew chief and line personnel were there three and four years without going home. And it was too bad that their work was taken for granted when pilots were receiving medals and awards. We owed so much to those mechanics.

"We also owe our wives, parents, grandparents, and those on the homefront—who sacrificed by doing without so many conveniences. They bought War Bonds, had scrap metal drives, and lived within their ration stamp allotment. They gave their energy, their resources, and their loved ones to support our nation's effort to achieve victory."

Floyd Penkhus received many accolades from Commanding Officers for his service to our country. He also received:
- The Asiatic-Pacific Theater medal with two stars,
- The European Theater of Operation Medal with two stars,
- The Air Medal with six oak leaf clusters, and
- The Distinguished Flying Cross.

And, after all these years, he still remembers where the hole next to the fourth fence post from the corner, on a side road in Carroll County, is located.

*Margaret and Floyd, after Floyd had returned from overseas.*

# BOOK NINE

# SINGER

*Lt. William A. Singer*

*B-17 Navigator*

*Eighth Air Force*

*94th Bomb Wing*

*384th Bomb Group*

*546th Squadron*

"Coming from one direction were a group of villagers armed with scythes, pitch forks, and a foul attitude. Coming from the other direction were seven soldiers from an anti-aircraft battery. The soldiers were a much safer surrender, and they protected us from the villagers."

—*Singer*

# SINGER
## CHAPTER ONE

Professor Percy Bordwell laboriously entered the classroom and shuffled to his desk. He set his well-worn leather briefcase on its side on the desk, sliding it to the front edge. He started to remove his tweed coat, unwrapping his woolen plaid scarf, then stopped and stared out the window, through the classroom building next door.

The class was Property, Bill Singer's favorite class. It was filled with the precedents of English common law, and represented several hundred years of refinement, reversal, and resolution. It was the culture and history that intrigued the young attorney-to-be. What started as the succession of noblemen, evolved into the transactions of rights and property of the common man, and the anecdotes of legal evolution which were the delicious whimsy of law.

It was 1941, and Bill was in his second year of law school at the University of Iowa. He had accelerated his undergraduate studies so that he might enter law school after three years of college. He had tested out of the Basic English requirement and was admitted to Honors English, which consisted of literature and philosophy. He was particularly intrigued by the two creative traditions of Hebrew and Greek. The Hebrews were an elitist state where ideas were handed down from the elders, while the Greek thought was democratic and ideas could be chosen for discussion.

Bill managed to cram all the basic core courses into three years, which cleared the way for entry into law school. He had always looked forward to this class on property, and the erudite instructor. It was on this frosty Monday morning that the students hesitantly entered the classroom, found their assigned chairs, draped their overcoats over the back of the chairs, and quietly eased into place with a minimum of noise.

Bill had graduated from Newton High School in 1935. For a year he worked at the Maytag plant in Newton in order to obtain funds for his advanced schooling. Maytag would come to his assistance three times during his formative years. Once he was in college in Iowa City, he worked in the Memorial Union at a board job, worked another job for his room cost, and was also a "clean-up boy" in a jewelry store in the downtown area. If there was an education to be had, Bill would have to earn it and pay for it.

John Andrew Singer was an "outside salesman," which meant that he traveled a good deal of the time. He was also a "front-man" for a violinist who performed concerts all over the world. Making the contacts, the contracts, the playbills, and travel arrangements took him away from home a good deal of the time.

Bill's mother, Francis Lettie Johnson Singer, was born in Monmouth, Illinois. She had received a degree from the Conservatory of Music in Monmouth. Bill had two brothers, Rollan who was two years younger, and Frank Budde who was eight years younger. The parents were very education-minded, and pushed hard for the young men to extend their education. Rollie became an M.D. and a psychiatrist, while (Frank) Budde received a master's degree in counseling and became a high school principal.

Bill's grandfather Singer had emigrated from Germany and was adamant that English be the language spoken at home. German was permitted only on two occasions: the evening dinner prayer, and singing Christmas carols.

The family lived in Lincoln, Nebraska, where young Bill was born April 24, 1917; they moved to Newton while Bill was quite young. Growing up during "the roaring twenties" was imperceptible to the young man; by the time he was old enough to comprehend his world, it was deep in an economic depression.

When Bill was in the sixth, seventh, and eighth grades, he got a summertime job working as a caddy at the Newton Golf and Country Club. The job introduced him to a game he would enjoy the rest of his life. His golf education really began when a member, Mrs. Bud Maytag, purchased some new clubs, and gave the young caddie a Spalding brassie club. He ultimately acquired several other hickory-shafted clubs, and learned to play at Newton's Westwood Course on sand greens. Bill has remained an ardent and enthusiastic golfer all of his life; he particularly loves the Hickory Hacker Open, played at Ames Golf and Country Club.

Mrs. Maytag's husband, Bud Maytag, was a local banker and sportsman—an expert in both golfing and skeet. Bud traveled the tour for a few seasons, before there was really a tour, and had the distinction one season of having Chi Chi Rodriguez carry his clubs. Maytag later sponsored Rodriguez on the professional tour. Maytag was instrumental in helping to design Broadmore Golf Course in Colorado Springs. The Broadmore remains one of the outstanding resort courses in the country.

As a banker during the depression, Bud Maytag was fearful that his bank might fold, as many banks did. When the threat of closing became imminent, Maytag called on some of his sportsmen friends, who loaded some silver bars on a railroad freight car and delivered them to the Newton bank. They were placed on display in the lobby of the bank, and when the bank clients lined up to withdraw their savings, which would have doomed the bank, they saw the ingots of silver stacked in full view in the lobby. Seeing what they thought was security, the line of customers dwindled and finally dissipated. There was no "run on the bank" and it continued to function with normal banking operations.

This lesson was not lost on the young caddie.

At the University, Bill was totally caught up in his literature and philosophy courses. At the end of the semester, Bill was required to write a term paper—in fifty words or less—on the topic of "Hebrew Elitism and Greek Democracy." Two weeks later, his professor, Seymour Pitcher, asked Bill to become his housekeeper for a free room. It was a wonderful opportunity to continue learning from this gentleman's challenging intellect.

Seymour Pitcher was also a political idealist, and active in national politics. In 1944, President Franklin Roosevelt rather cavalierly side-stepped his Vice President, Iowan Henry Agard Wallace, favoring a Senator from Missouri, Harry Truman, as his vice-presidential running mate. In 1948, the slighted Henry Wallace formed a third party, the Progressive Party, in a run for the presidency. This inspired Seymour Pitcher to run for the U.S. Senate on the Progressive Party ticket. In the election—by the narrowest of margins—President Harry Truman defeated Republican candidate Thomas Dewey in a surprise victory. The Progressive Party team was a distant third.

Bill Singer sat in the law school dormitory on December 7, 1941, and when the reports came in about the attack on Pearl Harbor, they didn't make any sense. He did not know where Pearl Harbor was, although he was aware that Hawaii was a territory of the United States. He dutifully went to classes the next day.

On this Monday morning, December 8, 1941, he sat in the law class on Property. Singer watched Professor Bordwell move woodenly from the window to his favorite stance behind the desk, leaning on both hands as though trying to push the desk slowly towards the students. He looked slowly, deliberately, around the room, with tears streaming down his face. He looked at the back row of students and said, "There comes a time when men lose their ability to reason together." More tears ran down his cheeks. "Look around. Only one-third of you will be back for the next class."

With that, Professor Bordwell slowly retrieved his briefcase and shuffled out of the room.

*Newton Daily News.*
*October 15, 1943*

## NEWS FROM THE BOYS
IN U. S. ARMED FORCES

News from Jasper county's boys in the U. S. armed forces, including army, navy, air force, marines, coast guard and selective service, will be carried in this column. Contributions of pictures and news items are appreciated.

### 3 Newton Boys Receive Aerial Gunner Wings

**KEITH WHARFF**     **SAM T. FLEMING, JR.**     **WILLIAM A. SINGER**

A-C Keith W. Wharff, son of Mr. and Mrs. C. M. Wharff, A-C Samuel T. Fleming, son of Mr. and Mrs. S. T. Fleming, and A-C William A. Singer, son of Mrs. Frances Singer, all of Newton, recently received their aerial gunners' wings at Harlingen, Tex. Army Air Field. The three were transferred from Gulf Coast Training Center's navigation schools to Harlingen Army Air Field.

*Bill Singer when he received his aerial gunner wings.*

# SINGER
# CHAPTER TWO

When the semester ended, Bill, like most young men, was caught up in the fervor to "Get the dirty b------s." He went to the Marine Air Corp Recruiting Office to enlist. He was turned down because he was underweight. He then went to the Navy Air Corp Recruiting Office. He was turned down because he was underweight. The solution was obvious. He went to the grocery store and bought a bunch of bananas and several bunches of carrots, and proceeded to stuff himself and—once full—ate three more bananas. He visited the Army Air Corp Recruiter and his enlistment was accepted on a waiver. Eight other law students were accepted as well.

His enlistment date was February 11, 1942. He started working once more for Maytag until October 1942, when he received his orders to report for duty.

Bill reported to Gunter Air Force Base near San Antonio, Texas, for processing, tests, and a medical examination. His observation was, "If you didn't have a hernia when you went into the exam, you had one when you came out."

After passing the required tests, he was given a form to list preferences in military roles. He listed pilot as first preference, navigator second, and bombardier third. He was selected for pilots' training and sent to Sikeston Air Force Base in southern Missouri.

Ten hours of instruction were intended to adequately prepare a cadet for his solo flight. If you had not soloed after ten hours, you were washed out. When it came time for Singer to take his solo flight, he had shin-splints so bad he could not walk, could not make it to the apron, and was forced to wash out.

All eight friends from law school were sent back to Gunter Air Force Base for reassignment. The free spirits created quite a stir by marching to mess, and other functions, in strict formation—as a joke.

Bill was next assigned to Navigator School, but since the incoming class was full, he had to sit out until the next class. He had an opportunity to go to Gunners School at Hondo, Texas, and get his flexible gunner's wings. He accepted the opportunity. In training, they shot skeet (with .30 caliber and .50 caliber guns) at both stationary and moving targets. At the completion of the training he earned his wings.

He attended Navigators' School at Ellington Field, near Houston, Texas, and completed training in February 1944. His mother and brother took the train to Texas for his graduation, and his mother pinned his wings and Second Lieutenant bars on his newly-tailored uniform.

Singer was next assigned to McDill Field near Tampa, Florida, attached to a contingent of Martin B-26 bombers. The B-26 was known as a "hot" airplane: hot to take off, hot to land, and difficult to fly in between. The standing joke was they, "lost one a day in Tampa Bay!"

Here they began an intensive B-17 transition, training in navigation, observation, ditching procedures, bailout, and techniques for surviving bombing runs. They flew over land and water, in both daylight and at night, in an effort to understand conditions they might encounter. Their training activities included search missions in the Florida Everglades, using "box search," "circular search," and "diagonal search" methods. These methodical approaches would assist them in locating targets and focus points, and developing a questioning mind for spotting the unusual. After one such exercise they returned for debriefing, and when questioned, reported seeing nothing unusual. The instructor asked if they had seen a Model T Ford on a mound in the middle of the Everglades. The crew said, yes, they had seen it. The instructor replied, "Isn't that unusual? How in the hell did a Model T get into the middle of the Everglades?" Point made.

Singer was finally assigned to a B-17 crew, and they reported to Savannah, Georgia, to pick up a brand new airplane. There were two routes overseas, the northern route and the southern route. This particular group of B-17s was assigned the northern route. The first two airplanes to leave the base were over the Atlantic when they burst into flames, losing all twenty personnel. Investigation showed that electric lines in the top turret were close to the oxygen lines, and grease on the turret track conducted electricity to the oxygen lines causing them to explode. The other crews had to "stand down" until corrections were completed.

Finally leaving Savannah, the crew flew north over the Statue of Liberty to Bangor, Maine, then to Newfoundland for a two-day layover before leaving for Ireland. Leaving Newfoundland early in the morning, the plane blew a manifold on one engine, and they had to return. Singer, as navigator, tried to retrace his steps. Fortunately, the bombardier had observed wind-drift off an iceberg using a Baby Ruth candy bar as a measuring device and—using those sightings—Singer found the base.

```
HEADQUARTERS
ARMY AIR FORCES NAVIGATION SCHOOL
HONDO ARMY AIR FIELD
Hondo, Texas                                CHC/bar

                                             8 October 1943

Mrs. Frances J. Singer,
518 East 2nd Street, North,
Newton, Iowa.

Dear Mrs. Singer:

This morning your son entered our school. He, along with a large group
of others, has now begun the course that will result, at the conclusion
of training, in a commission as Second Lieutenant in the Army of the
United States and the rating of Aerial Navigator.

The successful completion of the course will definitely establish him as
a qualified Aerial Navigator and provide him with the knowledge necessary
for him to assume his place as a member of the finest team in the world -
the Air Crew.

As an Aviation Cadet, your son is a member of a very select group, since
he has been chosen from the very best of American youth. It is an honor
to him that he has been chosen, and it is an added honor to have been se-
lected for navigation training, as the requirements for such selection are
the highest.

It is important now that you help him and keep him encouraged. Write him
often and keep him happy in order that his mind may be free to assimilate
the course of instruction. The staff will exert every effort to help him
through the course.

                                    Very truly yours,

                                    Cecil H. Childre

                                    CECIL H. CHILDRE,
                                    Lt. Col., Air Corps,
                                    Director of Training.
```

*Letter to Bill Singer's mom when he entered navigation school.*

Radar was just being developed, and the new technology would permit looking through clouds and undercast in both navigation and bombing. Singer was trained as a celestial navigator, relying on star sightings to determine location. This, of course, had its limitations when flying in fog and heavy weather. They had to use ground speed, compass heading, compass variation, wind drift, and several other factors to ascertain where they were on the globe. Navigation was still an imprecise science.

Leaving Newfoundland the second time found them flying in heavy weather, not being able to see either the stars or the sea. The radioman managed to get a third-degree fix on a radio station in Reykjavik, Iceland, and Singer felt comfortable that they were on course. When they reached Ireland, they discovered they were thirty miles south of Northern Ireland, and had violated Irish neutrality.

When they reached Belfast, the airfield was backed up with airplanes, and the B-17 circled over the ocean for two hours awaiting landing instructions. When they finally put down on the hardstand, one of the crew members put a measuring stick in the gas tank, and discovered they had one-quarter inch of gas remaining in the tank.

The crew was so elated that Singer had actually found Ireland and they had landed safely, they considered him a hero. They carted him off to a local pub, and each crew member bought him a drink. The next two days were rather a blur.

In Belfast, the bombardiers and navigators were placed aboard a B-24 and flown to Stone, England. There had been many vague rumors about a new technique for "seeing through clouds," but there were not many details. At Stone, they were introduced to—and lectured about—the new Loran Radar or G-box, a system about to be installed in bombers. The potential of bombing from five miles in the air, and being able to see the target in inclement weather, was an exciting prospect. Whether the accuracy of dropping bombs on the target would improve was another matter. Loran Radar did not anticipate the accuracy of anti-aircraft flak.

Back at the base, Singer joined his original crew. The crew was assigned to the Eighth Air Force, 94th Bomb Wing, 384th Bomb Group, 546th Squadron. Moving into the wooden barracks as assigned, Singer hauled his duffel bag indoors and started to look around. Finding an empty bed, he threw his duffel on it and began inspecting his new quarters, receiving very strange looks from his barracks mates. It seems that the occupant of that particular bed had been killed that very morning while on a mission, and his barracks mates were resentful the bed would be occupied so soon. They were reluctant to make new friends, since friendships tended to be short lived. Camaraderie and attachment were held at arms' length until they became resigned to the loss of a close friend, and it would be several weeks before Singer was accepted as "one of them."

# SINGER
## CHAPTER THREE

Bill Singer is an inveterate saver and stores most everything. However, the list of missions that he participated in is nowhere to be found. Keeping track of missions was not nearly as important to a navigator as it was to a pilot, whose pilot logbooks were sacrosanct. Somewhere in a file, in a remote location, the list of Singer's missions is gathering dust. Remembering certain key targets, and referring to "Memories of the 384th Bombardment Group (H)" by Ken Decker, has prompted Bill's recollection of some of the more memorable missions.

As navigator, Singer rose from squadron lead, to group lead, and finally to wing lead. Singer claims the progression was not because of skill but the attrition of available lead navigators.

The schedule of the lead navigator was to roll out of bed at 3:00 A.M., dress, and meet with the weather people, who would have data on the target. Cloud cover, wind direction for calculating wind drift, determining direction of approach to the target based on anti-aircraft deployment, and any other data pertinent to a successful mission were considered. After breakfast, all of the crews scheduled for the mission assembled in the briefing room. The huge map outlining the mission was covered with a drape; when the drape was removed, the crews would groan in unison. Usually, the more difficult the mission, the louder and longer their expression of dismay.

Operations would make most of the strategy decisions, but the navigator might make observations on the Initial Point (IP) and critical ground identification en route to the target. Once airborne, the navigator verified headings, drift, altitude, and path to the target. If they were exposed to flak, they tried to maintain their heading. As soon as the flak stopped, the navigator immediately reached for his mounted machine gun—as he knew fighters would soon pounce on them.

Singer's first three missions were with his original crew. After becoming a lead navigator, he flew with a number of other crews.

*July 4th.* Target: Dreux Airdrome, France. They took off very early in the morning. The target was Dreux Airdrome, about 30 miles west of Paris. It was very overcast at 25,000 feet, and unfortunately, the radar went dead on the final run. They dropped 100 lb. general-purpose bombs but missed

*After Singer was made lead navigator, he flew with a number of crews that lead group missions. This flight crew was on their way to Peenamunde, a site for launching V-2 rockets at England. Singer is standing second from the right.*

the target by 15 miles. The group navigator was very unhappy with the mission.

Note: On the way across the English Channel a group of B-24s crossed the intended path of the B-17 group, creating a turbulence causing the B-17s to drop 3000 feet. When the group finally regained their formation, the pilot asked members of the crew to check in on the intercom. Hugh Kidwell, the tail gunner aboard Singer's plane did not respond. A waist gunner discovered Kidwell was missing, as was his parachute, but his Mae West (floating device) was still in the tail turret. Later they learned Kidwell became alarmed at the change in altitude and jumped out of the airplane over water, fortuitously landing near a Belgian fishing boat. Rescued from the water, Kidwell was hidden by the sailors until making port, and concealed from the Germans for several weeks by the underground. They continued to move Hugh from house attic to house attic to avoid capture, and he was ultimately smuggled by boat back into England.

*July 18th.* Target: Peenemunde, Germany (Site of V-2 rockets). No flak or fighters were encountered. Eighteen aircraft made the mission with no spares and no aborts. The weather was good with scattered clouds. The 2d group had to make a second run on the target. On this mission Singer was checked out as lead navigator.

*July 25th.* Target: Lechatel, France. The 384th was to bomb Montreuil, La Chapelle, France. Weather was very bad, forcing selection of alternate target. 37 A/C took off with 25 actually bombing with 100 lb. fragmentary bombs at 13,000 feet. Flak was meager and inaccurate. The target was two miles from St. Lo, in support of ground troops. P-47s had knocked out the anti-aircraft emplacements.

*Aug 11th.* Target: Brest Peninsula, France (Submarine pens). Singers first group lead. 275 bombers over France. Gun emplacements, fuel depots, and railroad installations. Fighter escort comprised of 363 fighter aircraft, and only one bomber was lost with the crew landing in friendly hands. There were no losses to the 384th crews or aircraft.

*Aug 18th.* Target: Vise, Belgium. Primary targets were bridges at Leige and Namur, Belgium, to stop troop and supply movements of the Germans. Escort fighters strafed targets of opportunity. Success of bombing was unclear. No loss of aircraft nor serious wounds to crew members.

*Aug 26th.* Target: Anklem, Germany. One crew from the 547th did not return this day. Two Me-210s attacked and got one B-17. The crew bailed out, but the tail gunner's parachute caught on fire after bailout. One observer said, "There's a buddy out there in real trouble and you can't help him. All you can do is wait and watch."

*Aug 30th.* Target: Pas De Calais, France (Rocket launching sites). Rocket launching sites hit by over 800 bombers. Bomb load for the 384th was 20, 250 lb. bombs. Created a wider pattern than fewer and larger bombs, but still would damage the target. No losses to the 384th aircraft and no crew injuries.

*Note: On one mission, a Brigadier General was flying as mission commander in the co-pilot's seat. When the flight was attacked by fighters, the General opened his side window, drew his .45 caliber side arm, and started shooting at the incoming Me-109s, hoping to get a lucky shot. He was unsuccessful. He did manage to land a command responsibility at another airfield.*

*Sept 8th.* Target: Ludwigshafen, Germany (Synthetic Oil Plant). The 384th played a major roll in this mission. There was a good deal of exposure to flak both going and coming. The 384th reported no losses during this mission. Singer does not remember participating on this mission with his squadron.

*Sept 26th.* Target: Onasbruck RR Yards, Germany. The results observed were fair, with a bunch of 1000 lb. bombs hitting the town south of the rail yards. Flak was meager to moderate, but planes experienced some damage. No losses in the 384th.

*Oct 9th.* Target: Schweinfurt, Germany (Ballbearing Plant). The night before the mission Singer was in the Officer's Club, where he had just ordered a drink. Not scheduled to fly for several days, he decided to relax with friends. Bill was approached by the operations officer, who indicated they needed a group lead navigator as others were unavailable. Bill "volunteered" under pressure, left his drink on the bar, and started preparation for the next day's mission.

*Note: Schweinfurt was a dreaded target where early missions losses rivaled those at Ploesti. It proved not to be so bad this time. Fighter cover was excellent, which kept attacking fighters away. Flak over the target came up behind the formations.*

*Oct 11th.* Target: Wessling, a suburb of Cologne, Germany. (Synthetic Oil Plant) Cologne, with the IP at Coblenz, was one of the most protected targets in Germany. The need for oil and gasoline was an absolute necessity for the German military components. The Germans had installed 64 batteries of eight anti-aircraft guns around the industrial complex at Cologne. In addition, there were several fighter fields close by.

It was a mission that navigator Bill Singer will long remember.

# SINGER
## CHAPTER FOUR

It was Singer's seventeenth mission October 11, 1944. They were flying in the crew's plane named *Hell on Wings*. The target was a synthetic oil plant outside Cologne at Westling. Flying Deputy Group Lead put them in the second position and if the lead plane was shot down or aborted, they would take command of the mission. For the first time they were using the ultra-secret GH radar, new to the Eighth Air Force. As they neared the IP at Coblenz, they suddenly entered an intense field of flak. The lead plane dropped back in the formation since its GH radar stopped working. The Deputy Lead assumed their lead position and started on the final run.

*Hell on Wings* was piloted by Lt. John Peterson, with Second Lt. Robert McClelland as co-pilot, Second Lt. George Grady as bombardier, Staff Sgt. Oliver Wick in the top turret, Sgt. Frank Zink as radioman, Sgt. Irving Peckerar and Sgt. Arthur Rabe Jr. as waist gunners, and Sgt. Walter Woodruff as the tail gunner.

Singer, the navigator of the deputy lead—and now the lead—completed the run to target from the IP, and opened the bomb bay doors. Just as the bombardier hit the toggle to release the bombs, the airplane shook from two loud explosions. Two engines sputtered to a stop, and a third was trailing smoke. The plane started losing altitude in a long spiral. The pilot, Lt. Peterson, was shot in the hand and lost a lot of blood. Singer was hit with shrapnel in the left leg, and the co-pilot, Bob McClelland, was hit in the right foot. McClelland called to Singer to get into the cockpit. They managed to get the pilot out of his seat to the deck below, and Singer struggled into the pilots seat.

McClelland, with a bad right foot, controlled the left rudder pedal; Singer, with a bleeding left leg, managed to control the right rudder pedal. They attempted to guide the plane on its descent, just missing a church steeple. Using what little strength they had left, they pulled the nose up for a belly landing, and skidded to a stop in the middle of a potato field—without the plane breaking up. Expecting the plane to explode, they assisted each other out of the plane to a spot 100 yards away and tended to their wounds. The bombardier was not hurt, nor was the engineer.

The other crew members were nowhere to be found. It turned out that the "service door" between the pilot's area and the rear of the plane had jammed, and the gunners could not force it open. During the final run, the machine gunners had parachuted out of the airplane, just as cannon bursts hit the plane. They later learned that the men were captured by the Germans, spent time as prisoners of war, and returned home safely after being freed from the prison camp.

The plane did not explode, so Singer crawled back to the airplane and found a .45 caliber handgun. As instructed, he put a round through the GH radar box, the bombsight, and the compass. Looking out of the airplane, Singer saw a group of local villagers approaching with pitchforks, scythes, and a foul attitude. Having been bombed and strafed by the Allies, the villagers were quite brutal with downed airmen.

Coming from the other direction were six or seven soldiers from a nearby anti-aircraft installation, who were checking out the downed bomber. Singer immediately threw away the Colt .45 and crawled toward the soldiers, since it was a much safer surrender.

The patrol leader of the German soldiers was a Danish schoolteacher, a sergeant, who in civilian life had taught English classes, and joined the Luftwaffe rather than risk being sent to a labor camp. The Dane and the Americans immediately started a conversation. The Germans hid the prisoners in a nearby ditch to avoid strafing by P-51s patrolling the area in the skies overhead. Two of the German soldiers went to a nearby orchard and brought back apples for everyone. This was a breach of the German military standards—ordering they not steal from civilians—but a most welcome one.

The Americans convinced the Germans that the war would be over by the end of December, and most of them believed it from the advances the Americans were making. (This was before the Battle of the Bulge which occurred two months later.) Singer convinced the Danish teacher he would get "brownie points" if he had evidence he had helped the American pilots. They found a piece of cardboard, and Singer wrote his mother's name and address on it and gave it to the teacher. About a month later, the teacher was captured and, while he was in prison camp, wrote Mrs. Singer informing her that Singer was alive and a prisoner of war. He also returned the piece of cardboard.

The German soldiers managed to keep the townspeople at bay until dark, when a truck arrived to take them to Traben-Trabach near Trier. Singer was placed in a hospital and spent eight days having his wounds treated. They moved him to Oberursal where he spent twenty-two days in solitary confinement—exposed to intense interrogation. The German inquisitors attempted to glean any information that could describe technological advances, military strength, or intelligence to be used in the defense of the Reich. From Oberursal he was transported to Wetzlar, a processing camp for prisoners of war.

The American officer in command at Wetzlar was appalled at the condition and comportment of the men. Under the extreme circumstances they had not shaved, showered, or kept their uniforms in good condition. He demanded an immediate military cleanup. They showered, shaved, received new uniforms and shoes (Singer was still wearing flying boots), and stood for inspection. The ritual seems out of the ordinary because they were prisoners, but the "military way" restores the discipline, confidence, and teamwork necessary to survive.

At Wetzlar, 200 Air Force officers were separated from the rest of the prisoners and transported by train to Sagan (formerly in Poland), to Stalag Luft III. They walked the final thirty miles from the railroad station through the trees, to the camp—in foot-deep snow and mud "with very short tempers." The older Kreigies (short for Kriegsgefangner or prisoners of war) lined the entrance as they marched into the compound. Their tired, unsmiling faces reflected the many months of being denied food, freedom, and respect. The new men might bring news of the progress of the war, and recent news from home.

The prison camp consisted of several isolated enclosures: one for the Russians, one for the Americans, and one for the British-French-Polish prisoners. Singer was placed in the British camp which was called "Belaria." Stalag Luft III became famous for several escape tunnels that were dug in an attempt to get out of the enclosure, with one tunnel achieving limited success. Seventy-three prisoners managed to escape, and all but three were ultimately recaptured. As the seventy prisoners were being returned to the Stalag, they stopped for a toilet break. As they lined up in a field, fifty prisoners were machine-gunned, on the orders of Hitler, for having embarrassed the Germans by escaping. A movie describing the events entitled "The Great Escape" filmed in 1963, starred Steve McQueen, James Garner, and Richard Attenborough. The escape and subsequent events occurred prior to Singer's arrival at the camp, and had led to much stricter enforcement of camp rules.

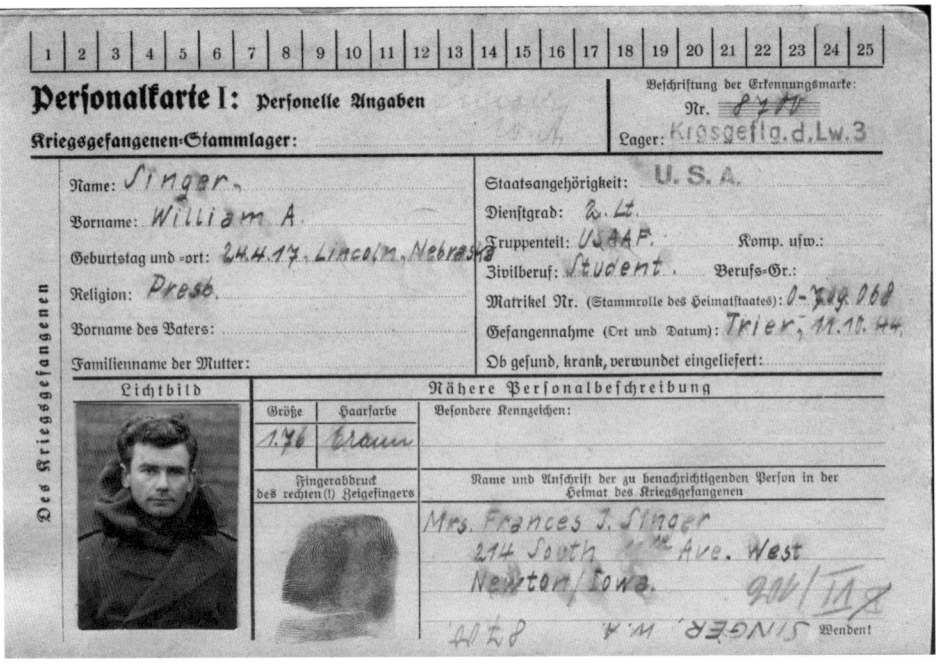

*Singer's prisoner of war identification card after being shot down.*

The camp consisted of crude wooden barracks, with a series of rooms holding ten to twelve men. Each room had bunks, a small heating-cooking stove, and a table with benches. The camp was enclosed with two twelve-foot-high barbed wire fences spaced ten to twelve feet apart, with coiled barbed wire in between. Every fifty meters around the camp was an elevated tower housing spotlights and machine guns. German guards constantly walked the perimeter of the camp. In addition, German guards, nicknamed "goons," patrolled inside the camp. "Ferrets" were Germans trained in English and slang, who attempted to overhear conversations to learn of prisoners' escape plans. With three or four thousand young men, eighteen to twenty-three-years-old milling about, there were always plans being developed to gain freedom.

When the 200 new prisoners arrived, they were taken to the mess hall for a meal consisting of a broth of barley, powdered milk, and some unidentifiable filler. The men were so tired, some fell asleep at the table. Prisoners received one meal a day of the broth, and sometimes received a crust of brown bread called kriegsbrot (prisoners bread). After their first meal they were handed a mattress cover and herded to a pile of straw, to stuff in the cover and use as their sleeping mattress. From the straw pile they were taken to barracks and assigned a bunk—where available. The rooms, designed to hold eight prisoners, now held twelve, and would ultimately hold fifteen or sixteen.

After several days in camp, Singer was called to a meeting with three American officers who interrogated him to be certain he was not a German "plant." One officer asked his hometown (Newton, Iowa) and another asked if he knew "Cozy Cole" who had been in his class at flying school. Singer indicated that Cole's parents' home was on his paper route, and Cole's mother worked at a dress shop next to the Savings and Loan where Singer's mother worked. The officer replied, "He's clean."

The "goons" carried thirty-inch-long screwdrivers and constantly probed for items hidden in the camp. They would poke every crevice, crack, and cranny hoping to discover where items might be concealed. The camp had radios, tools, documents, dyes, sewing equipment for making uniforms, and even piping for making an alcohol still. Most of the items were never detected.

The Germans called the men to the parade ground for roll call, or appel, twice daily. Regardless of the weather, the men fell in ranks and responded to their name when called. Early in the war, the prisoners were more playful, giving false names or cat-calling. However, the staff got quite tough with the prisoners, denying them privileges, and the number of "horsing-around" incidents dropped dramatically.

Singer was still being treated for his injury, and he had a reaction to the sulfa treatment for his wounds. His face began to swell, and he developed large, open sores. At first, the medics thought it was a reaction to powdered eggs they occasionally received. The first treatment for healing the sores was performed by a dental student, who tried to relieve the pressure in the swollen areas. It did not work. A British doctor asked the Germans for more medical supplies, but medicines were limited and none were forthcoming. The second treatment consisted of placing a plaster cast on Singer's face. It cracked from the heat of chemical hydration. It did not work, and it scared the hell out of Singer, who was quite claustrophobic. The third treatment was a liberal application of gentian violet, a purple ointment which gave some relief. It also caused Singer to sport a purple face until the skin regenerated itself several weeks later.

While in the camp, Singer enjoyed the company of the British and French prisoners. In order to keep his mind off food, or lack thereof, he spent time trying to learn German. He found an abandoned "Wartime Log Book," a sort of diary furnished by the YMCA to prisoners to occupy their mind and their time. Tearing out several pages of entries by the previous owner, Singer set about making his own entries. There are poems copied from other prisoners, entries copied from friends, and a recounting of incidents during his service. There are German language lessons and words to songs. It kept the young attorney's mind active, questioning, philosophical, and was an outlet for finding humor in the midst of deprivation.

As Christmas approached, the Brits decided to celebrate the event. Each man saved a small portion of dried fruit from his Red Cross rations, and contributed it to manufacturing some "Christmas Cheer." The brew ended up as half wine and half beer, and there was enough for one-third of a cup for each man. Because of their starvation diet, it proved to be too much of a good thing, and the men were soon reeling. It took several days for the camp to return to normal.

The aircraft Singer was navigating was shot down on October 11, 1944. He was held for interrogation from October 20 until November 11. He arrived at Stalag Luft III, the compound called "Belaria," on November 18, 1944. As the Russians approached from the east, the Germans were concerned about the release of the prisoners and decided to move them to another Stalag. In the American south camp on January 27, 1945, in the early evening, an appel was sounded. The prisoners formed in ranks, and they were told to pack their belongings, as they would be leaving the camp in a forced march in one hour.

When the American south camp was vacated, the prisoners from Belaria marched eight or ten miles, moving into the south camp for three days until they, too, would began a forced march.

A snowstorm had moved into the area with ten to twelve inches of snow accompanied by a biting wind. The men shuffled out of the camp into the darkness, attended by a few guards. They started the thirty-mile hike to the rail yards, marching continuously through the night. The next morning they stopped for a brief rest and toilet break, and the men flopped in the deep snow trying to catch their breath. The men had saved a few items to eat on the way, but the crackers and ersatz chocolate bars did little to generate warmth or energy. Singer had difficulty carrying his pack with the few possessions he had because of his injury. He had stored his belongings in a pair of summer pants with the legs tied at the bottom; this permitted him to carry it over his shoulder, but it was still difficult because of his wound. An Anglican chaplain carried the packs of several wounded soldiers in order for them to keep up with the forced march.

Once at the rail yard, the men were herded aboard boxcars, called "forty and eights" since they were built to house either forty soldiers or eight horses. The men were crowded seventy to a boxcar, with no room to lie down. One corner was designated as a toilet area, but because of the men's condition, some soiled themselves, making conditions in the enclosed space more intolerable. An occasional stop would release men for a toilet call, and the men would line up outside the train. It was a sorry sight to see a continuous line of men squatting in the snow with their trousers at their knees attempting to relieve themselves, when they had little or no food for four days. Passengers in the train stations laughed at the prisoners suffering this collective, yet personal, indignity.

The stop did permit cleaning of the lungs with the bitter cold air before returning to the stench and closeness of the railroad car.

They rode the trains for two and one-half days, finally arriving at the rail yards at Nurnberg, Germany. Here they disembarked, not knowing they would be marched for sixty miles to the next Stalag.

Although the Allied prisoners had been kept in separate compounds in Stalag Luft III, they were now mixed together as they formed new marching ranks. This mixture included British, Polish, Free French, Americans, and a few Russians. Most of the Russians in the camp were executed because the Germans had an intense dislike of them. As the men continued marching, the Germans refused to let the prisoners put out POW (prisoner of war) marker strips so American P-51s would not strafe them. Every so often an American fighter would make a slow pass over them and the men would take to the ditches. However, the prisoners were never fired upon.

Late one afternoon, a P-51 circled overhead with sinister intent, and the prisoners scattered. Singer and two other men found refuge in a deep ditch, and when the prisoners reassembled, Singer and the two men remained hidden until the long line had shuffled past. The three men decided to take their chances on finding food, and ultimately working their way west to the Allied lines. Near nightfall they left their hiding spot, and moved down the road to a large barn where they found refuge for the night. They found fresh hay in the loft, and, in spite of intense hunger pangs, enjoyed their first comfortable night's sleep since leaving camp.

They rested most of the day, and in the late afternoon began their quest for the Allied lines—avoiding the few visible city lights, finding little food, and wandering in circles most of the time. They usually found a barn to sleep in, but were wary of the local citizens and their antipathy toward airmen. On the third day, one of the POWs, named Champion, became violently ill with the dry heaves and fever. They were hiding in a wooded area and, after some discussion, the three men decided their flight was futile. They decided to turn themselves in to local authorities. There was a farmhouse near by, and Singer was elected to seek help, willing to suffer the consequences if they were German civilians.

Singer scouted the farmyard and—with some fear—approached the farmhouse door. He took a deep breath and knocked on the door. The door opened and peering out was a German soldier in full uniform. It turned out that he was an officer in the Hungarian SS (storm troopers). The officer accepted the surrender of the three POWs, and took them to the nearby city jail in Allersberg.

The city jail's main inhabitants were five Frenchmen who were forced laborers in the nearby farm fields. They had lived there for two seasons, helping the local Germans in their farming operations, since all eligible men were in the German military. The laborers were well known and accepted by the local citizens. The Frenchmen had managed to copy the keys to their cells, and moved about the community rather freely. In fact, they had established a steady routine of keeping company with a good number of lonely German women in the community, on scheduled nocturnal visits.

In the local jail they enjoyed regular meals and beds, out of the frigid weather. The Frenchmen were rather free-spirited, entertaining the exhausted POWs with their free-and-easy lifestyle. Singer taught them the "Star Spangled Banner," and from them learned "La Marseillaise," the French national anthem.

During the weeks that followed, the three prisoners were joined by more POWs captured in and around the countryside, and jail numbers swelled to ten or twelve prisoners. Caretakers of the local jail did not like providing food for that many prisoners and decided to move them out at the first opportunity.

A few days later, a column of American POW soldiers came marching into town. Most of the men were paratroopers captured on D-Day and were moving to a new camp. The prisoners in the local jail were forced to join the column. Escorting the POWs were very old German soldiers, who marched alongside with rifles and bayonets. One guard had severe blisters on his feet, and used his rifle as a crutch so he could keep up with the column, and the prisoners helped him along.

Marching along toward Bavaria, they took a rest in the town of Kell, Germany. Here they received word that President Franklin Roosevelt had passed away. They resumed marching to Closter-Gars on the Inn River, considered an "open city" that housed the

International Red Cross Regional Office and a hospital. All of the POWs received a food parcel, and special attention was given to emaciated prisoners and the wounded. It was a welcome break. The food parcels, which were meant to barely sustain life for a week, were immediately wolfed down by the starved men.

The German guards learned the Allies were in the process of negotiating surrender terms with the German military, but they continued the march of POWs to the next camp. The guards pushed the soldiers hard, trying to cross the bridge over the Inn River because the Germans intended to blow up the bridge at 1:00 pm. Consideration was given to marching the men to Berchtesgaden, Hitler's mountain retreat, to surround the community to keep the Allies from bombing and strafing it. The POWs refused to comply, so they continued on to Closter-Gars.

The prisoners were met at the entrance to the city by the Burgemeister, or town mayor. Some of the guards, recognizing that the war was almost over, took an expeditious exit, leaving the prisoners for the Burgemeister to deal with. The prisoners were divided into three groups for housing in the community; Singer was assigned to the Burgemeister's group, who housed them in a large barn on the edge of town. The men stretched out on the straw for a long sleep. Singer took off his shoes for the first time in over a week.

The prisoners were awakened by the clanking noise of approaching tanks, and welcomed a column of American soldiers—members of the Wisconsin National Guard—who handed out champagne and fresh fruit. The POWs were given K rations and a slit trench was dug for their use. The tanks and soldiers were looking for German soldiers to kill, since they had witnessed the carnage at Auschwitz and were seeking retribution. The few elderly German guards that remained were protected by the POWs, because of the humanity and consideration they had shown the previous two weeks of the march.

The next stop was a nearby airfield at Englstadt, where the men moved into cadet barracks that had not been damaged by bombing and strafing. Driving through the nearby town showed the prisoners the devastation caused by bombing, where not a single structure was left standing. While searching for a room in the cadet barracks, Singer and several other POWs found two bottles of Benedictine Brandy and a Very pistol which was used to shoot warning flares. That evening, the soldiers, with nearly full stomachs, drank brandy and shot flares in celebration of their imminent release.

The next morning, quartermaster trucks arrived and hauled the prisoners to a factory building outside Mooseburg, where they stayed for two days, out of the weather. Singer was billeted on the third floor, which was filled with metal lathes and manufacturing equipment. The "Red Ball Express" transport group brought several loads of K rations and C rations, which started to cure the hunger pangs of the last six months.

The airfield was crowded with a huge number of POWs waiting to be loaded on transport planes and flown to another field for processing. Between plane trips a lone Stuka dive-bomber attempted to surrender by landing at the airfield. Thinking they were under attack, the Americans put up a good deal of small arms fire to shoot it down. The plane circled one more time, waggled its wings, and landed on the field. As the pilot crawled out of the airplane he was mobbed by POWs looking for souvenirs, and they literally stripped him of his clothing.

Singer, along with others, was finally loaded on a C-47 transport and taken to another airfield. They were processed, interviewed, given butch haircuts, fumigated, and given hot showers. When they came out of the shower, they were handed a fluffy towel and two cigarettes. After his first two cigarettes, Singer was "hooked for fifty years." The soldiers were issued GI (government issued) clothes to use until they could buy their officers uniforms.

Their next move was to Camp Lucky Strike near Le Harve, France, for final processing. They lived in a "tent city," and could eat in the mess hall at any time. The mashed potatoes, chicken gravy, and fresh salads were a welcome treat.

POWs who were in traveling condition were permitted to visit Paris. The first trip, Singer stood in a mile-long line in order to get his pass. The second time, Singer did not want to get into a mile-long line to get a pass, and decided it was faster and easier to go AWOL (absent without leave). He found a paymaster, and received partial pay so he could acquire a new officer's uniform for his trip to Paris. He discovered a second paymaster and—again—drew partial pay, so he could have a good time in Paris. On the way to hitch a ride, he discovered a third paymaster, and drew a third partial pay that enabled him to stay in the best hotels and eat in the finest restaurants in the city.

Singer returned from Paris without incident, finished processing, and was transported to Le Harve, France, where they boarded the Liberty Ship Asa Grey, bound for Newport News, Virginia. The crossing was very rough, and most of the men on board went to the top deck to look at the horizon. They arrived in

Virginia with great fanfare, and spent three days in processing before being granted leave.

When they asked Singer for his residence, he indicated Monmouth, Illinois, his mother's birthplace. This would enable him to return via Chicago rather than St. Louis, where connections to Iowa were much more difficult. While processing, he caught a jeep ride to the officers' barracks, hopped out, opened the door, and found Bob Smith, a close friend from Newton. Singer wanted a pass to Chicago to see the city, and Major Bob Smith just happened to be the Adjutant Personnel Officer. The Major also happened to be the class president of Singer's Newton high school class, who just happened to process Singer's papers and just happened to route him through Chicago.

After a brief tour of Chicago, Singer climbed aboard a Rock Island Rail Road train headed for Newton. Green crops covered the rich Iowa soil, and breezes blew the willow trees that were along the streambeds. The rolling farmland was not as dramatic as the scenery marching through Bavaria, but he was really *seeing* the landscape for the very first time through a different pair of eyes, and it brought a lump to his throat. There was a strange quietness as the big steam engine rolled to a stop at the Newton Station.

The sight of his mother anxiously waiting on the railroad platform, watching for him to step down to the landing, is still very vivid in Bill Singer's memory.

*Prisoners at Belaria prison camp. They were rarely permitted to be this close to the fence.*

# SINGER
# CHAPTER FIVE

**TELEGRAM WESTERN UNION**

1944 OCTOBER 27 AM 7:44
MRS FRANCIS J SINGER
THE SECRETARY OF WAR DESIRES ME TO EXPRESS HIS DEEP REGRET THAT YOUR SON SECOND LIEUTENANT WILLIAM A SINGER HAS BEEN REPORTED MISSING IN ACTION SINCE 11 OCTOBER OVER GERMANY IF FURTHER DETAILS OR INFORMATION ARE RECEIVED YOU WILL BE PROMPTLY NOTIFIED J A ULIO THE ADJUTANT GENERAL

**TELEGRAM WESTERN UNION**

1944 NOV 25 AM 11:02
MRS FRANCIS J SINGER
REPORT JUST RECEIVED THRU INTERNATIONAL RED CROSS STATES THAT YOUR SON SECOND LIEUTENANT WILLIAM A SINGER IS A PRISONER OF WAR OF THE GERMAN GOVERNMENT LETTER OF INFORMATION FOLLOWS FROM PROVOST MARSHALL GENERAL = WITSELL ACTING THE ADJUTANT GENERAL

Francis Singer was a very strong and capable woman. When she received the telegrams that her son was missing, she immediately contacted as many of Bill's military friends as possible to see if they had any information about him. She received over forty responses from servicemen and the Red Cross who described the last time they saw Bill, giving encouragement that "somehow Bill would show up." Two months later, she received a letter and the piece of cardboard with her address on it from the Danish schoolteacher, assuring her that Bill was a POW, and was alive.

Singer's first letter home after being shot down, written while in the hospital:

Saturday-Oct 14th –44

Dear Mother

Well, your much traveled son is adding another spot to his itinerary. Not so much for the sake of future memoirs as per necessity. I am now a prisoner of war in Germany in a hospital recovering from a very slight wound. I have been treated very well and my companions and I are enjoying life and much more comfort than was expected. There is no need for money. The German Red Cross apparently functions much the same as our own and is providing us with our ration of cigarettes and this opportunity to write home.

Will you notify my commanding officer of my situation. You have his address. And if the parcels which you were going to send are already gone, don't worry about them for the boys in the barracks will use them as previously agreed among us. My other belongings will probably, in due time, arrive home safely—although who knows. I may beat them.

I had planned a big letter writing spree and had gotten off quite a few here & there. But I still owe letters to Val, Bill & Harry—to my friends in Chicago & to Virginia. Since my writing now is likely to be curtailed, all of my mail henceforth will be to you. Incidentally, you know the old story about compensations. My German was far from sharp & now I rattle it off like a veteran. Like all novices I had to begin with basic needs and wants like "bedpan," "match," and so forth. Now, however, I am beginning to use complete sentences with adjectives and other minor refinements. My French also serves when other tongues fail so when you next see Miss Franklin tell her that she didn't slave entirely in vain.

I never did get around to sending off that box of stuff to you. In addition to the things which I've mentioned, I also had some medical books for Rollo—technical stuff on paradontal diseases and bacteriology which he might conceivably be able to use. Also I had a copy of Harold Lamb's "Persian Mosaic," a fictionalized biography of Omar Kahayjam which I enjoyed very much. Also some newspapers for Bud—but I don't know whether or not all will be sent on. Anyway, none of it was so valuable or so rare but what it can be replaced.

After I get a permanent address, perhaps you can send a package including cigarettes, shaving equipment, candy & so on, OK?

My regards to all in Newton—Phyllis, Anna, and all my love to you, Katie & the family. I'll be with you before too long.
    Love, Bill

P.S. Fresh flowers every day-How do you like that? Today it's tea roses. B.

Prisoners of War were given a blank paged book titled "A Wartime Log," for use recording events and happenings during their incarceration; the International YMCA gave a logbook to each prisoner. They also furnished sports equipment to help the prisoners occupy their time. Though the diet of the prisoners did not permit great expenditures of energy, exercise was a device to keep their mind off their incarceration. Logbooks contained poems copied from other sources, personal reflections, diaries, artwork, and cartoons. Many POWs started making entries, then lost interest as boredom set in.

Singer had a year of law school, and was, perhaps, more disciplined in making entries in his logbook than other prisoners. His wounds limited his mobility, and he spent time writing, rather than walking the fence line for exercise. He had a broad interest and intellectual curiosity in many areas, as indicated by the variety of topics in his logbook. He was in Stalag Luft III only about three months before the forced march out of the compound.

Singer inherited a logbook another prisoner had started, then discarded. These selections are entries in a section of the book he titled "Episodes to Remember."

**Sagan**—march through the woods to north and back up to Belaria, on that cold snowing morning. The muddy roads and the short tempers. Our entrance to Belaria lined with old Kreigies, many of them yanks flying with the RAF—our greeting by G. C. McDonald at the cookhouse over barley soup, prunes and coffee. The many searches before we finally got to camp.

**Belaria**—Meeting our new zimmer mates & "the govnor"—not turning a hand for a week—the appels, outside aborts, and wash houses, the revier, library, barbershop, carpenter shop, boot shop, the bulletin boards, the delousing of block 17—the sports ground, parade field, goon boxes, fire pool, hockey pond, main road, perimeter lights, and search lights at night—the theater with their fine performances—Doc Montwee, Goeff, Geo, Mickey, Duncan, Mac, Bert, Jimmie, etc. The rumors & news, our "canaries" lost, the predictions of Lt.Col.Warford, S.A.O.—his B.S. at the hospital, Alex's friends…My first church service—the Christmas Bash.

Arguments with Hodge—navigation chats with Tungate—The Col., Jameson and Ginger Barlow—the games and plans for toys drawn up by Don and Vic. O.J.'s stories about Alabama. Frank and Bill at football—Frank on the guitar and accordion—Don, Vic, Jock and

Wally singing RAF songs—O.J. and myself learning "Gegen England"—Sam and "NJ was never like this"—Breakfast in bed—Wally's Kreigie Cake—Hodge's Rationing—Vic and Bill's "Brown Alerts" & the five page regulation—Jock, O.J., Vic, Sam & Don playing monopoly with cries of "Snake eyes"—"7's up" & "duovers"—Vic's stories of Egypt and France—Jock's exuberance, his stories of Calif. & how he got the V.C.—The bagpipe player on Xmas eve & New Years—the Evac. of Gorlitz—Jock of zimmer 7 being late at appel nearly getting the cooler—Maw's birthday on Jan 23 + my poor celebration in the hospital—The Russian Advance and the antics of Twee—Jimmies concerts on the accordion and his discussions on psychology and mysticism—the frantic disorder of camp and hospital block on Saturday of evacuation weekend—the method of notice the goons used for evacuation—the rifling of hospital stores—& delicious choc. And plum pudding confiscated by yers trooly for the Sabbath Bash—The notice of departure and march to the north compound—the Scotch Padre, Eric Rankin, helping out on the march—the wait outside the main gate in the snow and cold—the deserted tanks on the main street in Sagan.

**North**—Our assignment to block 106—Ben Boyle and myself building a sled—the scrounging in camp—the desolation of the whole place—the law and medical books—the wrecked musical instruments—the C.O. of our block, Col. Stevenson & and his excellent manners & gentlemanly treatment of his men—the meeting with Mac—D.P. duty—the good food—the inane conversations & later with Will Kamenisky—learning of Jim Brown being with Kammy and Jack Eley-ebe Atkins (Murgatroyd) & his snoring—His cadet training with Elmer Wolf at Victorville—Bob Hansell's cooking and the riding he got about the salt—Barney's "lights out" poetry—Murgatroyd's "big wheel" talk & threats to court martial his bombardier classmate Hansell—T.R Nielson's "flaps"—his adhesions & thus breadmaking activities—bridge with Ben, Barney, Ebe, Will, & Jack & the "3-B" system of bidding—the British Doc and everyone's estimate of him—the way my face cleared with his reversal of treatment—meeting Irwin Feld who studied at American Conservatory under Harrison and knew Bob Rayfield well—had heard of Marion Welle—his singing with the Milwaukee Opera Company and contract to appear with J.C. Thomas in S.A.—the sweating out of Uncle Joe's planes, tanks, & artillery—inside appels with 2 men in the sack—ration issue at 104 & the backbreaking labor as to toting bread—the early call to leave—the late departure—Ebe's klim whip—the march to the station supposedly 2 km & actually about 6 km—60 men in a 40/8 car the first night—later 56 men including 8 guards—Ebe's specially constructed, scientific, pail pack—my own effort.

**Transit**—the GI's, sleeplessness, grumbling, swearing, food flaps, crowded conditions. Paper shortage—Boyle's attempts, usually successful, at ironing out ugly situations—Niel's sickness—Kammy's GIs—Ebe's target practice from a moving base—the crowds of civilians, usually frauleins, at train stops checking out on POW toiletries—Eleey's acceptance—Kammy's humor—Neil's dry philosophy—Hansel's overwrought nerves—Ben's consideration—Young's boring monologues—Hansel's authoritative discourses on food, artillery, personnel movements & goon language—our conversations with the goons & and their nicknames (the proboscis, the lip, the dolt, the baker, the 4-eyes, Voss iss los, etc.) the bakers photos of our shoes at night & the flap with Hansell over his shot feet—the division of food parcels—our disgust with the English Doc's bedside manner—the five nights of this lousy situation & relief at arriving "home" behind barbed wire again.

**Nurnberg**—Langwasser: the sports field—bombed buildings—demolished hospital mixed awe, glee, and pity at the wreckage—the walk through the gate—the long wait beside the Rusky Hosp. & our greeting—the trading of cigs for souvenirs—the threats to fire on the Russ if they touched the wire and their utter disregard—the trampling over the little boy (nor more than 15 yrs old) on crutches and his momentary tears and recovery—the searches, waits, split-ups—meeting Alex again—the good looking "gepruft" gals at the censor office (our first thoughts in a long while which weren't about food)—the registry & entrance into the compound—the infantry boys who had been taken about Christmas & had no cigarettes or Red Cross food since—the "officer", no worse off than any one else, and no worse off than Alex & me, begging D-bars etc. from us—Our arrival at 117 & confiscation of food by those who didn't know the situation—Major ____'s untactful, accusatory & resented address—the RAF's flap over K.R. & search & seizure & how quickly it was ironed out—the the 1st appel—sleeping with Alex meeting Capt. Ed Bower, Griff & the others in the bay.—my discourteous answer to Ed's innocent questions about my flying, Alex's frying pan—My transfer to 106 & running into Pete, Morris & hearing about Stut being here. The St. Valentine day reunion of Mac, Pete, Stut & myself—Meeting Jim Brown—wondering about the main Belaria bunch and hearing they went to Meuseburg, near Munich—Introduction to Col. Alcair's command—his staff mess—

what the west boys complained about—His Saturday inspections derived from the usual G.I. misunderstanding of human nature & morale—

**2/20/45**—the perpetual, always daily, fligeralarms & the great raids on marshalling yards & city—the fort spinning in, on fire & two chutes—two fighters knocked out—the fort on fire—the waves in—contrails—smoke bombs—the haze—the parachuter who was in view 1/2 hour & the other so close that his body was visible. The night RAF raids & alerts—the 4000 pounder that lit 110 meters from our enclosure—the fires, smoke pall & clouds over Nurnberg following the raid—the rations continually being cut—43 2/3s% of potatoes—Allegedly 1200 calories per day—Col. Martin's fireside chat—his suggestion that we turn our thoughts from food to motorcars (ergo-Cadillacs with whipped cream)—Development of X from wool gathering to reality—Picture parades—The Oberst General's visit to camp & 105 & Kautz's description of the boy's efforts to please—How the bastard came in with a chip on his shoulder—the long appels when Hauptman Eiler miscounts & the shorts when Oberfeldstapfwebell (T/sgt) Eidemann takes over—The good humor (hubba-hubba) of Hauptman Glackowitz—The delousing program & its hardships to pay for 5 min of hot shower—The shower later—the reappearance of shorn, dilatory, hirsute growth—Shoick's inability to get along with others, & the way the others picked on him when, inevitably, he did something wrong—Jake's vagueness, confusion & lapses of memory in his cooking—the 3-man combine with Isley & Shearer—Teller's opinions—Bier's and McClouds' bunk fatigue—the shortage of cigarettes and tobacco Sanders being P.O.ed with the typical Amer. Officer (& my wholehearted agreement)—Kemp's, Bier's, Sander's & Turney's well functioning combine & their old Kreggie stories—The story of Sgt Cline C. Miles (Cameron, Mo.) of South Compound on 4/9/44 who was deliberately shot while standing in his doorway—Recollection of Don Tungate parachuting on top of a searchlight battery when captured—& Vic being blown out—The wanton and willful destruction of wash houses & aborts for firewood. Our construction of slit trenches between barracks for air raids & my determination not to sacrifice what comfort I might have for the safety of cold, wet trenches.

**Nurnberg**—3/5/45—Budde's birthday—Sweating out mail that never comes & parcels—My duties as liaison officer for contacts with Poles and Britishers—My carbuncle & Floto's solicitous

attentions—Reunion with Decker and Fetherstone (of Wetzlar days) over in the Sgt's camp—Fetherstone's early offer of cigs & me kicking myself for not taking them—How during alerts & raids not an enemy fighter would be in the sky, but my how they'd buzz around when there was no chance of meeting our 51s & 38s—Rumors, always rumors, of parcels, mail, & Rhine crossings, the meat & drink of Kreigies prayers—the gathering of recipes from states outside the localities by those masochistic individuals who loved to inflict self torture—The deals with the Russky—Our greetings to the French P.W.'s when we came in—Sanders' & Kemp's strategy in swiping the light bulb from the Vorlager during delousing & and how P.O.'d our bay was when we found out it was kaput—Nichts gute—Geoff & Cornish's interpretation of the communiqués & our own "wheels" ineptitude—The way rumors start, including my own relay on 3/9/45 & were pouring over in thousands: the way this spread like wildfire the A.M. of the 10th & my so sober decision to rely solely on OKW—Slogans of the day:
"Watch Ike's hike through the Reich!"
"C'mon Joe, let's go! C'mon Ike, let's hike!"
"Stone walls do not a prison make, nor iron bars a cage; but they never said nothin' about barbed wire!"
"Out of the gate in '48!"

**3/11/45**—Church services at Nurnberg in 79 of Sgt's camp—Had to be at the gate by 10:50 AM—the Padre's McVay excellent sermons & Col. Martin's reading of the Scripture, impressing me, as did G.C. McDonald of Belaria, of another responsibility taken by an intelligent & personable senior officer—the organ & the congregation on well known hymns—but the bitter cold & poor lighting especially during evening services—Conformation of Rhine crossing over flash news by Aschmann, the top interpreter of OKW. OKW confirmation of the Wesel bridgehead on Sunday 3/11/45 & our celebrating bash, the 1st time I'd been comfortably full, even temporarily, at Nurnberg—The wave of petty thievery of bread in the bay and our efforts to stop it.

**3/12/45**—The "lecture" with Ken Collins at night involving college education, philosophy, religion, vocational guidance, Engl. Lit. & Law. He being Jewish Reform Church, with Jake Shearer & Moe Skarloff, were abler to furnish interesting info on the Dietary Laws, Mosaic Code & Old Testament literature. Reminds me of the law chats with Jim Brown on subjects which I have yet to take in school & with Bill Young of J.A. of camp on Practice.—Seeing Col.

Hendricks, Lager "Entertainment" officer for permission to work with Erwin Feld on forming a vocal group—Details of organization falling to me, problems of personnel & music & direction to Erwin & to Bill Grogan—Bill turning out arrangement of "Stardust" sang piano between appel time & 7:00pm—The difficulties of getting piano, rehearsal room, & time etc. The philosophy discussions with Bob Kemp (his references to Prof. Whitehead of Harvard)—Getting the cooperation of Vic Besser who directed the chorus at West & his crack arranger Al Williams & instrumentalist Mott Williams.

3/14/45—The night alert—watching searchlights, flak, & flares from our slit trenches—My star lecture to all who would listen—Meeting Any Champion—My daily flaps with Morrie Kautz—Our Sun(day) bath which was interrupted by the entry of 3-6x6 GI trucks driven by Swiss civilians with French interpreter—containing 3600 parcels for our 5600 men, rumor of 2/3 per man, what with 570 parcels in reserve—No OKW for two days due to bombing of power plant in Regansburg—last nights communiqué as usual says nothing, even to mention the bridgeheads at Wesel and Bonn & Patton's drive down the Moselle—We always take goon communiqués in the light of "no news is good news."

3/16/45—Recalling Col. Alcair's letter to the protecting power setting out the conditions of our camp and asking for relief—The night RAF raids on Nurnberg and Furth with awe inspiring myriad of colors—Blue/white searchlights (dozens of them)—Red, Yellow, & green parachute flares cascading "Christmas trees"—Red flak bursts, AA fire on ground merging into incendiary fires of the target area—Deadly flamers with the whine of props winding up & the sight of exploding pieces—The 'chute' dropping under a green flare—The bomb release line (beyond which no bombs may be toggled or jettisoned) clearly demarked by flares—The whistle of falling flak & concussion and blast effect of the 4000 pounders—The cold & dampness of the slit trenches. The day ending with the announcement of full parcels as long as they last & as usual, my nightly contemplation of Ike's, Champ's and my plans for vacation.

3/21/45—First day of spring—sunny & warm—lazy spring fever—Chorus rehearsals for the past few days much better over first attempts to organize—GI trucks in on 19th, but due, allegedly, for Belgies and French—Ike promises "Mooseburgers" for dinner Thursday (invention of Moose Simler of West) constructed mit corned beef, liver pate', bread crumbs, oleo & klim in patties &

baked and/or fried with strips of cheese grilled in—Sehr tasty—Haven't hit the trenches for 2 nights (was ist los? RAF giving up?)—Communique shows Patton's 3rd at Kaiserlautern, supplies pouring through bridgehead at Remagen & Uncle Joe hammering at Stettin—What is the ETA's to Nurnberg & Berlin, navigator? Home Asthmann, Lager #1 interpreter still clings to Apr 1st.

4/4/45—Evacuation—using shirt pack—left at 0900 in Sec. 6 under Major Hammill—Next to last Sec. In first group of column—First let to Neumart, but fell short by 16 km—Slept night in barn in Obertierdon after passing through Feucht. Pfeifferhutte, Postbauer, Ochenbruck, got hot water & potatoes from farmer and family whose kindness I'll never forget—They thought our interpreter resembled their son who was, or had been a POW in Russia. Champ sick—got warmth & aid in the house—Ike and I doubled up in the barn, planning escape—Both of us having been appointed MPs, it was easy to rove the column for possibilities—Rear of column strafed by P-47s & varying reports gave several Sgts dead or casualties. Rumor that the sick party's train was bombed in Nurnberg & 100 were killed.

4/5/45—Left Obertierdon & hit Polling on the 2nd rest period (8km) holing up in a barn 10:30am covered up with straw until night waiting for the column to pass—Cold rain about 8pm fell through boards in loft & had devil of time opening the barred & locked doors in pitch blackness—Headed for fields with pack left in barn & only barest necessities plus all food with us—Stooged blindly to autobahn & then to wooded hill where Evac. train forced us to shack up till am in the cold & wet forest.

4/5/45—Awoke, chilled, to find a better spot at 0700 0 Found one at 0830—Slept & ate until 11:30 & then off thru woods heading west—Very enjoyable to me—Ike being a damned good woodsman—Dogs and wood choppers forced us into a very circuitous route—Left wooded cover for open field in daylight to escape dogs—Sighted by woman crossing R.R. & reached woods always climbing—Shacked up till 0430 in nice little nest of soft pine needles & bramble weed—left 0430 SW to edge of woods for rest to nightfall—0900 pm Took off on the worst night's travel of my young life—Headed west across fields—Pitch blackness, raining & blowing, muddy ploughed fields—Changed plan of attack a million times—Risked a cigarette under a tree about 11:00—Sighted road in westerly direction by headlights of trucks & so took off with frequent compass checks—

Fell into icy pond (presumably a cesspool by the smell) with Ike behind me in also—Both of us wet to the thighs—Almost lost sanity in the shock, couldn't see & no feeling below the hips—I gave up leading—Rested in woods for 15 minutes—Low spirits—Found a country lane going west—Walked to large tree for a break & a smoke—Mistook a crucifix for a sign post (not realizing it was the best sign post any of us could use, I guess—that is if you can draw nourishment from church symbolism as I can)—On the road—Stooging through a small town with barking dogs not being able to see us—Almost lost Ike who took a wrong turn, not being able to see us—Never so frightened in my life (like sweating out target time from an IP on a mission)—On the road, weaker, spirits low & the three of us at each others throats—Each blaming the others for wrong leads—Yet none having a better one—Another town & we have to had to have rest an shelter—Church door locked—Ike & Champ opposed to breaking in—Tried to read direction at cross roads but light poor—Compass has been sticking & we all suspect it but no one is willing to admit it to others—Take left fork in sloppy mud for about 2 km to another fork—Sight autobahn to right by lights but all pooped out & so head back up for 3 hours—My GIs terrific—Ike & I have chills & Champ as tuckered as we, but apparently over his attack—See to south a blinker code & R-G—Champ thinks he heard G. I. Trucks—We wonder where the hell the lines are—Surely wish we had a star or two to navigate by.

The entries in the logbook continued in haphazard fashion about the time spent in Allesberg. Inserted between pages was the following list of Iowans he found in the camp:

## IOWA CLUB
### At Nurnberg Langmasser
Lt. Morris Kautz (105)—216 W 10th St.—Newton—Pilot B-26—5/7/44 (day shot down)
Lt. James R. Brown (125)—219 S. Monroe—Mason City—Pilot B-17
Lt. Wm. G. Spangler (111)—Everly—Pilot B-17—9/2/44
Lt. Harry T. Long (106)—2427 Logan—Des Moines—Navigator B-17—6/22/43
Lt. O.G. Thompson—Schultz Apt #2—Ft. Dodge—
Lt. Ward L. McCombs—South English—Pilot P-38—
Capt. George Sterler—Ashton—
Lt. Leroy L. Adams—128 Highland—Ames—Bombardier B26—5/7/44
Lt. H. H. Kelley (126) 1956 W 7th—Waterloo—Navigator B-24—4/20/44 (St Omer, Fr)
Lt. Howard Erickson (124)—Apt #124 Butler Bldg—Ft. Dodge—Bomb. B-17—4/29/44

Lt. Owen D. Walton (124)—Ft. Dodge—Pilot B-17—4/29/44—Berlin
Lt. Victor Merryman—Ft. Dodge—Co-pilot B-26—10/12/44—Aachen
Lt. Edward Weiss—Ft. Dodge—Pilot B-24—(Italy)
Sgt. Vernon Johnston—Ft. Dodge—Radioman B-17 (Italy)—6/22/44
Lt. Frank Vratny (103)—Ft. Dodge—Pilot B-24—5/ /44—France
Lt. Esau—Davenport—Pilot P-38—
Lt. Fisher (95)—Meservey, Mason City
Lt. Albert Alsdorf (125)—312 N Holt—Ottumwa—Bombardier B-24—5/12/44—Ploesti
Lt. John Wittgreve (126)—529 10th St S.E.—Cedar Rapids—
Lt. Robert L. Lawrence (126)—804 S. 2nd St—Fairfield—Co-pilot B-17—8/15/44—France

The following telegram was received by Mrs. Singer:

1945 JUNE 22 AM 740
MRS FRANCIS J SINGER
THE SECRETARY OF WAR DESIRES ME TO INFORM YOU THAT YOUR SON 2ND LT SINGER WILLIAM A RETURNED TO MILITARY CONTROL 02 MAY 45
J A ULIO THE ADJUTANT GENERAL.

The following telegram arrived a few weeks later:

1945 JUNE 22 AM 740
MRS FRANCIS J SINGER
CHIEF OF STAFF OF ARMY DIRECTS ME TO INFORM YOU YOUR SON 2ND LT SINGER WILLIAM A IS BEING RETURNED TO THE UNITED STATES WITHIN THE NEAR FUTURE AND WILL BE GIVEN AN OPPORTUNITY TO COMMUNICATE WITH YOU UPON ARRIVAL =
J A ULIO THE ADJUTANT GENERAL.

As earlier indicated, POWs loved to write poetry, and much of the poetry written was shared with others who incorporated it into their logbooks. Singer had eight or ten poems in his logbook with titles like, "The Prisoner's Lament," "Heavenward," "The Kreigie's Song," and a few poems of a religious nature. One poem, written on the wall of a barracks, struck Singers fancy and he incorporated in his book:

# AN ESCORT OF P-38'S

## By A B-17 Radio Operator

Oh, Hedy Lamarr is a beautiful gal,
and Madelaine Carroll is too.
But you'll find, if you query, a different theory
Amongst any bomber crew;
For the prettiest thing, of which one can sing,
This side of the Heavenly Gates
Is no blond or brunette of a Hollywood set,
But an escort of P-38's.

It's quite true in the past, when the tables were massed,
With glasses of scotch and champagne,
That that very sight was a thing of delight,
Us intent upon "feeling no pain."
Now it's not the same, nowadays in this game,
When we head north across the Messina Straits,
Take the sparkling wine. Every time make mine
An escort of P-38's.

Now Byron, Shelley and Keats ran a dozen dead heats
Describing the views from the hills
Of the flowers in May, when the winds gently sway
An army of bright daffodils.
Take the daffodils, Byron, and the wild flowers, Shelley;
Yours is a myth, [my] friend Keats.
Just reserve me those cuties, those American beauties,
An escort of P-38's.

Sure, we're braver than hell; on the ground all is swell,
But in the air it's a different story.
We sweat out our track, through fighter and flak.
We're willing to split up the glory.
Well, they wouldn't reject us, so heaven protect us
Until all the shooting abates.
Give us courage to fight 'em, plus one other item;
An escort of P-38's.

# SINGER
# CHAPTER SIX

Bill returned to the comfortable confines of Newton, Iowa, enjoying his mother's cooking and renewing acquaintances. Many friends were returning from service, thrilled to be back. The town was in good cheer, with the conflict in Europe completed—but citizens were apprehensive about the cost in lives expended in winning the battle in the Pacific.

During high school, Bill had dated a young lady in his class, a banker's daughter named Virginia Russell. The acquaintance was casual because they usually hung out with a crowd of fifteen or so high school friends. They had communicated infrequently during Bill's stint overseas, but she was one of the first persons he contacted when he returned.

After high school Virginia, or "Ginny," attended the American Institute of Business in Des Moines, Iowa, for a year. She then went to Cornell College in Mount Vernon, Iowa, but did not have the resources to continue attending, so she took a job as the secretary to a dean at Cornell. She left Cornell to take a job as secretary to the Executive Director of the Council of State Governments in Chicago. When the executive moved to the head office New York City, Ginny went along as his personal secretary. As focus groups met, Ginny kept the notes of the meetings; she would then transcribe them over the lunch hour and give the attendees a copy of the proceedings when they convened the afternoon session.

One of the functions of the Council of State Governments was to publish the American Almanac for guiding state governments. Ginny was assigned the responsibility to write the section on County Government for the 1945 Almanac.

Virginia's father had worked in a bank in Newton, but lost his position when the bank closed. He worked for a period for the Reconstruction Finance Corporation (RFC) closing other banks in trouble. Mr. Russell then moved to Fort Madison, Iowa, where he was the Cashier at the Lee County Savings Bank. Bill found out that Virginia was home visiting her parents, and he immediately drove to Fort Madison to renew his acquaintance with her. Bill wasted no time in getting serious, and on August 5, 1945, Ginny and Bill were married. Fifteen or eighteen friends attended the wedding, held in the Russell residence in Fort Madison. Harry

Ryder, a friend from Newton, was the best man, and Ginny's sister was the maid of honor. The newlyweds traveled to New York City on their honeymoon, so Ginny could show Bill the community she had lived in for the last two years.

Walking down the street in New York City, they happened to run into a member of the 384th Bomb Group that Bill had known, and set up a meeting "under the clock" at Lexington and Third, a popular meeting spot; it was there that the friend informed Bill that he was promoted to First Lieutenant on October 7, 1944, just four days before he was shot down.

They returned from their honeymoon to discover Bill had to report to Miami Beach, Florida. When he checked in at Miami Beach, he learned he would be assigned to the Pacific Theater of Operations. He was slated to travel to San Antonio, Texas, for additional schooling before being sent overseas. He proceeded through processing, receiving his increase in pay from Second Lieutenant to First Lieutenant, and learned that he was still listed as single. In order to get married pay, Ginny had to be with him. He called Ginny, told her to sell what furniture they had, and get down there in a hurry, so he could get the marriage allowance. The other good news was he would be paid an additional seventy-five dollars per month for flying status.

They were still in Miami Beach in August 1945, when they received word of the atomic bomb dropped on Hiroshima. Bill realized he would soon be discharged and immediately called the Dean of the Law School at the University of Iowa. He learned he would be readmitted as the first returning veteran in law school. After a few days of processing and formal separation, he and Virginia were back in Iowa City in time for the fall semester.

Bill completed law school in February 1947, with good timing for the job market, since the majority of the class would graduate after the spring semester. He interviewed with legal firms in Newton, Des Moines, and with a Circuit Court Judge in Des Moines.

At that time, Bill had a pregnant wife and thirty-five dollars in the bank, and was not particularly interested in starting a law practice "from scratch." A classmate, John Miller, suggested that he apply as the Area Rent Director for the local Story County Rent Control Office. Housing was in short supply, and rent controls were necessary to keep costs within reason. Returning veterans were desperate for housing, as universities required proof of housing before permitting enrollment. The job was a civil service position with basis of selection made on a point system. Bill received five bonus points for being in service, five bonus points for being wounded, and five bonus points for being an attorney. With a fifteen-point head start, Singer was selected for the position.

The Singers moved to Ames where they found a small efficiency apartment—so efficient that when you pulled down the bed, it blocked the entrance to the bathroom. It was pure irony for a director of rent control to live in that quality of housing.

In 1949, Bill sent a housing form to a client of attorney Robert Pasley regarding rent control. Pasley contacted Singer to give a presentation on rent control to the local Story County-Ames Bar Association. No one particularly liked the law, and attorneys were often asked to interpret it. Bob Pasley was impressed with Bill's presentation, and contacted him to see if he would like to join Pasley's law firm. Since rent control was due to be discontinued, Bill accepted and joined the firm in September of 1949.

Bill remained in the Air Force Reserve, assigned as Adjutant of the 89th Troop Carrier Group out of Offutt Air Force Base at Omaha, Nebraska. When the Korean conflict erupted, Bill received orders to report to Offutt Air Force Base. Assigned to a B-29 bomber brought out of mothballs, Bill prepared to join a squadron on the west coast headed overseas. As they stood on the hardstand with bags packed, a jeep pulled up and asked for Captain Singer. He left the bag on the hardstand, got in the jeep, and was taken to the Judge Advocates Office in Offutt, and became a member of the Judge Advocates staff. This was good news, since Virginia and his young family could join him for his twenty-one-month tour of duty.

Bill remained in the Air Force Reserve after the Korean Conflict and was on Inactive Status during the Viet Nam War. He later retired as a Colonel after twenty-six years, receiving the Air Force Service Medal for his length of service.

After his twenty-one month commitment, he returned to active law practice in Ames and Story County. He was always interested in political activities, and ran in a primary election for County Attorney. He lost the opportunity to run in the general election by a narrow margin. Elected Chair of the Story County Republican Party in 1954, he served in that capacity for three years. In 1956, he ran for the Iowa Senate and lost that election by nineteen votes, with the greatest number of votes cast in a senate race in the district up to that time. He later reflected, "It was probably a good thing I was not elected. I would have made some bad mistakes."

The Singers' first child, Lynn, was born November 30, 1947. Son, William Andrew Singer Jr., was born March 6, 1949. When the children grew up and left home, Virginia took a position at the First

*Virginia Russell and Bill Singer's wedding picture, taken in Fort Madison, Iowa.*

National Bank in Ames, where she was initially a personal secretary to the president, Robert Stafford. She later became Cashier of the bank, and the first woman officer at First National Bank in Ames.

Bill was very active in the Boy Scouts, serving at several levels of scouting activity and recognized by state scout executives for his participation. He worked at every level of the organization and was richly rewarded seeing young men participate in scouting.

Two souvenirs Bill brought back from service were a German steel helmet and a bayonet. Bill presented them to his grandson, and they are his prized possessions.

Bill returned to England three times to attend reunions of his bomb group. Ginny accompanied him on the first return, he traveled alone the second time, and daughter, Lynn, and son, Andy, traveled with him the third time. Each trip was filled with memories, discoveries, and large dollops of nostalgia.

Bill has been an ardent golfer since he was a caddy in the sixth grade at Newton Golf and Country Club. When Bill returned to England the second time for the reunion of the 384th Bomb Group in Leicester, he arrived a few days early so he could play the Royal and Ancient St. Andrews Golf Course. Bill played it three times and relished every moment, from the pot bunkers, to the changing weather, and particularly the repartee of the aged caddies. Bill has a soft spot in his heart for things British—from early history learned in law school days in Property class, to his stint in Belaria at Stalag Luft III with British officers, to his return to Leicester and their delightful pubs.

While returning from St. Andrews, he was late for dinner at the reunion. Entering the dining hall, he was handed a note by the master of ceremonies to meet someone in the bar after the meal. When Bill entered the bar, he found one of their crew members who had bailed out of the tail section on the fateful day they were shot down. The airman recounted the events of that moment. When they were hit, the hatch door jammed and an alarm bell went off. The five airmen in the rear of the plane, hearing the alarm, bailed out without hesitation—and all survived as POWs. Bill and his crew member closed the bar that night.

After Virginia retired from working at the bank, her physical health diminished from a severe case of emphysema. Her health failed, and she passed away in of January 1987.

Bill then enjoyed the companionship of Darlene Osler Wagner; they were married in 1991. Darlene passed away in 1998.

The medals awarded to William Singer include:
- The Air Force Service Medal
- The Reserve Medal with Hour Glass cluster
- American Campaign Medal
- WWII Victory Medal
- The Prisoner of War Medal
- The Air Medal with One Oak Leaf Cluster
- The Purple Heart

Bill Singer continues to play golf at every opportunity and, as stated earlier, particularly likes the Hickory Hacker Open at Ames Golf and Country Club. He enjoys dressing the part of an early Scottish golfer, and still occasionally uses the hickory-shafted brassie given him by Mrs. Bud Maytag. Even though Bill's eyesight is failing, he remains a putter of absolutely uncanny accuracy from any distance.

In fact, had bombardiers used his hickory-shafted putter as a bombsight instead of the Norden variety, targets would have been hit with this same uncanny accuracy, and the WWII armistice would have been signed months earlier.

*On Singer's last trip to England for the bomb group reunion, he visited several friends who remain in England.*

# ACKNOWLEDGEMENTS

A big thank you to Donald Mangels (Col. USAF ret.) for his interest and encouragement in pursuing this effort. He loves the Air Force and Air Force stories.

A special thank you to Robert Underhill, Professor Emeritus of English and Speech at Iowa State University, who not only shared his story, but whose encouragement and advice were most helpful.

A monstrous thank you to Ann Andrews Rudi for several reasons. She walked around my very messy workspace for nine months without saying a word. She never complained about my working late into the night with classical music at full register. She once more applied her editing skills which are still irrefragable. And she is still my lovely wife.

# BIBLIOGRAPHY

Evie, Tom and Bob Powell. *The "Bluenosed Bastards" of Bodney: A Commemorative History.* Dallas, Texas: Taylor Publishing Company, 1990.

Woolnough, Lt. Col. John H. *The Eighth Air Force Album.* Hollywood, Florida: 8th AF News, 1978.

Freeman, Roger A. *The B-17 Fortress at War.* New York: Charles Scribner's & Sons, 1977.

*Reader's Digest Illustrated Story of World War II.* Pleasantville, New York: The Reader's Digest Association, 1969.

Freeman, Roger A. *The Mighty Eighth: The History of the U.S. 8th Army Air Force.* Garden City, New York, 1970.

Cooper, Brian. *The Story of Bombers 1914–1945.* London, England: Phoebus Publishing Company, 1974.

McManus, John. *Deadly Sky: The American Combat Airman in WWII.* Novato, California: Presidio Press, 2000.

Leuchtenburg, William E. and the Editors of Time Life Books. *The LIFE History of the United States.* Vols. 11&12. New York: Time Life Books, 1963.

Time Life Books. *Time Capsule 1939, 1941, 1944, 1945.* New York: Time Life Books, 1967.

American Map Corporation. *The Great World Atlas.* New York: American Map Corporation, 1994.

Slater, Harry E. *Lingering Contrails of the Big Square A.* Nashville, Tennessee: 94th Bomb Group Memorial Association, 1980.

# ABOUT THE AUTHOR

Norman Rudi has long been interested in World War II experiences. Rudi is a WWII veteran who served twenty months as a paratrooper in the 11th Airborne Division in the Army of Occupation in Japan, after hostilities ceased and before the Korean War started.

Rudi had three brothers each serve five years exposed to the worst conditions of the conflict. Brother, Edgar, served as a medical technician in an advanced surgical team with the 34th Division in North Africa, Sicily, and Italy. Brother, Fred, served in the 9th Armored Division, landing in Europe ten days after D-Day. He survived the Battle of the Bulge at Bastogne, and was in the first armored unit under General George Patton's command to cross the bridge into Germany at Remagen. Brother, Harold, regular U.S. Navy, served as a signalman in the Armed Guard aboard merchant marine ships. He made twelve convoy trips to England during the height of the Nazi submarine wolf-packs, two trips to Murmansk, Russia in, the middle of winter, and several trips to the South Pacific.

Norman Rudi is a native of Glidden, Iowa, and a graduate of the University of Oklahoma, where he received a Bachelor of Architecture. Rudi worked for architecture firms in Cedar Rapids, Iowa, before moving to Ames, Iowa, where he was an associate professor at Iowa State University in the Department of Architecture.

Rudi opened an architectural practice in Ames, Iowa, in 1966, and retired in 1994. Active in community organizations, he has served as president of the Ames Society for the Arts, the Ames Chamber of Commerce, The Ames/Story County Cyclone Club, Ames Rotary Club, Ames Golf and Country Club, the Iowa Architectural Examination Board, and served on the Board of Directors of the National Association of Architectural Registration Boards.

Norman Rudi's first writing effort, *An Iowa Pilot Named Hap*, was the biography of Hartley "Hap" Westbrook, a decorated WWII B-24 pilot, prisoner of war, airport operator for over fifty years, and a member of the Iowa Aviation Hall of Fame. *A Neighborhood of Eagles* is Rudi's second book. A third book about an American soldier who spent three years fighting the Japanese with the Filipino Guerrillas is underway.

# GLOSSARY

## A–D
A/C: Aircraft.
Allies: Countries who fought with the U.S. against the German military.
Appel: German word for "roll call."
Apron: Paved part of airport immediately adjacent to terminal area or hangars.
Axis: Countries who fought with the German military against the U.S.
Bd: Bombed.
Bomb Group: Thirty to forty planes.
Buzz Bombs: Self-propelled pilotless aircraft; crashed with their explosive load.
Calieche: Texas term for blacktop or dirt.
CE: Circular error probable.
CO: Commanding officer.
C rations: Field ration type containing meat, vegetables, hash, and/or beans.

## E–H
ETO: European Theatre of Operations.
ETO Newspapers: Included *Stars & Stripes* (among others).
Fat Man: Second nuclear weapon used in warfare.
Flying under a hood: Flying with no view of the outside.
GCI: Ground control intercept.
GFE depot: Government furnished equipment depot.
GH radar: Navigation system; more advanced version of the Gee (grid) system.
GI: Government issued.
GIs: Common soldiers; also, slang for diarrhea.
Gigs: Punishment for infractions.
Hardstand: Paved or stabilized area where vehicles are parked.
Hors de combat: Out of combat or disabled.

## I–L
IFF: Identify friend or foe.
IP: Initial point.
KP: Kitchen Police.
K rations: Field rations labeled as "Breakfast," "Lunch," or "Dinner."
Kreigie: Short for Kriegsgefangner, or prisoners of war.
Liberty Ship: Transported people and goods between Europe and the U.S.
Little Boy: First nuclear weapon used in warfare.
Luftwaffe: German airforce.

## M–Q
Marshalling yard: Railroad track-switching sites.
Mickey: Radar operator.
Nisei: Japanese word meaning "second generation Japanese American."
Non-com: Non-commissioned officer.
Norseman: Light transport and utility plane.
OCS: Officer Candidate School.

# GLOSSARY (cont.)

## P–Q
PX: Post exchange.
Quonset huts: a row of semi-circular steel ribs covered with corrugated sheet metal.

## R–Z
RDX: Rapid detonating explosion.
RON: Remain overnight.
Sorties: A mission or attack by a single plane or several planes.
Split "S": Aerial maneuver in which plane flies upside down for a moment before righting.
Squadron: (Aerial) Ten to twelve planes.
Strafing: Machine-gun fire from low-flying aircraft.
SAC: Strategic Air Command.
Target of Opportunity: An alternate, unplanned target.
V-E Day: Victory in Europe day.
V-J Day: Day of unconditional surrender; victory in Japan.
V-mail: Written on forms, photographed, flown across the world, and reproduced.
Very pistol: Flare gun used to send messages via different colors.